LUCK, LEISURE, AND THE CASINO IN NINETEENTH-CENTURY EUROPE

Gambling was central to the cultural, social, and intellectual history of nineteenth-century Europe. By tracing the evolution of gambling and investigating the spatial qualities of the casino, this book reveals how Europeans used gambling to understand their changing world. The development of resorts and the architectural qualities of casinos demonstrate how new leisure practices, combined with revolutions in transportation and communication, fashioned resort gambling in the Rhineland and Riviera. Jared Poley explores the importance of casino gambling in people's lives, probing how gambling and fate intersected. The casino impacted understandings of the body, excited emotions, and drove the "psychology" of the gambler, as well as affecting ideas about probability, chance, and luck. Ultimately, this book addresses the fundamental question of what gambling was for, and how it opened up opportunities to understand theories about aggression, play, and human development.

JARED POLEY is Professor of History at Georgia State University. He is the author of *Decolonization in Germany: Weimar Narratives of Colonial Loss and Foreign Occupation* (2005) and *The Devil's Riches: A Modern History of Greed* (2016) as well as coeditor of volumes on religious conversion, money, and migration in Germany.

NEW STUDIES IN EUROPEAN HISTORY

EDITED BY

PETER BALDWIN, University of California, Los Angeles
HOLLY CASE, Brown University
CHRISTOPHER CLARK, University of Cambridge
JAMES B. COLLINS, Georgetown University
KARIN FRIEDRICH, University of Aberdeen
MIA RODRÍGUEZ-SALGADO, London School of Economics and Political Science
TIMOTHY SNYDER, Yale University

The aim of this series in early modern and modern European history is to publish outstanding works of research, addressed to important themes across a wide geographical range, from southern and central Europe, to Scandinavia and Russia, from the time of the Renaissance to the present. As it develops the series will comprise focused works of wide contextual range and intellectual ambition.

A full list of titles published in the series can be found at:
www.cambridge.org/newstudiesineuropeanhistory

LUCK, LEISURE, AND THE CASINO IN NINETEENTH-CENTURY EUROPE

A Cultural History of Gambling

JARED POLEY

Georgia State University

CAMBRIDGE
UNIVERSITY PRESS

Shaftesbury Road, Cambridge CB2 8EA, United Kingdom

One Liberty Plaza, 20th Floor, New York, NY 10006, USA

477 Williamstown Road, Port Melbourne, VIC 3207, Australia

314–321, 3rd Floor, Plot 3, Splendor Forum, Jasola District Centre, New Delhi – 110025, India

103 Penang Road, #05–06/07, Visioncrest Commercial, Singapore 238467

Cambridge University Press is part of Cambridge University Press & Assessment, a department of the University of Cambridge.

We share the University's mission to contribute to society through the pursuit of education, learning and research at the highest international levels of excellence.

www.cambridge.org
Information on this title: www.cambridge.org/9781009393546

DOI: 10.1017/9781009393539

First published 2023

A catalogue record for this publication is available from the British Library.

Library of Congress Cataloging-in-Publication Data
NAMES: Poley, Jared, 1970- author.
TITLE: Luck, leisure, and the casino in nineteenth-century Europe : a cultural history of gambling / Jared Poley, Georgia State University.
DESCRIPTION: New York : Cambridge University Press, 2024. | Series: NSEH new studies in european history | Includes bibliographical references and index.
IDENTIFIERS: LCCN 2023016276 (print) | LCCN 2023016277 (ebook) | ISBN 9781009393546 (hardback) | ISBN 9781009393577 (paperback) | ISBN 9781009393539 (epub)
SUBJECTS: LCSH: Gambling–Europe–History–19th century. | Casinos–Europe–History–19th century. | Leisure–Social aspects–Europe–History–19th century. | Europe–Social conditions–19th century.
CLASSIFICATION: LCC GV1301 .P65 2024 (print) | LCC GV1301 (ebook) | DDC 795.09409/034–dc23/eng/20230425
LC record available at https://lccn.loc.gov/2023016276
LC ebook record available at https://lccn.loc.gov/2023016277

ISBN 978-1-009-39354-6 Hardback

For Robert L. Poley, 1943–2023

Contents

List of Figures   *page* viii
Acknowledgments   x

   Introduction   1

1 Gambling in the Nineteenth Century   10

2 Visiting the Resort   30

3 Experiencing the Casino   47

4 Probability and the Casino   89

5 Chance and Luck   111

6 Gambling and the Body   139

7 Gambling and the History of Emotions   153

8 The Psychology of Gambling   168

9 What Gambling Was   181

   Conclusion   199

Bibliography   204
Index   209

Figures

1.1   "Le Tir aux Pigeons" (Neurdein et Cie, ca. 1907–14)   *page* 25

2.1   "Etablissement Thermal, La Joie de l'Eau" (Giletta Freres, ca. 1907–14)   44

3.1   "Monte-Carlo – Le Casino" (Lucien Levy, ca. 1907–14)   49

3.2   "Monte-Carlo – Le Casino" (Lucien Levy, ca. 1907–14)   50

3.3   "Casino de Monte Carlo – Vue prise de la Mer" (Lucien Levy, ca. 1907–14)   51

3.4   "Monte-Carlo – Façade du Casino" (Giletta Freres, ca. 1907–14)   52

3.5   "Monte-Carlo – Les Terrasses pendant le Concert" (unknown, ca. 1907–14)   53

3.6   *The Salon d'Or, Homburg* by William Powell Frith, 1871   56

3.7   "Monte-Carlo. – Le Casino. Le Salon Rose" (Lucien Levy, ca. 1907–14)   58

3.8   "Casino de Monte-Carlo. Salle de Roulette. Salle Garnier" (Nuerdein et Cie, ca. 1907–14)   59

3.9   "Casino de Monte-Carlo. La Salle Schmidt" (Nuerdein et Cie, ca. 1907–14)   60

3.10   "Monte-Carlo. – La Nouvelle Salle de Jeux" (Lucien Levy, ca. 1907–14)   61

3.11   "Monte-Carlo. – Le Casino. – La Nouvelle Salle de Jeux. – Les Grâces Florentines" (Lucien Levy, ca. 1907–14)   62

3.12   "Monte-Carlo – Salle de Jeu Dans la Prairie, par Hodebert" (Giletta Freres, ca. 1907–14)   63

3.13   "Casino de Monte-Carlo. Salle Schmidt Table de Roulette" (Nuerdein et Cie, ca. 1907–14)   64

3.14   "Le Casino de Monte-Carlo. – La Salle de Trente et Quarante" (Lucien Levy, ca. 1907–14)   65

3.15 "Casino de Monte-Carlo. La Salle des Concerts"
(Nuerdein et Cie, ca. 1907–14) 66

3.16 "La Roulette de Monte-Carlo" (A. Sauvagio, ca. 1907–14) 72

3.17 "Tableau du Trente & Quarante"
(A. Sauvagio, ca. 1907–14) 73

3.18 Entry card, Monte Carlo (unknown, ca. 1907–14) 82

3.19 *At the Gambling Table* (first plate) by Jean-Louis
Forain, 1909 84

3.20 *At the Gambling Table* (second plate) by
Jean-Louis Forain, 1909 85

5.1 "La Fortune Monte Carlo" (unknown, ca. 1907–14) 125

5.2 "Monte-Carlo – Salle de Jeu (Veine et Déveine)"
(Giletta Frere, ca 1907–14) 126

Acknowledgments

There are many, many people and institutions who have nurtured this project, and to whom I am tremendously grateful. The College of Arts and Sciences at Georgia State provided financial support in the form of a semester-long workload adjustment, during which most of the manuscript was drafted, and Associate Dean Kathryn McClymond was very supportive of the writing process. I am fortunate to have a wonderful group of colleagues in the history department at Georgia State, and I am especially thankful for my friends Michelle Brattain, Denise Davidson, Nick Wilding, Rob Baker, Jeff Young, and Greg Moore. Portions of the project were tested at meetings of the Southeast German Studies Workshop, a warm and thoughtful community of scholars whose insights have been especially valuable at critical points. I also benefited greatly from presenting aspects of the work at German Studies Association (GSA) meetings, especially in seminars dedicated to emotions and to consumerism. The GSA remains a welcoming environment to explore new ideas, and I have greatly appreciated my friends and colleagues in that association: David Barclay, Dan Riches, Alexander Schunka, Heikki Lempa, Derek Hillard, Irene Kacandes, and Janet Ward. A special thank you to Suzanne Marchand and Jason Wolfe, who invited me to present on this topic at Louisiana State University, and to David Luebke, whose friendship, editorial eye, and advice are treasures. And of course, the incomparable Mary Lindemann has been equal parts inspiration and supportive mentor. I also need to highlight long-time friends Britta McEwen and Sam Keeley, whose support and encouragement of the project came at just the right juncture in the form of an international writing group. Jason Coy, Ben Marschke, Mike Sauter, and Claudia Verhoeven have been friends, allies, and co-conspirators for more than a quarter-century. Thank you for your many years of friendship. And last but not least, David Sabean continues to spur us on with his example, to teach us how to live and work as scholars, and to demonstrate the importance of community – both social and intellectual – in our lives. Thank you to both David and Ruth.

I also need to mention a large number of Decatur friends who provided an escape from academic pressures and have fostered levity and amusement for the past two decades: David Davis, Odile Ferroussier, Lisa Armistead, Christi Wiltse, Justin Wiltse, Bryan Downs, Nancy Downs, Duran Dodson, and Reagan Koski. Dan Kidder, John Ellis, Miguel Alandete, Geoff Koski, Joey Pate, Juan Guzman, Aaron Hilllegas, and Rob Baker have provided many memorable hours of agonistic play. Thank you all!

The book would never have made it to this point without the support of Peter Baldwin and the editorial board of the New Studies in European History series at Cambridge University Press. The anonymous reviewers have my gratitude, and the project is much better because of their feedback. Liz Friend-Smith deserves special attention – thank you for supporting this over many, many years. I am also grateful to the people who helped sort out the images that are included in the book: Christina Bleyer (Trinity College of Hartford, CT), Amanda Matava (Trinity College of Hartford, CT), Peter Huestis (National Gallery of Art), and Nicole Priedemann (RISD Museum). I am thankful to Berghahn Books for permission to include as parts of Chapters 7 and 8 portions of "Gambling and Emotion," which was published in *Feelings Materialized: Emotions, Bodies, and Things in Germany, 1500–1950* (Berghahn Books, 2020). Sections of Chapter 2 appear as "Visiting the Resort: Gambling, Medicine, and the Nineteenth-Century European Casino" in *Healing and Harm* (Berghahn Books, 2023).

Finally, thanks to my family, for their love and support. To my parents, Martha and Robert, and my mother-in-law, Sylvia, as well as Clint and Matt, Leslie and Matt, Cle and Tanna, and Josh and Jenn: I love you all. And to Felix, Vivian, and especially Laura: I love you.

Introduction

In his 1870 book *The Gaming Table: Its Votaries and Victims*, Andrew Steinmetz recounts the origins of gambling. Drawing on Greek allegory, Steinmetz claims that Gaming was the child of a union between the Goddess of Fortune – Tyche or Fortuna – and the God of War, Ares or Mars. Gaming was, at least in Steinmetz's retelling, a "misfeatured" child, a "wayward thing [who] could only be pleased by cards, dice, or counters."[1] Gaming, Steinmetz tells his readers, "was courted by all the gay and extravagant of both sexes, for she was of neither sex, and yet combining the attractions of each."[2] Gaming was also wooed by rough and violent men and has an "unnatural union" with one of them, later giving birth to two children: Dueling and Suicide. "These became their mother's darlings, nursed by her with constant care and tenderness, and her perpetual companions."[3] Gaming's mother surveyed her child's development, and "endowed her with splendid residences … magnificently designed and elegantly furnished."[4] All were allowed to enter, but exit required an escort. Some were led by her "half-witted son Duelling," while others were escorted by "her malignant monster Suicide, and his mate, the demon Despair."[5] Yet Gaming's calamitous reign was an extensive one. Steinmetz explains that "Gaming is a *universal* thing – the characteristic of the human biped all the world over."[6]

Steinmetz's recounting of the origins of gambling, like his assertions that gambling is a universal human trait or that it occasioned the creation of fantastic new spaces to enjoy this form of leisure, provides a hint of the central topic considered in this book: the history of European casino gambling in the nineteenth and early twentieth centuries. Steinmetz wrote

---

[1] A. Steinmetz, *The Gaming Table: Its Votaries and Victims*, 2 vols. (Tinsley Brothers, 1870), vol. 1, 1.
[2] Steinmetz, *The Gaming Table*, 1–2.   [3] Steinmetz, *The Gaming Table*, 2.
[4] Steinmetz, *The Gaming Table*, 2.   [5] Steinmetz, *The Gaming Table*, 2.
[6] Steinmetz, *The Gaming Table*, 3.

at a pivotal turning point in that history, just after the establishment of
legal gambling at Monte Carlo and just before the casinos in the German
Rhineland were shuttered in the wake of German unification. Casino
gambling of the type developed in the nineteenth century, which leveraged
new technologies and novel forms of leisure, was unlike the sort we are
now accustomed to seeing. These resorts were created at a moment of
possibility, a time when the politics of mass leisure were first felt and when
the casino offered a new way to socialize. Gambling – which was indis-
putably older and more universal than what we can consider in this book –
found itself in a new situation in the nineteenth century. New ways to
discuss luck and chance; new ideas about the body, emotion, and sensation; and new ways to understand health and morality coalesced in this
period to create a charged environment – the resort casino – in which
people experienced themselves and those around them in transformed
ways. Gambling provided the nineteenth century with a new vocabulary
that could be used to discuss the most intense and sharply felt events. Its
mechanical wonders provided scientists and mathematicians with a built-
in experimental space that was used to probe the meaning of likelihood,
luck, and chance. And gambling's emotional intensity drove the creation
of new ways to understand impulse, behavior, and feeling. Furthermore,
gambling – especially when experienced in the context of the resort
casino – presented nineteenth-century patrons with an opportunity to
engage in new ways of historical thinking, to consider the meaning of
causation and correlation, and even to contemplate the ability of humans
to intervene in history or to exert influence on their world. In short,
gambling ushered in new ways to understand what a human was and
how it acted. Describing the historical evolution of these ideas is the goal of
the book.

Readers familiar with Jackson Lears's *Something for Nothing: Luck in
America* will see parallels with that great work. While Lears's subject – the
history of luck – is focused on a related topic, many of the themes
entertained there appear in transformed ways in this text. Lears explains
that central elements of American cultural history may be explained as an
oscillation between two poles. One consists of the self-made man whose
"success comes through careful cultivation of (implicitly Protestant) virtues
in cooperation with a Providential plan," while the other is characterized
by the "speculative confidence man" whose eye is always on the "Main
Chance."[7] This duality means that gambling and luck are especially

---

[7] T. J. J. Lears, *Something for Nothing: Luck in America* (Viking, 2003), 3.

freighted cultural systems in the United States, in part because of the notion that good fortune is deserved by the fortunate. Lears also emphasizes what could be called the secularization of chance, in which the category moves from an emphasis on Providential theories of design and fate to secular notions of "management" and chaos. The overall arc of his narrative may be summed up in his suggestion that a "culture of chance" dominating the eighteenth and nineteenth centuries was insistently supplanted by a "culture of control" in the twentieth. There were gaps in this shift, to be sure, but the overall suggestion is that an ephemeral existence dominated by fate or by Providence was replaced with a logic of management and controlled design that sought to relentlessly preclude chance from reattaining any kind of dominant cultural position. Managerial attempts to understand, balance, and mitigate chance, especially applied within the context of the Cold War and as part of a geopolitical nuclear strategy, were a hallmark of mid-century Americanism.

While Lears proposes a historical trajectory that moves from chance to control, sociologist Gerda Reith argues for a different view of historical change in which an assumption of certainty crafted during the enlightenment gives way to an "age of chance" dominating the twentieth century. Play and gambling are central pillars of this argument. Tracing the history of play, Reith argues that the eighteenth-century theory of play saw it as unproductive and irrational, but not directly sinful. By the nineteenth century, however, gambling represented to moralists a loss of both money and time and, according to Reith, was criminalized at this historical juncture because it represented a failure to adopt the basic demands of work discipline.[8] In the twentieth century, gambling was still a problem, but that problem was understood in a "medical rather than an ethical sense."[9] Gambling and play were directly related to larger attempts to understand fate and causation. Reith, suggesting that the universe was apprehended by faith in the early modern period, reason in the eighteenth century, and chance in the twentieth, explains that in the "twenty-first century, chance is understood as a constituent part of the world, codified in the rules of probability theory and, in the branches of quantum mechanics and chaos theory, an irreducible feature of modern science."[10] In this way, chance – and not, as Lears would argue, control – is the dominating principle of our time.

---

[8] G. Reith, *The Age of Chance: Gambling in Western Culture* (Routledge, 1999), 5–6.
[9] Reith, *The Age of Chance*, 6.   [10] Reith, *The Age of Chance*, 13.

Lears and Reith provide us with two different ideas about the history of human perceptions of the world. While they both suggest a kind of secularization of indeterminacy that characterized modernity, Lears and Reith reach different conclusions about where we are today. Lears ends his book with a gesture toward the advancing ubiquity of control; even chaos theory represents an attempt to separate signals from noise, to use Nate Silver's memorable formulation.[11] Reith argues that the Enlightenment represented a collapse of indeterminacy. In the "Age of Reason, everything had a cause, whether material or transcendental, and so chance had no place in the world. It was an irrational aberration which could be banished by the application of reason and the advance of knowledge. Chance thus had no real *being*, and existed only in an epistemological sense as a deficit, a lack of knowledge."[12] One of Reith's conclusions is that with the rise of indeterminacy, uncertainty, and then chaos theory we can see the primacy of chance as the dominant intellectual fact of the twentieth and twenty-first centuries. We have order, but no certainty. Things instead are governed by orders of probability. Despite their differing conclusions, both Lears and Reith indicate that the nineteenth century was a pivot point in our understanding of these issues. And there was no realm more central to the discussion of determinacy than gambling, thus requiring a deeper focus on this period and the intellectual forces at work between 1840 and 1925.

My understanding of the period and of the issues at hand is framed by the work of four historians of gambling. David Schwartz's *Roll the Bones: The History of Gambling* provides a wonderfully complex look at the trajectory of gambling in a global context and over millennia.[13] Tracing the history of gambling from the ancient world to its current incarnations in Las Vegas and Macau, Schwartz illustrates both the ubiquity and the variability in our approach to gambling. Schwartz's central argument in that text, that "gambling unites humanity," is borne out through his compelling retelling of what he calls the evolution of gambling.[14] Schwartz defines gambling as a human practice that transcends temporal periodization, cultural affiliation, and social stratification. His project is an expansive one, bridging 5,000 years of human history and all the continents. This book has a narrower focus: the creation of industrial forms of

---

[11] N. Silver, *The Signal and the Noise: Why So Many Predictions Fail – But Some Don't* (Penguin Press, 2012), 118–22.
[12] Reith, *The Age of Chance*, 30.
[13] D. G. Schwartz, *Roll the Bones: The History of Gambling* (Gotham Books, 2006).
[14] Schwartz, *Roll the Bones*, xviii.

casino gambling and their proliferation within the ecology of the European spa resort in the nineteenth and early twentieth centuries. Schwartz provides a panoramic view of gambling; my aim is more modest: a dive into the social, cultural, and intellectual frameworks generated by European casino gambling in a critical time of change and transformation.

Other scholars of gambling have produced similarly focused studies to useful effect. Thomas M. Kavanagh's *Enlightenment and the Shadows of Chance: The Novel and the Culture of Gambling in Eighteenth-Century France* connects gambling, the origins of probability theory, and the birth of the novel in the French Enlightenment.[15] Kavanagh's argument – that a juxtaposition of enlightenment thinking and a mania for gambling presents a paradox that continues to inform how we orient ourselves in the world – is supported through his rich analyses of literary texts, joining them in valuable ways to social practice and cultural position. The resulting study, which connects "the emergence of the novel to the problematics of chance, gambling, and probability theory," makes a strong case for a cultural history of gambling that is connected to the social, economic, and political dynamics of a particular time.[16] In Kavanagh's view, Enlightenment France and the court society of Versailles produced a dramatic reconfiguration of how people understood probability and chance. Kavanagh notes the existence of a perplexing paradox: eighteenth-century France was obsessed with gambling, and it was also obsessed with "coherent systems of reason, law, or nature."[17] Examining the interplay between these two ways of understanding the operation of the world allows Kavanagh to frame gambling as something more significant than a mere pastime or type of leisure. Gambling – and its representation in cultural forms like the novel – provided new ways to probe questions about chaos, order, and meaning. Kavanagh pursues this line of inquiry in another valuable text, *Cards, Dice, and Wheels: A Different History of French Culture*.[18] While confining his analysis to francophone texts, Kavanagh embarks on a longer historical view of gambling in France, positioning it as a way to understand larger shifts and transformations in French life. His source material ranges from

---

[15] T. M. Kavanagh, *Enlightenment and the Shadows of Chance: The Novel and the Culture of Gambling in Eighteenth-Century France* (The Johns Hopkins University Press, 1993).
[16] Kavanagh, *Enlightenment and the Shadows of Chance*, xi.
[17] Kavanagh, *Enlightenment and the Shadows of Chance*, 1.
[18] T. M. Kavanagh, *Dice, Cards, Wheels: A Different History of French Culture* (University of Pennsylvania Press, 2005).

medieval texts to contemporary ones, allowing Kavanagh to produce a transformed vision of the contours of French history.

Schwartz's panoramic view of the history of gambling is one strategy to understanding its importance. Kavanagh's focus on French gambling is another. Other historians have pursued the issues in different ways. Mark Braude focuses narrowly on Monte Carlo, producing a wonderful account that combines business history with social, political, and cultural analysis.[19] By focusing on Monaco and its relationship to resort gambling, from its inception in the mid-nineteenth century to today, Braude is able to do more than just provide the history of a "gambling town."[20] Instead, he writes the history of gambling at Monte Carlo as just one part of a larger story about place-making in the Mediterranean. Everett John Carter's equally illuminating dissertation, "The Green Table: Gambling Casinos, Capitalist Culture, and Modernity in Nineteenth-Century Germany," uncovers the development of Rhenish casino gambling and positions it as a sign of the "legitimation of a credit economy" and a significant element within a "culture of corporate and finance capitalism."[21] I have benefited from reading each of these works. Carter illuminates critical aspects of German casino gambling in the nineteenth century; Braude's work carries that story into the Mediterranean zone and into the twentieth century.

One of the crucial insights coming from the work of these scholars is that gambling is not something peripheral to historical change; it is central to it. As Kavanagh explains, "Rather than a curious underworld set apart from the larger society, gambling brings with it a hidden and ignored, yet rich and provocative history of the tensions and conflicts that prevailed with the broader culture."[22] In short, gambling is not something on the margins of cultural or historical significance; it is instead uniquely positioned to open a window onto fundamental questions such as how we understand time and causality, how we experience our bodies and the visceral pleasure of play, and how we navigate the constraints and possibilities of intervening in the world. Gambling lets us wrestle with big questions, and I argue that this intellectual, social, and cultural process was inflected in the nineteenth century with questions that arguably remain

---

[19] M. Braude, *Making Monte Carlo: A History of Speculation and Spectacle* (Simon & Schuster, 2016).
[20] Braude, *Making Monte Carlo*, 4.
[21] E. J. Carter, "The Green Table: Gambling Casinos, Capitalist Culture, and Modernity in Nineteenth-Century Germany," PhD dissertation, University of Illinois at Urbana-Champaign 2002, 3.
[22] Kavanagh, *Dice, Cards, Wheels*, vii.

leading ones in our world as well: What is democracy? What is the basis of society? What is luck? How do we change the world?

I argue that gambling is central to the cultural, social, and intellectual history of the nineteenth century. Studying casino gambling provides a way to see how nineteenth-century Europeans understood their changing world, even as it also reflected those changes itself. In this way, gambling was used in an explanatory capacity, one that let contemporaries probe the inner workings of the machine and the creation of knowledge. Gambling has only attracted serious scholarly attraction since the 1990s, but it is increasingly clear that if we want to understand the intricate dance of society, culture, politics, and ideas, then gambling is a useful tool to pry open these different stories, allowing us to see better large historical transformations.

Readers will be introduced in the course of this book to a varied cast of characters and modes of analysis. The source material for this book gives voice to diverse perspectives related to gambling. While much of the material comes from the European context, I have also included North American sources when they spoke in interesting ways to the issues at hand. Some of the sources are ephemeral publications that no doubt had a small readership; others were mass publications that enjoyed popular acclaim and stimulated review and discussion. Novels, memoirs, biographies, pamphlets, newspapers, travel reports, and scientific and mathematical materials are treated as equally indicative of the culture of the time even if they require different modes of analysis and interpretation. In the course of this book, readers will consider how contemporary biographies of key people were used to shape understandings of the narrative history of casino gambling. We will also consider emerging genres of travel writing – travel guides as well as didactic texts that not only served to locate gambling in specific contexts but also gave readers an education in gambling that would allow them to participate knowledgeably in the practice. Other contemporary sources – from newspapers and diaries to letters and postcards – provide evidence of the growing culture of leisure associated with resort casinos. Pro-gambling texts produced a range of laudatory descriptions of the practice, while moralizing ones warned of the dangers of casino gambling. Fictional accounts – by authors as well known as E. T. A. Hoffmann and Fyodor Dostoyevsky and less-familiar ones like Margaret de Vere Stacpoole – set in resort casinos allow analysis of the cultural meanings associated with gambling in the nineteenth century. The work of social scientists like Georg Simmel and Thorstein Veblen is placed alongside mathematical and philosophical texts (from figures as varied as the industrialist Hiram Maxim, the eugenicist Karl Pearson, and the mathematician John Venn) in order to pull back the curtain on the ways gambling and the casino were integrated into late nineteenth-century analyses of social and human development. Through an analysis of a range of psychological, pedagogical, and medical texts we explore how gambling produced new ways of understanding human behavior and agency.

The analysis of gambling in this book is focused on the nineteenth and early twentieth centuries. Other scholars, notably Thomas Kavanagh, have provided detailed analyses of eighteenth-century developments, a period in which gambling reached new heights of popularity and critical concern. This book focuses on the nineteenth century, in part because this was a period of time when new developments in communication, transportation, politics, and intellectual life permitted the development of a mass form of gambling. This is not to say, of course, that gambling was not richly and widely enjoyed in earlier periods. Rather, I argue that the nineteenth century was a critical period when gambling was institutionalized in novel contexts and when gamblers participated in the wholesale transformation of European society and culture.

The book consists of three sections. The first – Chapters 1–3 – traces the evolution of gambling in the nineteenth century and then investigates the spatial qualities of casino gaming. Moving from the outer to the inner, chapters in this section consider the development of resorts and resort towns and the architectural qualities of casinos and gambling rooms. We consider in this section how new leisure practices that developed after the Napoleonic Wars, combined with revolutions in transportation and communication, rejuvenated gambling in the resort towns of the Rhineland and the Mediterranean. The next sections initiate an analysis of what casino gambling was thought to mean to people at the time. The second section (Chapters 4 and 5) probes the ways that gambling and fate intersected in the nineteenth-century casino, looking at the ways that gambling inflected ideas about probability, chance, and luck. I argue in this section that refinements in the field of probability, coupled with the use of the casino as an experimental space for mathematicians and then amplified through popular culture, provided a way for people in the nineteenth century to ruminate on the meanings of history, chance, and luck in especially pointed ways. The third section focuses on the body, again following a trajectory that moves from the outside in. We consider in Chapters 6–8 how gambling affected the body, how it excited emotions, and how the "psychology" of the gambler was evaluated. The chapters in this section use the work of social scientists, psychologists, novelists, and even educators to evaluate the ways that gambling was both cause and symptom of the changed ways that people experienced their bodies, understood emotion and behavior, and assessed compulsion and pleasure. The final chapter considers the larger question of what gambling was, contemplating the ways that gambling was deployed as a heuristic device that opened up opportunities to understand in fresh ways theories about aggression, play, and human development.

The book unfolds in a particular way: moving from narrative history to a discussion of the mechanics of gambling in the nineteenth century. Along the way, it also dives into the questions that contemporaries posed of the practice, but which were anchored in a basic problem: what is gambling doing to us? Each section may be read independently, and while there is a logic to the development of the argument across the chapters, it is not necessary to read them in order.

CHAPTER I

Gambling in the Nineteenth Century

Gambling in its modern form was invented in the nineteenth century. The resort casino, built in an environmentally or politically desirable location, attracted a wide range of people from around the world to an atmosphere of luxury, leisure, and cultural cultivation. Visitors to European casinos in the nineteenth century traveled there by steamship or by locomotive; they stayed in hotels and ate meticulously prepared foods; they listened to music performed by artists on tour and caught up on global and regional affairs by reading newspapers from around the world. And of course, they lost money in immense quantities in the gambling rooms. Built upon an existing network of health-conscious spa towns in the Rhineland, and then relocating to the Riviera in the 1860s, nineteenth-century casino life gave expression to bourgeois demands for leisure, luxury, and levity. This system was the product of two French men – twin brothers – Louis and François Blanc. The innovations developed by the Blancs transformed the experience and logic of gambling in Europe.

Louis and François Blanc were born on December 12, 1806. Their father died before their birth. The brothers left their village as early as was practical and were itinerant workers and con artists. One of their early initiatives included opening a bank in Bordeaux and using the capital to invest in the stock market. The Blancs developed an intricate – and illegal – communications system with Paris that involved bribing semaphore operators to insert coded trading instructions into official messages in which agents in Paris relayed information about the Parisian bond market from the capital. Using this system, the Blancs earned 100,000 francs between 1834 and 1836. When their system was inadvertently discovered (an attempt to correct a coded misspelling led to the unraveling of the scheme), the Blancs were arrested for bribery and corrupting officials. The trial revealed all sorts of information about the methods at work on the Bourse, and the Blancs, although convicted, were given light sentences. Stock market manipulation, while lucrative, was only an appetizer for the

Blanc brothers. Stung by the experience, the brothers relocated to Paris and began to frequent the Palais-Royale, the center of vice and gambling in both the city of Paris and Europe as a whole.[1]

The Palais-Royale, which served as the official residence of the Orleans dynasty, grew by the early nineteenth century to include a range of commercial and leisure spaces open to the general public. These suites included spaces in which visitors could play various games, lay a wide variety of bets, and mix with social types of their choosing. These casinos, modeled on older forms like those found in Venice, also reflected an expansion of gambling out of court society and into other social arenas.[2] The segmentation of the palace matched the segmentation of the gambling trade in Paris. Once in the capital city, the Blancs joined forces with Jacques Bénazet, a club owner who instructed the twins in the intricacies of dealing, banking, and casino management after he hired them to oversee operations at his Palais-Royale casinos (Bénazet, like his protégés the Blancs, would also relocate to the Rhineland, taking the casino concession in Baden-Baden). The apprenticeship in casino management that Bénazet gave the Blanc twins proved indispensable when they later launched their own enterprise. The Palais-Royale's dominance over the European gambling market was to be short-lived, however, a victim of political revolution.[3]

Ascending the French throne after the revolution of 1830, King Louis-Philippe banned gambling in France beginning January 1, 1838, perhaps in part to reclaim his family's dynastic residence from the public. Egon Corti, a biographer of François Blanc, notes that Louis-Philippe responded to gambling at the Palais-Royale in vexed ways. "Even at the beginning of the king's reign it had been a thorn in his side that in the Palais-Royale, so closely connected with the House of Orleans, all kinds of human passion had opportunity for satisfaction."[4] This change in the legal status of gambling in French territory had important ramifications. When the

---

[1] See M. Braude's rich history of Monte Carlo for a detailed account of the Blanc brothers' activities. *Making Monte Carlo: A History of Speculation and Spectacle* (Simon & Schuster, 2016), 1–11.

[2] D. G. Schwartz, *Roll the Bones: The History of Gambling* (Gotham Books, 2006), 95. Historian David Schwartz explains that the first state-run casino was established in Venice in 1638. Later iterations of the institution included a dress code as well as a heterosocial clientele. When the Great Council of Venice voted to close the Ridotto in 1774, gambling was simply driven into other underground spaces.

[3] Braude, *Making Monte Carlo*, 11–14. For a general overview of the July Revolution, see D. H. Pinkney, *French Revolution of 1830* (Princeton University Press, 1972); S. Kroen, *Politics and Theater: The Crisis of Legitimacy in Restoration France, 1815–1830* (University of California Press, 2000).

[4] E. C. Corti, *The Wizard of Monte Carlo* (E. P. Dutton, 1935), 30.

gambling halls were closed in France, casinos and gamblers relocated to Switzerland and the Rhenish territories under German control – places where gambling remained legal and in which the "passion for gaming could be indulged in undisturbed by the State, and continued to exert its attraction over all."[5] Indeed, the Rhineland had developed a reputation for a permissive attitude toward gambling during the Napoleonic Wars. The warfare that engulfed central Europe, and the migrations of opposing armies across the region, brought new cultural influences and social forms in their wake. The Napoleonic Wars, as one critic notes, "with their comings and goings of soldiers devoted to gambling, had spread the passion for games of chance to such an extent that they had become a part of everyday life."[6]

Bad Homburg's growth as a spa town and resort developed in the wake of Louis-Philippe's ban on gambling in France. The Blanc brothers, no longer able to ply their new skills in Paris, moved along. They stopped first in Luxembourg, where François Blanc met his wife Magdeleine-Victoire Huguelin (with whom he later had two children). Soon after, the Blancs left to settle in the Rhineland, at Bad Homburg, where they quickly sought to arrange a concession that would permit them to open their own casino. The Landgrave of Hesse-Homburg, Ludwig, ruled over a tiny and impoverished polity along the Rhine River. The territory, which had lost its independence in 1806 only to regain it again thanks to the Congress of Vienna in 1815, had little in the way of infrastructure, commerce, or agriculture. Faced with these economic constraints, the Landgrave sought new forms of revenue that could produce economic stability, if not livelihood. A gambling concession and an improved space for a casino provided an answer, and the Blanc twins proved to be willing partners. The initial plan called for a partnership between the Blancs and Landgrave Phillip, who took the title in 1839 upon his brother's death. A deal was struck in July 1840: the Blancs would construct a pump room (costing 100,000 francs), which would become the property of the Landgrave when it was completed in 1842; the Blancs would lease the facilities from the Landgrave and have a gambling concession in effect until 1871. The deal was signed in August 1839, and construction began in 1841.[7]

[5] Corti, *The Wizard of Monte Carlo*, 32.   [6] Corti, *The Wizard of Monte Carlo*, 31–32.
[7] Corti, *The Wizard of Monte Carlo*, 27–44. E. J. Carter, "The Green Table: Gambling Casinos, Capitalist Culture, and Modernity in Nineteenth-Century Germany," PhD dissertation, University of Illinois at Urbana-Champaign, 2002, 36–38.

The partnership marked the beginning of a symbiotic relationship between the ancestral lords of Hesse-Homburg and the Blancs, as well as a rejuvenated Bad Homburg. The *Homburger Kur- und Bade-List*, which recorded visitors to the town between 1834 and 1918, indicates that 829 visitors came in 1839, the year Phillip took the title (this does not include hundreds of other "strangers traveling through" whose names appear in the text).[8] The *Kur- und Bade-List* records 870 visitors in 1841 (when the casino opened partway through the year) and 1,732 in 1842, the first full year of operations. Some 5,137 visitors came in 1847, the year before the 1848 revolutions impeded travel. This growth in the number of visitors was due in part to changes that the Blancs introduced, innovations like the practice of keeping the resort open for a longer season, which attracted an aristocratic Russian clientele who fled the bitter Russian winters for the comparatively mild ones in the Rhineland. These successes encouraged the Blancs to take their business public, selling shares of stock in the concern on the stock exchange.[9] This promising start would be tarnished in 1852. First Louis Blanc died, and he was followed by François's wife, Magdeleine-Victoire Huguelin. François hired a governess, the German Marie Hensel, to whom he was married in 1854. The two had a child soon after.

The Blanc twins were central to the development of gambling in Europe in the nineteenth century, a period during which, Gerda Reith argues, Europeans saw the development and proliferation of games that possessed a "highly numerical nature."[10] The innovations that the two Blancs brought to bear on the logic of gambling once they were established in the Rhineland were nothing less than transformative. The brothers developed the use of print advertising to promote the spa and its casinos, and a range of subsidiary industries developed alongside the casino that catered to the influx of new visitors, including a robust hospitality industry.[11] The Blancs also began to think about gambling in a new way. They sought to

---

[8] "Homburger Kur- und Badelisten: Die Quellen im Faksimile: LAGIS Hessen," www.lagis-hessen.de/de/klhg/browse. The Homburg archives have digitized the texts and made them publicly available. There is also an impressive data visualization and digital humanities site that allows exploration of the data published in the *Kur- und Bade-List*: www.lagis-hessen.de/de/klhg.

[9] Braude, *Making Monte Carlo*, 23.

[10] G. Reith, *The Age of Chance: Gambling in Western Culture* (Routledge, 1999), 80.

[11] The *Kur- und Bade-List*, for instance, included advertisements for new books, Havana cigars, foreign-language education, as well as artistic representations of scenes both local and further away. Regarding the growth of hotels in Bad Homburg, the initial lists of visitors from the 1830s indicated that people stayed in private homes. By the 1840s, however, visitors were often categorized by the hotels in which they stayed.

use luxury and a suite of correlated pleasures (excellent restaurants, reading rooms with free international newspapers, musical performances, and so on) to bring people to the casino. While gambling may have been the primary lure, a trip to the spa could be represented as a sumptuous cultural experience. The Blancs envisioned their casino, in other words, as an institution that should exist as something more than just a gambling hall. The resort should seek to entertain and amuse in a variety of ways, all of which cost money. Attracting the right type of clientele was a key to success in the endeavor. Egon Corti explains that the Blancs sought to build a resort at which "the stay in Homburg must be pleasurable and so attract distinguished, but above all, rich foreigners."[12] Advertising the resort was therefore a key principle to the development of its reputation and of its money-generating potential. And of course, the resort was also presented as a wholesome oasis for restoration. The healthful benefits of Bad Homburg's water were promoted by the Blancs' colleague Dr. Gardey, based on the results of a chemical analysis done at the Sorbonne.

Construction on the casino began in May 1841. The foundation-laying was a spectacle. Although the Landgrave did not appear, he did send representatives. Corti explains that the Landgrave felt that the entire show was somewhat undignified, and he also was worried about potential embarrassment in the event the casino enterprise failed. Seeking further capital to support the construction and expansion of the infrastructure at Bad Homburg, the Blancs sought to secure a loan from the Rothschilds, who demanded transparency and government subvention. Privy Councilor Heinrich of Hesse-Homburg, however, was stunned at the profits already generated and urged the state of Hesse-Homburg to simply loan the Blancs the capital, thereby cutting the Rothschilds out of the deal. The casino was completed in August 1843 and opened on the night of August 16. While some gambling in the small pump room that the Landgrave had built earlier was already underway, the grand opening represented a shift in the way spa gambling would be carried out. To mark the occasion, the Blancs provided a huge celebration feast – which, unlike the foundation-laying ceremony, the Landgrave attended – but the Blancs maintained modesty, donating all proceeds to charity. Visitors to the casino on that opening night would have been surveyed by staff; those who presented themselves at the door poorly dressed, looking obviously like a worker or a peasant, were forbidden entry. Those appearing rich or of high birth were treated with extreme deference. The Blancs set table limits to ensure that no run of

---

[12] Corti, *The Wizard of Monte Carlo*, 45.

misfortune ruined the opening of their casino. One could bet 4,000 gulden on even chances and 120 gulden on single numbers at the roulette table.

Prior to the arrival of the Blancs and the creation of the casino at Bad Homburg, gambling in the spa towns of the Rhineland was relatively unrefined. The gambling at Baden-Baden and Ems remained primitive, operating according to a set of principles unfamiliar to us today. "The strange thing about spa gambling," historian Mark Braude explains, "was how little money, or at the least gaining of it, seems to have figured into the practice. Instead, this wagering formed part of a larger and more elaborate social ritual of aristocratic privilege."[13] It is important to note the continuation of eighteenth-century social forms – gaming – in nineteenth-century social spaces. Thomas Kavanagh explains that for France, at least, gambling's heyday was located in the period from Louis XIV to the Revolution, when aristocratic forms set the tone for other social classes.[14] When those social forms were no longer expressed within court society, but within the space of the nineteenth-century casino, new possibilities emerged. Gambling did not serve a primarily economic function. Instead, Braude argues, gambling functioned as an ersatz warfare that a defanged nobility could use to demonstrate the qualities of aristocratic bearing in a tamed way. Kavanagh's work on eighteenth-century gaming in France demonstrates that aristocratic gambling practices – such as the highly developed gaming at the court at Versailles – were implicated in the larger dynamics of court intrigue and noble competition. The social life of courtly gambling, dominated by the nobility, provided tangible markers of wit, status, and wealth. The competitive nature of the games, in which players competed against one another, stands in contrast to the social dynamics of nineteenth-century casino gambling, which tended to be of an aleatory rather than an agonistic nature.[15] In other words, players did not compete directly against one another; instead, they played against the house.

No longer able to assert social dominance by virtue of their battlefield victories (and no doubt reeling from the implications of the French Revolution and the democratic movements of the early nineteenth

---

[13] Braude, *Making Monte Carlo*, 19.
[14] T. M. Kavanagh, *Dice, Cards, Wheels: A Different History of French Culture* (University of Pennsylvania Press, 2005), 68.
[15] Kavanagh, *Dice, Cards, Wheels*; T. M. Kavanagh, *Enlightenment and the Shadows of Chance: The Novel and the Culture of Gambling in Eighteenth-Century France* (The Johns Hopkins University Press, 1993).

century), mid-nineteenth-century members of the nobility sought alternate avenues to demonstrate their social validity. Braude notes that gambling was especially useful to the nobility as a way of instigating duels that could be used to demonstrate physically the aristocratic bearing of the participants. François Blanc, however, changed the social environment of Bad Homburg in key ways to transform this aspect of spa life. As we will see, Blanc exploited a new population of middle-class resort-goers who sought access to the rhythms of aristocratic life, and who might play new games for higher stakes, thus replacing aristocratic hierarchies based on birth with bourgeois ones centered on economic exchange and monetary value. In response to this social demand of his bourgeois customers, Blanc made the casino at Bad Homburg focus exclusively on games like roulette and Trent et Quarante, which were "communal games" in which players played against the house (and not against each other). He also eliminated the double-zero on the wheel, which meant that he could publicize Bad Homburg as having the best odds in Europe, allowing his casino to compete directly with Ems, Baden-Baden, and Wiesbaden for customers.[16] It is significant that Blanc's casino was anchored in roulette, which despite its earlier figurations as a mere "wheel of fortune" had by the nineteenth century developed into a highly engineered and finely calibrated machine. Like other aspects of nineteenth-century life, roulette represented an industrial form of an earlier design. Perhaps part of the attraction of these games existed partially in the fact that roulette, as one critic from the early twentieth century notes, is a game of "intellectual mediocrity ... which required practically no thought," and so was suited to a highly social environment.[17] The Blancs also instituted rule changes for Trente et Quarante (a card game with betting rules similar to roulette) that made the odds better for visiting gamblers. By losing some of the margins associated with gambling, the Blancs sought to overcome that problem by attracting a greater volume of gamblers to the casino at Bad Homburg.

Part of the same social class as his bourgeois clientele, Blanc was a careful businessman. Profits from the casino were reinvested into other areas of resort life that spoke to its new status as a locus of leisure: better food, free hunting, scientifically quantified curative waters, talented orchestras, and so on. Needless to say, these improvements were carried out with an eye toward meeting the goal of keeping the clientele at the casino as long as possible. The result, as one critic in the early twentieth

---

[16] Braude, *Making Monte Carlo*, 22.   [17] Corti, *The Wizard of Monte Carlo*, 32–33.

century put it, was that in the Rhineland people "gambled with passionate enthusiasm."[18] The passion for gambling was cultivated in precise ways. While some critics, like Karl August Varnagen von Ense, depicted Bad Homburg as being little more than a "nest of vagabonds, adventurers, cut-purses and disreputable women," most saw the resort in a much more positive light.[19] Russians were drawn to Bad Homburg, especially the aristocrats, who Corti argues were "immensely rich, luxurious and plea-sure-loving." Furthermore, "as was only natural, the mania for gambling found easy victims among them, the women being especially addicted to it."[20] The opportunity for rubbing shoulders with rich Russian aristocrats that Bad Homburg presented provided a key to understanding the attrac-tions of the resort more generally. Indeed, Blanc transformed gambling by infusing it with a sense of democratic opportunity. In the opinion of one observer in the early twentieth century, Blanc "was the first man to democratize the vice of gambling, which before his time had been almost the monopoly of the idler and the aristocrat."[21] The same critic declares that the social environment of the casino gave concrete expression to the characteristically nineteenth-century bourgeois myth of the self-made man: "The great clubs which provided gilded youth and moneyed age with opportunities for demonstrating their inherent stupidity black-balled the self-made man and disdained the society of social inferiors. Blanc created a club for the whole world and charged no entrance fee. He threw it open to both sexes and made no inquiries as to the antecedents of his clients."[22] The heterosocial space of the casino in Bad Homburg – the mixture of social classes and genders – helped generate its appeal.

The casino and resort that Blanc crafted at Bad Homburg was spectac-ularly successful. In 1847, the *Kur- und Bade-List* reported that 5,137 people visited Bad Homburg. Profits for the half-year ending March 1, 1848, totaled 273,514 gulden (double what was earned in 1842–43).[23] The result was economic tranquility and social peace in Hesse-Homburg. Indeed, an early biographer of François Blanc remarks that "from the Landgrave down to the least of his subjects, everybody in this little principality, which had been wretched not long since, could live in perfect indifference to the rest of the world, with their eyes fixed upon the casino,

[18] Corti, *The Wizard of Monte Carlo*, 31.   [19] Quoted in Corti, *The Wizard of Monte Carlo*, 53.
[20] Corti, *The Wizard of Monte Carlo*, 54.
[21] C. Kingston, *The Romance of Monte Carlo* (J. L. the Bodley Head, 1925), 49.
[22] Kingston, *The Romance of Monte Carlo*, 49.   [23] Corti, *The Wizard of Monte Carlo*, 62.

the success of which was producing such a magical revival throughout these territories."[24]

The tranquility of success was imperiled again by political developments in Europe. If the Blancs were ingenious builders of bourgeois sociability and culture, those same qualities exposed their enterprise to the stress and strain of the 1848–49 Revolutions that swept France and the German-speaking territories of the Rhineland in different ways but with similar intensity.[25] The 1848 Revolutions were serious threats to the stability of the casino at Bad Homburg. The Frankfurt Parliament (which sought to unify Germany according to bourgeois principles) debated outlawing gambling in the German-speaking lands. The Landgrave, incensed at this threat to his sovereignty (a sentiment widely shared among European nobles), vigorously defended his right to ordain legal gambling in his territory. A legal ban on gambling that affected all the spa towns in the Rhineland was passed by the Frankfurt Parliament in January 1849, and this – at least for the Blancs – raised important legal questions about the status of a concession granted by a sovereign prince but then revoked by the national assembly without compensation. When the Blancs vowed to keep the casino in Bad Homburg open despite this change in its legal status, the Frankfurt Parliament resorted to military might to enforce its will. The Parliament sent a column of Austrian troops to close the casinos; when they faced no military opposition (the Landgrave lacked an army), the Austrian troops demanded the closure of the casino. The Landgrave's Privy Councilor was forced to concede the reality of the situation, and he ordered the casinos closed. The *Kur- und Bade-List* indicates that the closure spurred a steep decline in the number of visitors to Bad Homburg. More than 5,000 people visited the town in 1847. That number dropped to 4,029 in the revolutionary year of 1848. The record shows that 3,628 came to Bad Homburg in 1849 before rebounding to 6,624 in 1850. The Blancs demanded compensation for their losses, and they also began converting the casino from a public institution to a private, "closed" one that required an entry ticket. Once the Assembly collapsed (when it too was confronted with a military force that sought to close its doors in the spring of 1849) and its authority was absent, Bad Homburg reverted to business as usual. The Revolutions of 1848 are often described (at least in some phases of the turmoil) as "bourgeois revolutions" in that

---

[24] Corti, *The Wizard of Monte Carlo*, 62.
[25] For an overview of the 1848 Revolutions, see P. N. Stearns, *1848: The Revolutionary Tide in Europe* (Norton, 1974).

they gave voice to the political aspirations of an emergent social class that sought to craft a legal regime based on legal equality and the rule of law. As socially mobile as they were entrepreneurial, the Blancs fit this mold. Indeed, early biographers of François Blanc note that while he was a gambler, "there was this difference between him and his clients, that, whereas they were the slaves of a passion, or of one of those 'infallible' systems which have never yet triumphed over chance, and the fortune depended upon the chance of the cards, Blanc succeeded in shaping his own fate by bold foresight, clever organization and skillful modifications of the rules of play when he found that he was losing."[26] Blanc embodied, in other words, a suite of bourgeois cultural values.

Writing in 1860, George Sala noted the impacts of the 1848 revolution on gambling in the Rhineland. "It is due to the fierce democrats who revolted against the monarchs of the defunct Holy Alliance," Sala explains, "to say that they utterly swept away the gambling-tables in Rhenish-Prussia, and in the Grand Duchy of Baden."[27] While Bad Homburg dodged the threat of permanent closure, other spa towns had a different experience. Aachen was controlled by the Kingdom of Prussia, and therefore experienced a different legal environment. Having evaded the risk that the German states would make gambling illegal, the Blancs soon were faced with another problem: that the new French government might reverse its stance on the legality of gambling. Thus, a major question facing the Blancs during the 1848 revolution was whether or not Louis Napoleon would authorize gambling in France after he took power in December 1848. Realizing that if France relegalized gambling, the profitability of their casino would be endangered, the Blancs tried to arrange a nationwide concession or to keep the ban in effect as a way of creating a monopoly or at least diminishing the risk of competition for the casino at Bad Homburg. As the varying experiences of Paris, Bad Homburg, and Aachen demonstrate, the legal environment – and the patchwork of various polities making up the Rhineland – generated vastly different outcomes.

After the collapse of the Frankfurt Parliament and the continuing illegality of gambling in France removed the most tangible threats to his growing business, François Blanc expanded his operations in Bad

---

[26] Corti, *The Wizard of Monte Carlo*, 93.
[27] G. A. Sala, *Make Your Game, or, The Adventures of the Stout Gentleman, the Slim Gentleman, and the Man with the Iron Chest: A Narrative of the Rhine and Thereabouts* (Ward and Lock, 1860), 192, see n.

Homburg. Even when experiencing misfortune, he sought to use those experiences to expand the reputation of the casino at Bad Homburg.[28] For instance, when Prince Charles Lucien Bonaparte (one of Napoleon I's nephews) came to Bad Homburg in September 1852, he experienced a run of good fortune that nearly broke the bank on several occasions. Indeed, Bonaparte had at one point won 560,000 francs, forcing Blanc to consider lowering the betting limits, and reintroducing the double-zero (on the roulette wheel) and the double refait (in the card game Trente et Quarante). Even this episode was used to heighten the allure of Bad Homburg. Because the winner – Prince Bonaparte – was famous, he could be used as good press for the casino, thereby generating more traffic through its doors. Blanc's ability to create publicity from bad fortune was legendary, and the casino's stature as the premiere gambling resort was unparalleled. Appearing in novels like Fyodor Dostoyevsky's *The Gambler*, Bad Homburg was depicted as the high point on a gambler's journey through the Rhineland. As one character in that novel explains, "and then – then straight to Homburg. I won't go to Roulettenburg, except maybe next year. Indeed, they say that it's a bad omen to try your luck twice in a row at the same table, and the real gambling is in Homburg."[29]

Despite its international reputation as a place where "real gambling" could be found, Bad Homburg was still subject to larger geopolitical forces developing in the 1850s and 1860s. Of these, none were perhaps as potent as the desire for German unification.[30] While German unification had been a dream of German nationalists since the late eighteenth century, it was only first expressed in concrete political terms in the course of the 1848 Revolution. During the revolution, there was a debate among German nationalists about how to unify the country, and which political entities would be included. One proposal from the Parliament came in the form of an offer to the King of Prussia, Frederick William IV, that he take the crown of a unified Germany. The offer was summarily refused (and Frederick William IV made no secret of his feelings about accepting a "crown from the gutter"). More importantly, the offer generated an impression that if German unification were to occur, it would come

---

[28] Corti, *The Wizard of Monte Carlo*, 98–99.
[29] F. Dostoyevsky, *The Gambler and Other Stories* (Penguin, 2010), 263.
[30] For the winding path and competing visions of German unification, see O. Pflanze, *The Unification of Germany, 1848–1871* (R. E. Krieger Pub. Co., 1979); C. M. Clark, *Iron Kingdom: The Rise and Downfall of Prussia, 1600–1947* (Allen Lane, 2006); H. Walser Smith, *Germany: A Nation in Its Time: Before, during, and after Nationalism, 1500–2000* (Liveright Publishing, 2022).

through Prussian – and not Austrian – leadership, in part because German nationalists did not wish to include non-German Habsburg territories (Hungary, for instance) in a unified Germany. And if Prussia was to engineer German unification, as they did over the course of the 1850s and 1860s, culminating in the creation of the German Empire in January 1871, that meant that Prussian legal standards would likely be extended to other German states.

After facing the threat that his casino in Bad Homburg could be closed by political authorities over whom he exercised little control, François Blanc began seeking alternate locations to expand his gambling enterprises. He was particularly drawn to undemocratic and authoritarian places to relocate, apparently feeling that they provided a safer environment. One of his biographers asserts that Blanc "had learnt many lessons since his arrival at Homburg, and the principal one was that an ideal gambling den must not ruin the locals but must take its toll entirely from visitors. That meant his next patron must be in a position to ignore the sentiments of his subjects, and as nearly all Europe had become either uncomfortably democratic or superficially moral his choice was limited."[31] Blanc correctly perceived that the extension of Prussian law would threaten gambling in the Rhineland, prompting him to investigate other European locations where his casinos could continue to operate free of interference. The Principality of Monaco – an isolated and economically distressed backwater far from the centers of European power – beckoned.

Monaco endured a slow decline over the course of the first half of the nineteenth century. Like Hesse-Homburg, the principality faced economic turmoil, and it was in many ways cut off from the centers of European commercial and political action. One analysis of Monaco posits that the area had long been a "robber state" that had survived in the medieval and early modern periods by levying tolls on passing ships. Because this was ultimately unsustainable by the nineteenth century, new extractive practices needed to be developed. If nothing else, Monaco and its leaders recognized that the polity needed to adapt if it was to survive. Threatened with absorption into either France or Italy, the tiny state needed a secure economic basis if it was to remain independent. François Blanc helped provide a key to that particular problem.

In 1855, Caroline of Monaco sent emissaries to the Rhineland to observe the resorts and determine if gambling and spa living might provide a way out of the death spiral facing the principality. Caroline sent the

[31] Kingston, *The Romance of Monte Carlo*, 7.

lawyer Adolphe Eynaud to Bad Homburg to see what opportunity looked like.[32] According to historian Mark Braude, Eynaud told the ruler, Prince Florestan, that once gambling was made legal in Monaco the fusion of spa resort and casino gambling could extricate Monaco from its predicament. "The bathing establishment [in Monaco]," Eynaud explained to the Prince, "should in a sense act as a façade for the gambling establishment."[33] Despite its host of other problems, Monaco enjoyed certain geographical attributes: situated alongside Cannes and Nice on the Mediterranean coast, it was the only spot with a legal casino in the area, and it was also an early adopter of the spa resort mentality that was beginning in cities all along the Mediterranean coast.

If resort gambling offered Monaco a way to prosper, the question that remained was how casino gambling could be organized and encouraged in the tiny state. In 1855 Eynaud and Prince Florestan put together a plan for a new company that would administer gambling in Monaco and encourage an economic revitalization of the area.[34] The Sociéte Anonyme des Bain de Mer et du Cercle des Étrangers à Monaco (usually shortened to SBM) would facilitate the sale of gambling concessions on the market, and then oversee the operations of any casinos that were put into place. The plan was enacted, and a gambling concession was sold. Two Parisians took the concession, and when Florestan died in 1856, his son, Charles III, took the throne. Monaco's first casino opened in December 1856. Blanc – always attuned to the development of new threats to his business – sent several of his trusted croupiers to work at the new casino at Monaco and to report back to him on the situation. According to Braude, Blanc's spies found the situation to be dire, and boring. Very few people came to gamble, and the casinos were on the brink of bankruptcy. The concession changed hands, ending up in the control of Pierre August Daval, who poured his limited resources into the concession and quickly found himself two million francs in debt. Hostilities associated with Italian unification damaged business, and Daval transferred his rights to the concession to the Duc de Valmy.[35]

Charles recognized that the hoped-for revenue from casino gambling was pathetically small, so he began to think about ways of attracting someone like Blanc – who had the financial resources and casino

[32] Braude, *Making Monte Carlo*, 34.   [33] Braude, *Making Monte Carlo*, 35.
[34] G. Saige, *Monaco, ses origines et son histoire; d'après les documents originaux* (Impr. de Monaco, 1897), 487–89.
[35] Corti, *The Wizard of Monte Carlo*, 137–74.

experience to make the concern viable – to Monaco. Charles explained to Eynaud that "Blanc knows that everything still remains to be done at Monaco, but he performed a similar feat at Homburg twenty years ago; for he found it a little out-of-the-way country town, and transformed it into an attractive spa. He knows that in order to attract visitors we must offer them comfort and amusement."[36] Eynaud echoed these sentiments back to Charles, telling him that "M. Blanc is colossally rich; he created Homburg as it is to-day and he is a past master in the art of dissimulating the green cloth of the gaming-tables behind a veil of luxury, elegance and pleasure. In five years' time, Monaco will have changed out of all recognition."[37]

Despite his reputation as a miracle worker whose casinos could transform the economic and social character of a region, François Blanc had reservations about the viability of gambling in Monaco. Braude reports Blanc initially dismissed Monaco as a poor choice for a casino and spa, in part because of how difficult it was to get there. A traveler could get to Monaco from Nice – the closest town with a rail line – but the voyage took three hours by carriage, followed by an hour-long hike down the hill to the settlements along the coast. Travelers coming to Monaco by sea could expect a two-hour voyage in what was described by contemporaries as a very "shaky craft."[38] Nonetheless, Blanc saw Monaco as a Wild West, free from political interference, and therefore a valuable hedge against the political fallout from potential events like the unification of the German states under Prussia. When imagining the benefits of a casino on the Riviera, Blanc expressed a vision for Monaco that moved it in the direction of a high-class resort. And yet, if gambling was going to develop in the Riviera, Blanc recognized the value in controlling it, so he sought to outmaneuver rivals from Wiesbaden who took an interest in Monaco, outflanking them in negotiations with the Duc de Valmy over the ownership of the concession.

Blanc made a low offer to Valmy for the concession and stipulated a two-day time limit for a decision. Then he took the deal off the table so he could make the voyage to the city of Monte Carlo in Monaco, meet with Charles III, and survey the properties. Blanc went to the Riviera in March 1863, and he was pleased enough with what he saw that he upped his offer to 1.5 million francs, again giving Valmy a short window of opportunity to accept or reject. Valmy seized the opportunity to rid himself of the

---

[36] Quoted in Corti, *The Wizard of Monte Carlo*, 171.
[37] Quoted in Corti, *The Wizard of Monte Carlo*, 177.   [38] Braude, *Making Monte Carlo*, 37.

gambling concession that had borne so little fruit, and on April 1, 1863, Blanc took control of the concession.[39] Despite the obvious benefits that the partnership with Blanc would bring to the tiny state of Monaco, Charles III remained skeptical due to the moral questions raised by gambling; he forbade his subjects to enter the casino except for work and he was cognizant of the ways that legalized gambling would transform the reputation of his principality. As one early twentieth-century biographer of Blanc noted, "The evil reputation which Monte Carlo acquired almost as soon as it had become the home of the greatest casino in the world was due to some extent to the equivocal policy of François Blanc and the long trail of ruined men and women he had left behind him at Homburg."[40] The prince was aware of Blanc's somewhat dubious reputation but relished the financial security that casino gambling would bring to this territory, a sentiment also expressed by the palace historian in 1863:

> We do not approve of gaming houses, and the governments who suppress them act wisely. Established in large centres of the population, they [stimulate] the spirit of cupidity, and bring about … demoralization and ruin.… But when established far from large cities, and when the distance is such that the cost of the journey can only be met by rich foreigners, one may accord such games the benefit of extenuating circumstances, for they do bring an element of prosperity to the native population, itself severely barred from entering.[41]

Blanc's vision for Monaco aligned with what he had accomplished at Bad Homburg, namely that gambling and all sorts of other non-gambling activities should coexist side by side. The luxuries of the resort setting, in other words, should help form, as Braude puts it, "an emotional bond between visitors and the resort, with the hope of turning casual gamblers into long-term clients more devoted to the ideas of his gambling town than simply to its gaming rooms."[42] To this end, the resort at Monte Carlo operated through a kind of psychology of isolation – the setting of the town and the resort, populated with foreign plants and a grand architectural style, was meant to produce a feeling of other-worldliness in visitors that would then encourage greater spending. These feelings were then reinforced with a feeling of social exclusivity maintained not only by the elite activities (as in when visitors were given the opportunity to "hunt" pigeons, for instance; see Figure 1.1) but also through the dress codes and

[39] See Corti, *The Wizard of Monte Carlo*, chapter 10, for a description of the negotiating process.
[40] Kingston, *The Romance of Monte Carlo*, 109.   [41] Quoted in Braude, *Making Monte Carlo*, 53.
[42] Braude, *Making Monte Carlo*, 57.

1738 — MONTE-CARLO.   Le Tir aux Pigeons.   ND Phot.

Figure 1.1   "Le Tir aux Pigeons" (Neurdein et Cie, ca. 1907–14). Courtesy of Watkinson Library at Trinity College, Hartford, George Watson Cole European Postcard Collection.

exclusion lists that were adopted by the casino. The surveillance of clientele and employees alike generated an impression of honesty and fairness. Having a "fair" casino was of paramount importance for bringing in rich people who merely wanted to gamble and have fun without the added risk of being fleeced or taken advantage of in ways that were not transparently clear. The entire spectacle – Thomas Kavanagh calls Blanc's Monte Carlo a "dream space" – produced an illusion that was a key to the success of the casino, and it bore resemblance to other central locations of consumerist display critical to nineteenth-century bourgeois culture.[43] "As in department stores and exhibition halls," Braude notes, "the casino put clients on display as much as the things they consumed."[44]

The quality of display was critical to Monte Carlo's success, and as we will see, Blanc exerted tight control over the resort's image. To this end, Blanc spent heavily (and engaged in back-channel wheeling and dealing) on print advertisement and friendly relationships with the editors of prominent regional, national, and international publications. His marketing genius paid off immediately. Braude reports that in Blanc's first year as director, Monaco hosted 30,000 visitors and the casino grossed 640,000 francs. One way of manufacturing the consent of the local population who had to deal with the influx of visitors was through a series of generous concessions; income tax for Monégasque citizens was abolished in February 1869.

For a ten-year period after assuming the gambling concession in Monaco, Blanc operated two casinos: Bad Homburg and Monte Carlo. The casinos were promoted as sister organizations, encouraging the clientele to shift from one to the other depending on the season. The system was an effective one, at least until Blanc's intuition about the impacts of German unification and the extension of Prussian legal norms into the Rhenish states began to seem more tangible. In comments published in 1863 in *Journal de Monaco* on the issue of gambling in Germany and its reported ban, Blanc noted that there "are growing rumors that Germany, for reasons of what can only be described as hypocritical morality and sham humanitarianism, will shortly abolish gambling. All the worse for Germany, then! And all the better for Monaco, which will not be so stupid as to commit financial suicide in order to please a few moralists whose opinions will not bear serious and impartial examination."[45] Indeed,

[43] Kavanagh, *Dice, Cards, Wheels*, 193.   [44] Braude, *Making Monte Carlo*, 66.
[45] Quoted in Corti, *The Wizard of Monte Carlo*, 189. The *Journal de Monaco* has been digitized; this edition is available at journaldemonaco.gouv.mc/Journaux/1863/Journal-0261.

Blanc's anxiety about the future of his German gambling empire was not unwarranted.

When Landgrave Ferdinand of Hesse-Homburg died heirless at the age of eighty-three in 1866, the territory was incorporated into the holdings of the Grand Duke of Hesse-Darmstadt, Louis III. Following the calamitous defeat of Austrian forces at the hands of the Prussian army in the Austro-Prussian War of 1866, the territory was included in the North German Confederation. The Prussian Reichstag did not delay in taking up the question of gambling in these newly acquired territories along the Rhine. The issue was debated in the Reichstag in December 1867, and a law banning gambling was introduced in February 1868. The bill, which was passed by a large majority, stipulated a ban on gambling that was to go into effect on January 1, 1873. Compliance with the law would be enforced by the Prussian state.

Surveying the landscape of European gambling in 1870, Andrew Steinmetz not only noted the declining number of locations where visitors could gamble legally, but he also dismissed Monaco as a somewhat dubious replacement. "The only existing continental gaming houses authorized by government," Steinmetz wrote, "are now the two Badens, Spa (of which the lease is nearly expired, and will not be renewed), Monaco (capital of the ridiculous little Italian principality, of which the suzerain is a scion of the house of 'Grimaldi'), Malmöe, in Sweden, too remote to do much harm, and HOMBOURG."[46] Steinmetz also indicated the ways the legal framework of a particular German state affected the experience of gambling: "By the Prussian Code all games of chance, except when licensed by the state, are prohibited."[47] Bavaria had a looser standard, and allowed a variety of games to be played legally, but under state observation. Cheating was punished. "Although, therefore, cheating gamblers are liable to punishment in Bavaria, it is evident that gambling is there tolerated to the utmost extent required by the votaries of Fortune."[48]

Between 1845 and 1865 the number of visits to Bad Homburg increased dramatically; visitors went from roughly 4,500 per year to more than 12,400, as reported in the *Kur- und Bade-List*. The pace accelerated until the casino at Bad Homburg was closed. To be clear, Bad Homburg was not the only German casino that felt the sting of Prussian law. The casinos at Ems and Wiesbaden were shuttered in October 1872, and Bad

---

[46] A. Steinmetz, *The Gaming Table: Its Votaries and Victims*, 2 vols. (Tinsley Brothers, 1870), vol. 1, 140.
[47] Steinmetz, *The Gaming Table*, 414. [48] Steinmetz, *The Gaming Table*, 417.

Homburg – subject to the law of 1868 – saw the last spin of the roulette wheel at 11 pm on December 31, 1872. By New Year's Day, 1873, gambling was eliminated in Bad Homburg, and the locus of action – and François Blanc's gambling empire – shifted definitively to Monaco. The *Kur- und Bade-List* demonstrates the impact of the casino closures on the number of visitors to Bad Homburg: nearly 21,000 people went to Bad Homburg in 1872; only 9,287 came the following year.

François Blanc died on July 27, 1877; Prince Charles III followed him twelve years later. Blanc's life is indicative of many important elements of nineteenth-century European history. From his sketchy start in the French financial markets to his apotheosis as the premier resort builder in Europe, we see how Blanc – with his wife and his brother – seized a set of nineteenth-century opportunities. Recognizing the value of heterosocial environments to the conceptions of bourgeois self-worth, he built casinos that allowed non-nobles to rub shoulders with nobility. Seeing the ways that money and social capital intersected in tourism and leisure, he built resorts that cultivated cultural sensibilities at the same time that they extracted vast amounts of money from customers. Sensing the ways that mechanization transformed human relationships and intellectual horizons, Blanc not only leveraged the new transportation networks of the European rail system to lure visitors to his resorts, but he also promoted games like roulette that were in their essences demonstrations of highly engineered random number generators. Blanc, over the course of his peripatetic life, provides an example of a highly mobile and transnational type of European. He lived in four different European states and had bank accounts in three. A French citizen, he married a German woman. If nothing else, his example should remind us of the opportunities and transformations that Europeans experienced in the nineteenth century.

Mark Braude argues in his history of Monte Carlo that that city-state exemplified the ways that one could leverage dreams of social mobility.[49] Blanc's example surely validates that insight. And yet social mobility is something that needs to be manufactured; it requires human effort to craft a system in which people can experience the types of freedom that Blanc exemplified. Indeed, Blanc recognized the ways that Monte Carlo repre-sented a novel form of social organization. Writing to SBM shareholders in 1875, Blanc explained that "I am convinced that it is not gold that brings the rich, and artists, to Monte Carlo, but rather the desire to free

---

[49] Braude, *Making Monte Carlo*, 209.

themselves from everything, to tempt chance, to bet against fate, and this is why we must give them dreams, pleasure, and beauty."[50] We turn to these issues in a more specific way in the following chapter, investigating the ways that tourism, health, and leisure were embedded in the experience of the resort.

[50] Quoted in Braude, *Making Monte Carlo*, 69.

CHAPTER 2

Visiting the Resort

In her 1913 book *Monte Carlo: A Novel*, Margaret de Vere Stacpoole describes the arrival of a character to the sensuous luxury of Monaco. "But now," Stacpoole writes,

> just as life carries swiftly fools and wise men, the virtuous and vicious, the painted, the tainted, and the pure to the great terminus of each generation – so the Rapide was bearing its crowd to their destination. Nice, burning in the afternoon sun, Beaulieu, Villefranche, the blue sea, castellated Monaco, passed Julia's eyes in succession. La Condamine: Monte Carlo! Julia stepped from the train into a blaze of sunshine. She felt as though the great warm golden god of day had taken her in his arms and kissed her on the cheek. Palm-trees were waving their fronds in the wind; the crowd was nothing, the journey a bad dream over and done with; this was realization in full measure of all her visions of the south.[1]

Spa towns experienced a boom with the creation of rail lines that brought tourists by the thousands to their area. These customers, beckoned by the climate and environment, sought healthful cures and leisurely activities. Resorts like those crafted by François Blanc at Bad Homburg and Monte Carlo exploded in part because they offered gambling, but they also grew because they were able to take advantage of the mechanization of travel in the mid-nineteenth century to open access to middle-class urban populations seeking leisure.[2]

We see in the passage from Stacpoole's novel one way that the resort town was built by its connections both to a pleasant atmosphere and climate but also to the rail lines that connected Europeans in Paris or

---

[1] M. de V. Stacpoole, *Monte Carlo: A Novel* (Dodd, Mead and Co., 1913), 24.

[2] The classic account of the cultural, psychological, and social implications of industrial travel can be found in W. Schivelbusch, *The Railway Journey: The Industrialization of Time and Space in the Nineteenth Century* (University of California Press, 2014); S. Kern's equally fascinating *The Culture of Time and Space, 1880–1918* (Harvard University Press, 2003) also provides an overview of how mechanization transformed the perceptual and cognitive frameworks of travelers.

Berlin to the centers of luxury and leisure at Bad Homburg or Monte Carlo. Writing more than fifty years before Stacpoole's book was published in 1913, George Augustus Sala produced in his book *Make Your Game* an extended travelogue that described, as the front piece to the book mentions, a "narrative of the Rhine and thereabouts."[3] The book purports to tell the story of three friends – known simply as the stout one, the slim one, and the Man with the Iron Chest – as they travel from London to Amsterdam, and from there up the Rhine River in search of gambling. Sala's 1860 text – written for an Anglophone traveling public – is useful at this juncture for its depictions of Rhenish spa towns and for what it can tell us about the ways in which a transnational class of tourists and gamblers traveled to their destinations at a point in time when travel by rail was not yet universally accessible. Nineteenth-century casinos were represented in a variety of formats. They were incorporated into pulp novels and travelogues, depicted in guidebooks and in moralizing texts, and they served as a location for romances and high intrigue. The representational power of the nineteenth-century casino, in other words, demands investigation. Spanning genres, representations of the casino served as the locus for a type of creative nonfiction that included highly didactic sections that served both to advertise the casino to potential customers and to carefully explain how the games worked and how the social life of the casino functioned. In this way, depictions of nineteenth-century casinos served as a type of etiquette guide for the uninitiated. And importantly, over time the casino became a recognizable setting on its own terms, allowing it to function partially as a set-piece that could serve as the backdrop or mise-en-scene for romance, excitement, glamor, espionage, or "luck story."

The three travelers described in Sala's book make their way from Amsterdam up the Rhine, arriving in Cologne, Mainz, and Frankfurt. They meet a dwarf, who counsels them to visit Homburg-von-der-Höhe, which one of the characters describes as "as a place situated amidst some of the most charming scenery in Europe, and only eight miles distant from Frankfort – as an Armida's garden of dainty and delicate dalliance, where life was a round of feasting, singing, dancing, and merrymaking."[4] We see, in other words, that the spa town was described as being a place geared

---

[3] G. A. Sala, *Make Your Game, or, The Adventures of the Stout Gentleman, the Slim Gentleman, and the Man with the Iron Chest: A Narrative of the Rhine and Thereabouts* (Ward and Lock, 1860).
[4] Sala, *Make Your Game*, 128.

toward the production of pleasant sensations.[5] Bad Homburg was presented as a location that conformed to the pattern of leisure and health
found at spa resorts such as those nearby at Wiesbaden or Mainz. The
travelers go to Homburg via coach from Frankfurt (a rail link between
Homburg and Frankfurt was finished in 1860, the same year Sala's book
was published), but they find the outskirts of the spa town unimpressive:
"'Upon my word this is a pretty place to bring people to,' the stout
gentleman remarked, half humorously, half savagely. 'This comes of
knowing red-nosed men, who pick up promiscuous acquaintances in
stable-yards, dwarfs and monsters, and pig-faced ladies and children with
two heads. I see it all now. Hombourg is a mere country village.'"[6] But the
town itself was far more impressive than its surroundings. Bad Homburg
comes into view as a place buzzing with activity. The entrance to Bad
Homburg is

> a broad, handsome, well-paved street, of seemingly interminable length. No
> gas-lamps on the pavement, but a profusion of big oil *revérseres* hung from
> ropes stretched high across the thoroughfare; plenty of shops, however,
> brilliantly lighted with gas – shops, too, gaily decorated and handsomely
> stocked. There were jewellers, watchmakers, milliners, stay-makers, confec-
> tioners, tobacconists, stationers, print-sellers, venders of toys and knick-
> nacks. Jewels gleamed, waxen "dummies" simpered from hair dressers'
> shops; the air was redolent of the fumes of expensive cigars, the odour of
> genuine *eau-de-Cologne* and patchouli; and the foot pavement was thronged
> with groups of dandies, in waxed moustaches and patent leather boots, and
> ladies with ravishing bon nets and cavalier-hats, and whose crinoline rustled
> in the autumn night breeze. So many large white buildings, too, with
> jalousied windows, on whose entablatured friezes you might read
> "Banque de Commerce," "Banque du Landgrafschaft," "Banque
> d'Escompte," "Banque et Bureau de Change."[7]

Unlike the depiction of rural idiocy that Sala included in his description of
Homburg's hinterlands, the town itself is shown as a commercial nexus.
Not just some backwater "mere country village," Homburg bustles,
stocked with a deep supply of luxury goods catering to a well-heeled
bourgeois clientele. The built environment – well kept, well lighted, and
well organized – presents a pleasing view of a clean and commercially
viable resort.

[5] H. Lempa, *Spaces of Honor: Making German Civil Society, 1700–1914* (University of Michigan Press,
   2021). Lempa provocatively argues that spa towns were places in which the norms of bourgeois civil
   society were forged.
[6] Sala, *Make Your Game*, 150.   [7] Sala, *Make Your Game*, 151.

The three travelers in Sala's book, impressed with Homburg's environs, seek the source of its prosperity: the casino. "Midway in this grand street," Sala writes,

> the road receded some hundred paces, forming a quadrangular area. Bounded by a gravelled carriage-drive, the area itself was laid out in grass-plats, and parterred, and was pierced in the midst by a broad avenue, lined by a double row of splendid orange-trees in tubs, and laden with fruit. And at the bottom, parallel with the street, was a vast and sumptuous edifice – a *corps de logis* – and wings of Grecian architecture. The lofty windows were blazing with gas; and before the portal stood carriages, while liveried lacqueys, and more dandies, and more ladies, in crinoline and cavalier-hats, hurried in and out. "Kursaal," said the postilion, pointing as usual with his whip.... So many vast, lofty, handsome mansions there were too, with large court-yards and *portes cocheres*, and whose lower floor seemed to be occupied as cafes, for the travellers could see bearded and moustached loiterers smoking, drinking – card, domino, and billiard playing. The balconies, too, were full of idlers, ladies and gentlemen, puffing, cool-drink sipping, and flirting in the calm evening. What could these mansions be?[8]

The Kursaal, or casino, like the "mansions" surrounding it (the text identifies them in fact as hotels filled with vacationers), is dominant and luxurious. Its landscaping – filled with orange blossoms and organized by orderly paths – is "sumptuous" and brightly lighted. The people there – rich, attractive, well dressed – derive their "idle" pleasures from drinking, smoking, flirting, and gambling. If nothing else, Bad Homburg is described as a fun place to be.[9]

Sala's description of Bad Homburg makes clear the ways that spa towns developed in tandem with a culture of tourism among well-off Europeans.[10] We see the creation of a transnational elite who crossed borders in search of novel sensations, new experiences, and a chance to rub shoulders with others of the same social position.[11] European tourism in the mid-nineteenth century was not simply a recreation of aristocratic *Bildungsreisen* or grand tours. The novel mode of tourism that developed

---

[8] Sala, *Make Your Game*, 152.

[9] See Y. B. Alaluf's *The Emotional Economy of Holidaymaking: Health, Pleasure, and Class in Britain, 1870–1918* (Oxford University Press, 2021) as a model of how to apply the history of emotions to social practices like tourism.

[10] See R. Koshar, *German Travel Cultures* (Berg, 2000); A. Confino's *The Nation as a Local Metaphor: Württemberg, Imperial Germany, and National Memory, 1871–1918* (University of North Carolina Press, 1997) describes the development of German tourism as a way of forging national identity after German unification.

[11] R. Koshar, *Histories of Leisure* (Berg, 2002).

in the mid-nineteenth century was enabled, in part, by the creation of a new market for tourist-related guides. Baedeker began publishing its famous travel guides in 1839.[12] Baedeker guides published in the 1860s, as was Sala's *Make Your Game*, included English-language guides to Switzerland, France, Germany, Italy, Belgium, and the Netherlands. Travel guides like these performed important cultural work by setting tastes and curating what came to be a tourist canon. Baedeker, for instance, noted that Homburg "is one of the most popular watering-places in the Rhine-land," and conveyed to readers the pleasures of the Kurhaus, or resort, and the grounds, noting natural features of the environment, notable hotels, and dining establishments.[13] This stands in contrast to earlier editions, which indicated that most activity centered on the Kurhaus but that "independently of the baths, [it is] a place of no importance."[14] Works like Sala's, however, performed equally significant ideological work and functioned as a didactic text. Sala's text offered readers long passages of descriptive prose that described the environment and taught them the basic rules of the casino and the games played there.

Sala issued a veiled warning to his readers seeking guidance on how to locate, travel to, and then participate in the social life of spa towns. "Consider all these things, my son," Sala counseled, "and be wise ere you steam up the Rhine towards Hombourg-von-der-Höhe; for if you go there, and be made of ordinary flesh and blood – I am not writing for oysters or icebergs – you must play, and will in all human probability leave your skin behind you."[15] Sala's reference to "steam[ing] up the Rhine" here is significant. While river-going steamships had been in operation since the 1780s and used in efficient ways to move passengers up the Hudson River beginning in 1807 with the *Clermont*, European rivers like the Thames, the Seine, the Rhine, and the Danube – not to mention fjords in Scandinavia or lakes in Switzerland – were obvious targets for the mechanization of transportation. Sala's characters traveled up the Rhine to Bad Homburg by steamship; other visitors to spa and resort towns like those on the Rhine or, later, Monte Carlo came by railroad. In this way, the creation of rail lines and the use of steamships along river routes facilitated European tourism and helped build the gambling resorts of

[12] See Koshar, *German Travel Cultures*, for a history of Baedeker Guides, 19–64.
[13] Karl Baedeker (firm), *The Rhine from Rotterdam to Constance: Handbook for Travellers* (Karl Baedeker, 1882), 215.
[14] Karl Baedeker (firm), *A Handbook for Travellers on the Rhine, from Holland to Switzerland* (K. Baedeker, 1864), 170.
[15] Sala, *Make Your Game*, 220.

the nineteenth century. Indeed, the nineteenth-century casino should be seen as an industrial space, a pleasure factory. Thomas Kavanagh explains that "the term most frequently used in dictionaries and encyclopedias of the last quarter of the nineteenth century to describe the new kind of gambling epitomized by Monte Carlo is 'industrial.'"[16]

These new modes of transportation provided a key to the success of places like Bad Homburg or Monte Carlo. As the locus of the gambling industry in Europe shifted to the Mediterranean, areas like Monte Carlo were integrated into a European rail system. A rail line from Paris to Cannes was established in 1863 (the year François Blanc began to build his Monégasque empire), and a connection between Cannes and Nice was completed the following year. Knowing that a rail connection to Monte Carlo was imperative, Blanc gave land for a connection and a station to encourage the extension of the line to Monaco (thus making it easy for Parisians to travel entirely by rail to Monaco). The link was completed in October 1868. The effect of the rail line was felt immediately: 173,865 visitors came to Monaco by rail in 1869. By the 1890s, 500,000 train passengers were coming to Monte Carlo annually; that number doubled by the first decade of the twentieth century.[17]

The arrival of all these new tourists was transformative. Hippolyte de Villemessant, the editor of *Le Figaro*, was treated by Blanc to a press junket to Monte Carlo in 1865, about which he wrote glowingly: "M. Blanc has transformed this region, once pleasing rather than rich, into a veritable California; only he does not discover gold mines, he creates them. M. Blanc is a bold, sagacious gambler, self-controlled and never out in his calculations; he has both vision and judgment.... It is as though Monaco had been touched by a fairy's magic wand."[18] Later observers were equally in awe of the transformative effects of the resort. Corti writes that "It was François Blanc who created this unreal and magic world, this atmosphere of escape from every-day contingencies. He built his fortunes on the most ineradicable of passions, that of gambling."[19] Part of the attraction to Monaco existed in its climate and environment, but this element was itself only part of the package. In these descriptions of the

[16] T. M. Kavanagh, *Dice, Cards, Wheels: A Different History of French Culture* (University of Pennsylvania Press, 2005), 191.

[17] M. Braude, *Making Monte Carlo: A History of Speculation and Spectacle* (New York: Simon & Schuster, 2016), 100. The *Journal de Monaco* published transit totals, typically in January. Scans of the *Journal* are available at journaldemonaco.gouv.mc/Journaux.

[18] Quoted in E. C. Corti, *The Wizard of Monte Carlo* (E. P. Dutton, 1935), 194–95.

[19] Corti, *The Wizard of Monte Carlo*, 268.

environment, of the built environment, and of the cognitive and cultural processes that took a backwater and allowed it to be converted in the imagination into a fairy land, we see the ways in which the resort town affected the class of transnational tourists who descended upon it.

We also need to consider the ways that the presence of all these tourists – and the money they brought with them – changed resort towns.[20] Integrating these areas into regional and in some cases global economic structures, life in these villages was radically transformed. Reflecting on the changes that the resort had engendered in Monaco, one writer of a 1920 guidebook called *Riviera Towns* noted the transformations that had taken place since the 1860s. "In blood," Herbert Gibbons explains,

> the Monégasques are affiliated to the Provençal and Italian neighbors. What one sees in the old town of Monaco is a confirmation of the assertion of many historians that nationality, in our modern political sense of the word, and patriotism, as a mass instinct shared by millions, are phenomena of the nineteenth century. Steam transportation, obligatory primary education, universal military service, are the factors that have developed national consciousness, and the exigencies and opportunities and advantages of the industrial era have furnished the motive for binding people together in great political organisms.[21]

A remarkable anticipation of Eugen Weber's famous argument about the creation of a modern French identity and consciousness contained in *Peasants into Frenchmen*, Gibbons's assessment is useful here for its concise description of quick and dramatic change in the most obscure of European territories.[22]

Gibbons was right to describe these changes as coming from the influx of new people and new wealth. The rise of international tourism and the promotion of the Riviera as a destination spot and as a place for transnational connections to form is a central factor in the development of gambling in nineteenth-century Europe. Contemporary observers also commented on the ways that Monte Carlo changed the territory around it. Writing in 1890, W. Fraser Rae argued that "at few places has the transformation been greater than at Monaco within the like space of time, the whole being due to the building and success of the casino."[23] Rae was

---

[20] Alaluf, *The Emotional Economy of Holidaymaking*; Koshar, *German Travel Cultures*.
[21] H. A. Gibbons, *Riviera Towns* (R. M. McBride & Co., 1920), 94.
[22] E. Weber, *Peasants into Frenchmen: The Modernization of Rural France, 1870–1914* (Stanford University Press, 1976).
[23] W. F. Rae, "Play and Players on the Riviera," *The Nineteenth Century*, 27/February (1890), 240–57, 246.

quick to suggest, however, that this transformation came with a dark side: "This success is believed in some quarters to have been obtained at a terrible price. The present condition of Monte Carlo is said to be deplorable. Men of high position in the Church of England declaim against its infinite wickedness. According to them it is the 'plague-spot' of the Riviera."[24] One way to imagine the underlying logic of the transformations wrought by international tourism is to consider the Riviera as a contact zone in which the Northern power elite learned to take pleasure in the climate, the food, the wines, and the resort-like qualities of the area. What is important is that the Riviera was not really a destination until the last third of the nineteenth century, and only then because it could take advantage of rail lines connecting Nice and Menton. Industrialized transportation networks promoted industrialized forms of leisure such as the casino at Monte Carlo.

If one way of considering resort life is to focus on its social porousness and the heterosocial connections that it fostered, another aspect of the issue is to note the exclusivity of spa towns.[25] Aside from obvious anti-Semitism, it is not incorrect to note the racial segregation that characterized spa society. While historian Julian Hale mentions the *pied noir* community (and its affiliation with right-wing political movements) in his study of the Riviera, the African or Mediterranean perspectives are rarely included in studies of the region.[26] The only Black person who seems to have ever visited the Riviera was Josephine Baker. In a way, this is not surprising, but it is worth mentioning that the social and cultural history of the Riviera is one that is based on racial separatism in a very real way.

Resort life was built in part through a process of racial exclusion, hinting at the existence of new mechanisms of social differentiation characteristic of the nineteenth and twentieth centuries. The social life of nineteenth-century casinos unfolded in a historical context much different from the social norms characterizing the ancien régime. The social forms found in the *nouveau régime* that German observers characterized as *Gesellschaft* were organized not only through class but also through race. An element of the cultural work of race on the Riviera was to conceive of Mediterranean populations in racialized ways. Counseling tourists in a book published in 1920 to avoid the boring museums found in Monaco,

---

[24] Rae, "Play and Players," 246.   [25] Lempa, *Spaces of Honor*, 90–114.
[26] J. A. S. Hale, *The French Riviera: A Cultural History* (Oxford University Press, 2009).

travel guide Herbert Gibbons remarks that "'doing' museums is the last word in tourist folly."[27] Gibbons continues,

> Yes, I know that skeletons and the cutest little fish are in those museums. I am not ashamed to confess that I never darkened their doors. Life is short, and while the Artist revels in his subjects, I find more interest in studying the living Monégasques than their – and our – negroid ancestors.... For there is a separate race, with its own patois, in Monaco. You would never spot it in the somewhat Teutonic cosmopolitanism of the Condamine and Monte Carlo tradesmen and hotel servants. It is not apparent in the impassive *croupiers* of the Casino. But within a few hundred yards, in half a dozen streets and lanes, the physiognomy, the mentality, the language of the people make you realize that regarding Monaco as a separate country is not wholly a polite fiction to relieve the French Government of the responsibility for the Casino. These people are different, children as well as grown-ups. They are neither French nor Italian, Provençal nor Catalan, but as distinct as mountain Basques are from French and Spanish. It is not a racial group distinction, as with the Basques.[28]

Gibbons acknowledged and then denied that the Monégasques possessed a racially separate status. The hybrid qualities of the local population – so different in demeanor, physiognomy, and mentality from their guests – indicates Southern Europeans could be assimilated into the racial structures beloved by Northern Europeans, but only to the degree that other groups (like the Basques in this example) could be ruthlessly excluded.

To be clear, race was never a simple issue in spa towns, and an African American like Josephine Baker was as welcome in Monte Carlo as she was in Berlin or Paris. That said, the social environment of the casino was overwhelmingly white, and the cultural norms of white supremacy hardly required comment. One character from a novel published in 1913, for instance, says when betting on black at the roulette table and losing: "'Ugh!'.... 'What a swindle! My beautiful five francs!' 'Gone where the good niggers go.'"[29] Other forms of exclusivity based on class were also important elements in the culture of mystique surrounding these resorts. Fyodor Dostoyevsky, writing in his 1866 novella *The Gambler*, describes how class, reputation, and style were managed in spa towns like Bad Homburg or Wiesbaden: "At spas – and, it seems, throughout Europe – hotel administrators and managers, when assigning rooms to their guests, are guided not so much by their guests' demands and wishes, as by their own personal view of them; and, one should note, they are rarely

---

[27] Gibbons, *Riviera Towns*, 93.   [28] Gibbons, *Riviera Towns*, 93–94.
[29] Stacpoole, *Monte Carlo*, 34.

mistaken."[30] This feeling of exclusivity could be imagined in other ways as well. One rumor about Blanc published in 1890 suggested that he sought to craft a gambling environment at Bad Homburg that could be socially differentiated. One room, the story goes, would be restricted to men who would gamble only with gold.[31] Even a practice as banal as suntanning (which proliferated in Monaco beginning in the 1920s) took on class connotations. During the Great Depression and after the French Popular Front established holidays for French workers, "The Duke and Duchess of Windsor were advised against renting Maxine Eliot's Château de l'Horizon near Cannes [in 1936] because, they were told, the Côte d'Azur was full of communist red flags."[32] More distressing, perhaps, were the crowds of working-class sunbathers: "I saw people crowded together on beaches," Eileen Gray remembered, "and it was dreadful."[33] The resort casino – built on the premise that it was at once obtainable *and* exclusive – constantly wrestled with the dynamics of exclusion and inclusion. Casinos depended on a certain volume of customers to ensure profitability, but they also required that an illusion of private privilege be manufactured and maintained.

As Gray's passage demonstrates, not everyone fell in love with spa life. The Russian writer Anton Chekhov complained in a letter written in April 1891: "How contemptible and loathsome this life is with its artichokes, its palms, and its smell of orange blossoms! I love wealth and luxury, but the luxury here, the luxury of the gambling saloon, reminds one of a luxurious water-closet. There is something in the atmosphere that offends one's sense of decency and vulgarizes the scenery, the sound of the sea, the moon."[34] But these sentiments were certainly not uniform, and many visitors – despite the inconveniences of too many sunbathers or the presence of communists (even Karl Marx visited Monte Carlo, after all) – responded in emotionally positive ways to the beauty and luxury of the spa towns. Writing fifty years before Chekhov, Nicolai Gogol, visiting Nice in December 1841, explained simply: "Nice is a paradise. The sun spreads over everything, like a layer of oil; there are countless butterflies and flies, the air is like summer. Utter peace."[35]

Gogol's contemplative celebration of the Mediterranean climate provides a clue to another critical element of the success of nineteenth-century

---

[30] F. Dostoyevsky, *The Gambler and Other Stories* (Penguin, 2010), 189.
[31] Rae, "Play and Players," 255.
[32] M. Blume, *Côte d'Azur: Inventing the French Riviera* (Thames & Hudson, 1992), 119.
[33] Quoted in Blume, *Côte d'Azur*, 119.
[34] A. P. Chekhov, *Letters of Anton Chekhov to His Family and Friends* (Macmillan and Company, 1920), 249–50.
[35] Quoted in Hale, *The French Riviera*, 85.

spa towns: the role they played in promoting cures to various health complaints. Especially in the Rhineland, where the mineral springs promised all sorts of restorative powers, resort towns had for centuries courted a traveling class seeking to boost their vitality through access to the environmental attractions of a region. Like Rhenish water cures, the climate of the Riviera was marketed as an ideal one for promoting a healthy and vigorous body. Travelers to resort towns could blend the curative process with the other social and cultural attractions of a particular region. In other words, it did not all have to be cold water and wheat germ; as Sala's description of Bad Homburg shows, there were plenty of diversions and amusements for those who were inclined. It is important to note, however, that the health and leisure industries could function as separate enterprises. Even after gambling was prohibited in the Rhineland, the health spas continued to attract customers. And yet the conflation of these two systems at various points indicates something important about the historical trajectories of the nineteenth-century health and leisure industries. Both exhibited the logic of an enterprise that projected exclusivity but still required a steady stream of customers for financial stability.

We see evidence for this dual logic in the ways that Rhenish casinos were marketed. François Blanc used Bad Homburg's water as a way of marketing the resort throughout Europe. Submitting samples of the water for chemical analysis, he promoted its healthful benefits as a way of making Bad Homburg more attractive to his international clientele, and it is useful to see this development as a part of Blanc's strategy of building up peripheral activities that served the larger purpose of funneling people into the gaming rooms. There is also evidence of a reverse marketing strategy at work in the Rhineland, one in which the various springs (and their medical benefits) were included in books dedicated to describing the mechanics of the various games. Health-enabling water brought customers to the casinos; gambling brought people to the waters. Indeed, the promotion of Bad Homburg as a health resort was carried out at the highest levels of the Landgrave's court and in close coordination with the Blancs. Frederick Müller, personal physician to the Landgrave, wrote the *Treatise on the Use of the Mineral Waters of Homburg* (the text went through multiple editions in the 1850s and 1860s), to describe more precisely how the waters from the various springs around Bad Homburg could be used for healthful effect.[36] The text, which was also published in multiple languages, offers insight into the ways resorts leveraged their natural environment to expand

---

[36] F. Müller, *Treatise on the Use of the Mineral Waters of Homburg*, 3rd ed. (Louis Schick, 1865).

the circle of potential visitors and to promote visits to the casino. Müller –
as the reader is told in the preface – suffered from recurring constipation.
Luckily, "the sufferings inseparable from those ailments and the relief
afforded by the use of the waters strongly impressed him with the duty
of making known the valuable properties of the Homburg springs."[37]

Müller sought to highlight how the springs might help potential visitors.
Obstructed circulation brought on by "sedentary habits and free living"
was the root cause of the problem.[38] The result was a "superabundance of
blood, its accumulation in the vessels of the abdominal organs, and morbid
distention of the latter are the inevitable results of such a mistaken mode of
living. Excess of nutrition induces excessive sanguinification, and sedentary
habits, by obstructing (even occasionally) the large ascending vein, bring
on impeded circulation and venous congestion."[39] Sadly enough,
obstructed circulation ultimately culminates in even worse disorders than
constipation: "The natural consequence of obstructed circulation is vascu-
lar congestion, which, when occurring in the veins of the rectum, is termed
Hemorrhoids, an ailment which usually generates new disorders."[40]
Fortunately, Müller reports, "This abdominal plethora and morbid state
of the blood are directly and efficaciously combated by aperient invigorating mineral waters."[41] Dr. Müller, seeking balms to salve the various
"derangements of the digestive canal," prescribes the mineral waters drawn
from four wells in Bad Homburg.[42] One spring combats indigestion, he
claims, while another is helpful in the fight against hemorrhoids, both
suppressed and those "profusely flowing."[43] Hemorrhoids of the bladder,
mucous hemorrhoids, undeveloped hemorrhoids, and anomalous hemorrhoids were similarly attacked with the "judicious use" of mineral waters
from the area springs.[44] Dr. Müller also describes cases of hypochondria –
both with liver complaint and without – that were solved with a mineral
water cure. One man, Müller reports, felt himself "born again" after six
weeks of water.[45]

The digestive tract was not the only source of concern. "Hysterical
affections," even those "without derangement of the menstrual evacua-
tions," could also be cured by the local waters, in part because the waters
"exercise a special influence on that organ [the uterus]."[46] All sorts of other
nervous maladies – affecting both men and women – were subject to the

[37] Müller, *Mineral Waters of Homburg*, iv.   [38] Müller, *Mineral Waters of Homburg*, 2.
[39] Müller, *Mineral Waters of Homburg*, 2.   [40] Müller, *Mineral Waters of Homburg*, 2.
[41] Müller, *Mineral Waters of Homburg*, 3.   [42] Müller, *Mineral Waters of Homburg*, 7.
[43] Müller, *Mineral Waters of Homburg*, 16.   [44] Müller, *Mineral Waters of Homburg*, 15.
[45] Müller, *Mineral Waters of Homburg*, 21.   [46] Müller, *Mineral Waters of Homburg*, 28.

healing powers of the water. Sufferers of asthma, rheumatism, gout, scrofula, and ringworm were similarly likely to find relief from the waters around Bad Homburg. Aside from providing a list of counterindications, Dr. Müller produced a description of how and when the waters should be ingested, and he also described the ideal diet likely to assist in producing a cure. Perhaps the most interesting element of Dr. Müller's pamphlet, however, is the detailed chemical analysis of the water. According to the Giessen chemistry professor Dr. Justus von Liebig, Bad Homburg's celebrated waters included minerals ranging from muriate of soda to carbonic acid. The unique combination found in the waters, Müller notes, allowed it achieve efficacy for patients when the waters of other spas – like those around Kissingen – did not.[47] The book concludes with a description all the wells – the depths and the degree of effervescence that the waters enjoy – and then readers are treated to a list of other titles published by the same press, including three iterations of a text called *Trent-et-Quarent und Roulette* that introduces readers to the intricacies of the games played at the casino.

Müller's text tells us much about the ways that resorts like Bad Homburg could frame an appeal to health in ways that did not preclude one's enjoyment of the casino. Indeed, the text serves as a lengthy advertisement not only for the waters around Bad Homburg but also for books that would serve to educate would-be gamblers on the rules, norms, and customs of casino games. Even after imperial German authorities banned gambling in resorts like Baden, gaming and health were conflated in popular opinion, demonstrating the importance of the shift in the location of gaming from the eighteenth-century court to the nineteenth-century spa. When British doctors held a Congress meeting at Baden in 1879, they made sure to explain that the *absence* of gambling did not detract from the suite of healthful interventions available at the resort. Reporting in the *British Medical Journal* of October 4, 1879, one doctor explained that

> We cannot conclude without a word as to the advantages of Baden as a health-resort. Now that the gambling tables are abolished, there is no possible objection as regard the character of visitors. The air and surroundings are admirably suited to those invalids who, on account of nervous diseases, or affections of the heart or lungs, require sedative influence; and the bathing establishment, Friederichsbad, is perhaps the most perfect in Europe. Marble swimming baths at various temperatures of running water

---

[47] Müller, *Mineral Waters of Homburg,* 58.

from thermal springs, vapour baths, and douches of all kinds, and the most scrupulous cleanliness, unite to make the establishment as great a luxury as it is useful in a sanitary point of view.[48]

The doctor's stated concern with the quality of the character of potential visitors to the spa – and his worry that the character of his medical colleagues might be impugned by a visit to the resort – is characteristic of moral critiques of gambling circulating in the last quarter of the nineteenth century. Even Monte Carlo's climate was used to highlight its healthiness, although in a way that was tinged with a certain salacious quality. Figure 2.1, which shows a postcard circulating before World War I, depicts a collection of ten female bathers purportedly enjoying the thermal waters near Monte Carlo. Those who purchased the card may have possessed motives other than an interest in hot springs for doing so. Nonetheless, what concerns us here is the way the healthful "luxury" of an establishment was highlighted both in texts and visually, clues that help us understand how spa towns cemented their reputations as a place not only of luxury and sanitation but, more importantly, of leisure.

While both gambling and spa towns were associated with leisure, the connection only became more pronounced over the course of the nine-teenth century. Writing in 1819, E. T. A. Hoffmann described in his short story "Gambler's Luck" (Spielerglück) the ways in which leisure activities like gambling came to be affiliated with spa towns.[49] "Who does not know," Hoffman writes early in the story, "that the magical attraction of gambling can become irresistible, especially during the season in watering places, where everyone has stepped out of his normal surroundings and is deliberately devoting himself to the enjoyment of leisure and freedom."[50] Hoffmann intuited something significant in this story: the spa town generally and the casino specifically existed as a place apart – normal rules did not apply – and in this case he provided a key to understanding how leisure would be theorized in the nineteenth century. On one hand, the built environment provided a location for novel experiences and for a suspension of normal rules. This builds on older ancien régime style of gambling, in which the physical seclusion of eighteenth-century court society was inherently exclusive. With the nineteenth-century spa casino we no longer see a difference in kind from the older forms, but rather a different effect of isolation and exclusivity that was significantly more open

---

[48] "The Congress at Baden," *The British Medical Journal*, 2/979 (1879), 556, 556.
[49] E. T. A. Hoffmann, *The Tales of Hoffmann* (Frederick Ungar Publishing Co., 1963).
[50] Hoffmann, *The Tales of Hoffmann*, 213.

Figure 2.1 "Etablissement Thermal, La Joie de l'Eau" (Giletta Freres, ca. 1907–14). Courtesy of Watkinson Library at Trinity College, Hartford, George Watson Cole European Postcard Collection.

44

than that of court society. But the casino – especially when it came to specialize in games like roulette that operated according to probabilities and not the skill of the player – created a highly routinized environment full of rules. And by virtue of the change in the types of games that were played – from competitive games to "social" ones in which players competed against the house – the social life found in the nineteenth-century casino was dramatically altered.[51]

This contradiction between exclusivity and sociability did not escape the eye of sociologists working around the turn of the twentieth century. In his 1910 essay on "Sociability," Georg Simmel argues that play is a critical element in the building of sociability. "It is an obvious corollary," Simmel argues at one point in the essay, "that everything may be subsumed under sociability which one can call sociological play-form." Continuing, Simmel notes that,

> above all, play itself ... assumes a large place in the sociability of all epochs... For even when play turns about a money prize, it is not the prize, which indeed could be won in many other ways, which is the specific point of the play; but the attraction for the true sportsman lies in the dynamics and in the chances of that sociologically significant form of activity itself. The social game has a deeper double meaning – that it is played not only *in* society as its outward bearer but that with its help people actually "play" society.[52]

Playing games, arguably the raison d'être of a casino, allowed the players to create society, and these novel forms of sociability were spatially, politically, and economically different from what had come before. Everett John Carter argues that nineteenth-century casinos did important cultural work, as they "created an entirely new form of sociability," one he describes as "modern."[53] What that society looked like, and how it functioned, was the process of deeply historical trajectories that brought together a new transnational social class, a new transportation system based on steam, a new culture of leisure and play, and a set of new political circumstances that permitted legal gambling in only a few circumscribed places. Simmel's argument about the significance of play in the creation of sociability

[51] T. M. Kavanagh, *Dice, Cards, Wheels: A Different History of French Culture* (University of Pennsylvania Press, 2005). Kavanagh explains that this shift in the style of play was also critiqued by one French observer as a form of "industrial exploitation."
[52] G. Simmel, *On Individuality and Social Forms* (University of Chicago Press, 1971), 134.
[53] E. J. Carter, "The Green Table: Gambling Casinos, Capitalist Culture, and Modernity in Nineteenth-Century Germany," PhD dissertation, University of Illinois at Urbana-Champaign 2002, 42.

demands that we investigate more closely the ways in which the casino operated. Having now explored the logic and function of the spa town, we turn to consider the casino, an institution that held dueling possibilities for its clientele. For some a source of fun; for others, the casino may have been best described by inventor Hiram Maxim, who wrote in 1904 about Monte Carlo: "This institution must live; it feeds off the players, and as in the case of the lamb, is disastrous to them. It lives on disasters; without them it could not exist."[54]

[54] H. S. Maxim, *Monte Carlo: Facts and Fallacies* (Grant Richards, 1904), 173.

CHAPTER 3

Experiencing the Casino

Thirty years before he was identified in Havelock Ellis's *Sexual Inversion* as Case XVIII, John Addington Symonds visited Monaco.[1] Married in 1864 in a futile attempt to "suppress his strong desires for other men," the scholar visited the Riviera and was an early visitor to the casino at Monte Carlo.[2] His diary entry from March 22, 1866, records his impressions of the visit in dramatic detail.[3]

> After dawdling about Monaco itself we went round to the "Jeux" – a large gambling-house established on the shore near Monaco, upon the road to Mentone. There is a splendid hotel there, and the large house of sin, blazing with gas lamps by night. So we saw it from the road beneath Turbia our first night, flaming and shining by the shore like Pandemonium, or the habitation of (some) romantic witch. This place, in truth, resembles the gardens of Alcina (? Armida), or any other magician's trap for catching souls, which poets have devised. It lies close by the sea in a hollow of the sheltering hills. There winter cannot come – the flowers bloom, the waves dance, and sunlight laughs all through the year. The air swoons with scent of lemon groves; tall palm trees wave their branches in the garden; music of the softest, loudest, most inebriating passion, swells from the palace; rich meats and wines are served in a gorgeously painted hall; cool corridors and sunny seats stand ready for the noontide heat or evening calm; without are olive gardens, green and fresh and full of flowers. But the witch herself holds her high court and never-ending festival of sin in the hall of the green tables.[4]

[1] S. Ledger and R. Luckhurst (eds.), *The Fin de Siècle: A Reader in Cultural History, c. 1880–1900* (Oxford University Press, 2000), 307–14.
[2] Ledger and Luckhurst, eds., *The Fin de Siècle*, 314.
[3] J. A. Symonds and H. F. Brown, *John Addington Symonds, a Biography*, 2nd ed. (Smith, Elder, & Co.; Charles Scribner's Sons, 1903).
[4] Symonds and Brown, *John Addington Symonds*, 202.

Symonds's description of the physical space of the casino in Monte Carlo identifies the ways the casino attacked all the human senses.[5] His eyes take in the blazing brightness, his nose is attuned to the scent of lemon, his skin is warmed and cooled, and his taste buds relish the "meats and wines" that are served. His ears listen to passionate music. Lording over this sensory assault, this "large house of sin" is a "romantic witch." Later observers like Charles Kingston echoed this assessment of the casino's allure. "Indeed," Kingston quipped, "Monte Carlo, with its subtle appeal to all the senses except, perhaps, commonsense, is rapidly attaining the dignity of a necessity."[6] Visitors to Monte Carlo, in other words, could expect to be enveloped in a new world that had the casino and its pleasures at its core. External views of the casino at Monte Carlo are shown in Figures 3.1–3.5.

And yet the casino at Monte Carlo represented an evolution of the form developed in the Rhineland in the mid-nineteenth century. In Sala's description of Bad Homburg in 1860, he called the casino there a "Greek edifice, with wings which loomed large and white, opposite the Hotel de France, the structure which was approached by an avenue of orange trees, and before whose portals carriages were forever standing."[7] Sala notes that this impressive structure exerts a special lure, and he compares the casino to a light that attracts insects: "Thus, like moths fluttering round about a candle, our three travelers had hovered about the precincts of the Kursaal, without venturing into its confines. But the time was come for them to be drawn within its all-absorbing vortex."[8] Like Symonds's description of the casino as the location of a "festival of sin" that attracted gamblers, Sala's "vortex" provides an important clue as to how people approached the casino in the nineteenth century. As we will see, the psychological dimensions of gambling contributed to the attractiveness of the casino generally. And while casinos have a longer history, the novel forms that the institution assumed in the nineteenth century represent a change in the structure as a whole.

There is evidence for this claim about the novelty of the nineteenth-century casino in contemporary descriptions that contrasted resort casinos with neighboring cities. William Henry Wilkins and Herbert Vivian described the differences between Cannes and Monte Carlo in a cowritten

---

[5] See M. M. Smith, *Sensing the Past: Seeing, Hearing, Smelling, Tasting, and Touching in History* (University of California Press, 2007), for approaches to sensory history.

[6] C. Kingston, *The Romance of Monte Carlo* (J. L. the Bodley Head, 1925), v.

[7] G. A. Sala, *Make Your Game, or, The Adventures of the Stout Gentleman, the Slim Gentleman, and the Man with the Iron Chest: A Narrative of the Rhine and Thereabouts* (Ward and Lock, 1860), 168.

[8] Sala, *Make Your Game*, 170.

41 MONTE-CARLO. — *Le Casino*. — LL.   SELECTA

Figure 3.1   "Monte-Carlo – Le Casino" (Lucien Levy, ca. 1907–14). Courtesy of
Watkinson Library at Trinity College, Hartford, George Watson Cole European Postcard
Collection.

Figure 3.2   "Monte-Carlo – Le Casino" (Lucien Levy, ca. 1907–14). Courtesy of Watkinson Library at Trinity College, Hartford, George Watson Cole European Postcard Collection.

164. Casino de MONTE CARLO. Vue prise de la Mer. N.D. Phot.

Figure 3.3   "Casino de Monte Carlo – Vue prise de la Mer" (Lucien Levy, ca. 1907–14). Courtesy of Watkinson Library at Trinity College, Hartford, George Watson Cole European Postcard Collection.

727. MONTE-CARLO – Façade du Casino

Figure 3.4 "Monte-Carlo – Façade du Casino" (Giletta Freres, ca. 1907–14). Courtesy of Watkinson Library at Trinity College, Hartford, George Watson Cole European Postcard Collection.

MONTE-CARLO — Les Terrasses pendant le Concert

Figure 3.5 "Monte-Carlo – Les Terrasses pendant le Concert" (unknown, ca. 1907–14). Courtesy of Watkinson Library at Trinity College, Hartford, George Watson Cole European Postcard Collection.

novel of 1894 called *The Green Bay Tree*. "Cannes is an inconvenient place for those who want to play at Monte Carlo," one character states. "It is a long day's excursion, involving a barbarously early breakfast and a return in the small hours of the next morning, if you mean to play seriously.... Most of our friends, however, flitted to and fro between the two places, coming to Cannes for their society and returning to Monte Carlo for their dissipation."[9] Later in the novel, Wilkins and Vivian bluntly compare the casino to Paradise, noting that the "terrace at Monte Carlo is a pleasant lounge at noon in winter. There are not enough people about to be exacting in the matter of dress; you can give yourself over to the full enjoyment of your surroundings. And such surroundings! Assuredly the world contains no other such favoured corner, where art and nature have so conspired to erect a paradise."[10] A product of human ingenuity and natural beauty, the casino presented – in the minds of Wilkins and Vivian – a heaven on earth.

Contrasting sharply with Symonds's more diabolical representations of the casino, Wilkins and Vivian produced a vision of the casino that highlighted its paradisiacal qualities. Indeed, the divine sanction of gambling at Monte Carlo was in debate by visitors. After an earthquake struck Monte Carlo on February 23, 1887, these questions surfaced in the minds of visitors. Charles Kingston, a historian of Monte Carlo writing in the 1920s, asserts that "The superstitious, believing that the rock was about to be devoured because an offended God could no longer delay His vengeance, shrieked their prayers and howled for mercy, and the hardened sinner, thinking only of this world, roused himself from his frozen lethargy and made for the railway station."[11] Kingston continues, noting that God's plan for the region seems to have been confirmed by the fact that the "huge building seemed to lend itself to sudden destruction in such a disaster as this, but Nature was cynical enough to destroy several churches and leave the casino unscathed. Ecclesiastical buildings toppled down but the Temple of Chance stood erect, and the moralists were dumbfounded."[12] The casino – both embedded in fantasy and a locus of debate about secular and profane – did important cultural work in the imaginations of nineteenth-century observers. And if the casino sat at the "vortex" of the spa town, the gambling room sat at the heart of the casino.

The gambling house had long been represented as a topsy-turvy world. One description of the space written in 1669 complained that "Blaspheming,

---

[9] W. H. Wilkins and H. Vivian, *The Green Bay Tree: A Tale of To-day* (Hutchinson & Company, 1894), 1–2.
[10] Wilkins and Vivian, *The Green Bay Tree*, 18.   [11] Kingston, *The Romance of Monte Carlo*, 190.
[12] Kingston, *The Romance of Monte Carlo*, 191–92.

Drunkenness, and Swearing are here familiar, that Civility is by the Rule of contrarieties accounted a Vice."[13] By the nineteenth century, however, such displays of revelry and chaos were largely confined to illegal underground gambling dens and blind pigs in favor of a series of more civilized interactions in the resort casino.

While the motivations of gamblers were understood to be framed by financial passions, the surrounding environment shaped an experience much different from that of the early-modern gambling den. George Sala described the gambling rooms of the casino at Bad Homburg as a refined architectural attempt to infuse the gambling room with a certain religious sensibility. "Through a vast and lofty vestibule," Sala writes, one sees "a carved and panelled ceiling supported on Seagliola columns. Lightly fall the footsteps of the many passers-by. Solemnly hushed are the whisperings of vanity and the murmurs of folly. Distinct above all is heard the chinking of money. Be reverent, O ye worshippers! for this is the vestibule to the temple of Mammon – the ante-chamber where is set up on high the effigy of the Golden Calf."[14] Sala continues, producing a description of the interior of the Kursaal that focuses on its sumptuousness, but also does not neglect to remind readers of the activities that take place in the room: "In the Kursaal is the ball or concert room, at either end of which is a gallery, supported by pillars of composition marble. The floors are inlaid, and immense mirrors in sumptuous frames are hung on the walls. Vice can see her own image all over the establishment."[15] In short, the nineteenth-century casino produced a different experience of space than earlier itera-tions of the form. Architectural grandeur, spatial volume, and references both to classical traditions and to religious space informed the logic of casinos in the nineteenth century. And central to this logic was the construction of voluminous space that could accommodate crowds of gamblers and observers, recalling but transforming similar courtly gam-bling locations characteristic of the eighteenth century.

William Powell Frith's 1871 depiction of a gambling room at Bad Homburg (*The Salon d'Or, Homburg*; Figure 3.6) shows a crowded room of well-dressed players gathered around a table. Some are seated, playing what appears to be Trente et Quarante, a card came that allows betting in a form similar to roulette, while a large standing crowd watches the action. The central figure is a woman who has risen from seat with a stunned look on her face. The scene is notable, as we will discuss in later

---

[13] *The Nicker Nicked, or, The Cheats of Gaming Discovered*, 3rd ed. (1669), 97.
[14] Sala, *Make Your Game*, 174.   [15] Sala, *Make Your Game*, 177.

Figure 3.6　*The Salon d'Or, Homburg* by William Powell Frith, 1871. Courtesy of the RISD Museum, Providence, RI.

sections, for its depictions of sociability. But equally important is the representation of architectural grandeur: the room is voluminous, the walls are covered with monumental paintings, and ornate chandeliers illuminate the table.

Photographs of the gambling rooms at Monte Carlo depict a similar style of ornamental grandeur. Postcards of the Salon Rose (Figure 3.7), for instance, while showing a roulette table surrounded by twenty chairs, also show a tall-ceilinged room, brightly lighted by the tall windows on one side of the space. Intricately ornamented walls and a tromp l'oeil ceiling contribute not only to the sense of spatial volume but also to its grand appearance. The Salle Garnier (Figure 3.8) contains similar evidence of the ways that gambling rooms – large and voluminous – nonetheless gilded the borders while maintaining a focus on the site of the action: the tables. The Salle Garnier featured two roulette tables, each with seats for about a dozen players (others would stand in second and third rows to place their bets). Large paintings adorned the walls and intricate entrance ways signaled to visitors the splendor of the room within (see the images of "Les Grâces Florentines," Figure 3.11, and "Dans la Prairie," Figure 3.12). La Salle Schmidt (Figures 3.9 and 3.13), which contained four roulette tables that each seated fourteen gamblers (again, with more arranged standing behind), was an enormous space. It allowed crowds to gather: socializing, watching, and betting. The Nouvelle Salle de Jeux (Figure 3.10) was a similarly spacious and opulent location. The rooms dedicated to card playing (mainly Trente et Quarante) evinced a similar style (Figure 3.14). Even though the games being played were less automated, the architectural style remained equally grand, luxurious, and lofty.

The nineteenth-century casino recalled but transformed other social spaces, from the court to the church. But it also offered a contrast to other locations associated with nineteenth-century modernity: the hotel and the train station. While the focus is on the gambling hall, Sala also reminds his readers that there are other ways to spend one's time in comfort and surrounded by the gilded trappings of luxury. Describing the reading room at Bad Homburg, Sala remarks, "When I say that this room is more splendid in its decorations (the work of Belgian artists) than the great *salle a manger* of the Hotel du Louvre at Paris, you may form some idea of its magnificence. There is a sumptuous reading-room, warmly carpeted, and on whose inlaid tables lie the chief newspapers and periodicals of the civilized world."[16] Images depicting the "Salle des Concerts" (Figure 3.15) at Monte Carlo

---

[16] Sala, *Make Your Game*, 178.

Figure 3.7 "Monte-Carlo. – Le Casino. Le Salon Rose" (Lucien Levy, ca. 1907–14). Courtesy of Watkinson Library at Trinity College, Hartford, George Watson Cole European Postcard Collection.

Figure 3.8 "Casino de Monte-Carlo. Salle de Roulette. Salle Garnier" (Nuerdein et Cie, ca. 1907–14). Courtesy of Watkinson Library at Trinity College, Hartford, George Watson Cole European Postcard Collection.

59

555 — Casino de MONTE-CARLO. La Salle Schmidt. ND Phot.

Figure 3.9 "Casino de Monte-Carlo. La Salle Schmidt" (Nuerdein et Cie, ca. 1907–14). Courtesy of Watkinson Library at Trinity College, Hartford, George Watson Cole European Postcard Collection.

50 MONTE-CARLO. — La Nouvelle Salle de Jeux. — LL.

Figure 3.10 "Monte-Carlo. – La Nouvelle Salle de Jeux" (Lucien Levy, ca. 1907–14). Courtesy of Watkinson Library at Trinity College, Hartford, George Watson Cole European Postcard Collection.

Figure 3.11 "Monte-Carlo. – Le Casino. – La Nouvelle Salle de Jeux. – Les Grâces Florentines" (Lucien Levy, ca. 1907–14). Courtesy of Watkinson Library at Trinity College, Hartford, George Watson Cole European Postcard Collection.

Edition Giletta

735. MONTE-CARLO – Salle de Jeu
Dans la Prairie, par Hodebert

Figure 3.12 "Monte-Carlo – Salle de Jeu Dans la Prairie, par Hodebert" (Giletta Freres, ca. 1907–14). Courtesy of Watkinson Library at Trinity College, Hartford, George Watson Cole European Postcard Collection.

947 — Casino de MONTE-CARLO. Salle Schmidt Table de Roulette. ND. Phot.

Figure 3.13 "Casino de Monte-Carlo. Salle Schmidt Table de Roulette" (Nuerdein et Cie, ca. 1907–14). Courtesy of Watkinson Library at Trinity College, Hartford, George Watson Cole European Postcard Collection. The image actually appears to depict La Nouvelle Salle de Jeux.

52 *LE CASINO DE MONTE-CARLO.* – *La Salle de Trente et Quarante.* – LL

Figure 3.14 "Le Casino de Monte-Carlo. – La Salle de Trente et Quarante" (Lucien Levy, ca. 1907–14). Courtesy of Watkinson Library at Trinity College, Hartford, George Watson Cole European Postcard Collection.

529 — Casino de MONTE-CARLO. La Salle des Concerts. ND Phot.

Figure 3.15 "Casino de Monte-Carlo. La Salle des Concerts" (Nuerdein et Cie, ca. 1907–14). Courtesy of Watkinson Library at Trinity College, Hartford, George Watson Cole European Postcard Collection.

demonstrate that the opulence of the gaming rooms spilled out into other areas of the casino.

The gambling rooms were the central points of the casino. Even those architectural elements that were not directly related to gambling (the concert halls, the landscapes, the stairwells, the reading rooms, and so on) had the subsidiary purpose of keeping people within the physical confines of the building so that they would – eventually – return to the gambling tables. Dr. Gardey, who touted the mineral water of Bad Homburg in one publication from 1851, confirms the argument that the logic of the entire casino was to funnel people toward the tables. "From morning till night," Gardey wrote,

> the powerful lure of the tables is felt, dazzling piles of gold and heaps of banknotes, these thrilling games in which, by abandoning some of its advantages, the casino has given players an equal chance against the bank … Thus life in Homburg can be briefly summed up as passing one's time in the pleasantest possible fashion, restoring one's health, resting from the cares of politics and business worries, meeting the most distinguished people from every capital in Europe and making friendships which will be a pleasant and enduring memory.[17]

Contemporary descriptions of Baden-Baden focus on similar themes, not only noting the "seductions" of the place, but also indicating the socially diverse nature of the gambling hall: "But among the seducing attractions of Baden-Baden, and of all German bathing-places, the Rouge-et-noir and Roulette-table hold a melancholy pre-eminence, – being at once a shameful source of revenue to the prince … and a vortex in which the student, the merchant, and the subaltern officer are, in the course of the season, often hopelessly and irrevocably ingulfed [*sic*]."[18]

The tables themselves exerted, as Gardey notes, a "powerful lure" over visitors. Charles Baudelaire, describing gaming in Paris in "The Gaming Table" (included in *The Flowers of Evil*, 1857), produces a remarkable image of the central focus of the casino.

The Gaming Table
On tarnished chairs the pale old harlots quiver,
Sly fatal eyes under the eyebrows painted
Dreadfully mincing: as their lean ears shiver
With hateful jewelled peal the air is tainted.

[17] Quoted in E. C. Corti, *The Wizard of Monte Carlo* (E. P. Dutton, 1935), 86.
[18] A. Steinmetz, *The Gaming Table: Its Votaries and Victims*, 2 vols. (Tinsley Brothers, 1870), vol. 2, 156–57.

Round the green tables a frieze of lipless faces,
Of blue-cold lips, if lips, of toothless gums,
And fingers, fevered with Hell's last disgraces,
Fumbling in pockets – or in deliriums.

Dull chandeliers in the soot-mottled ceiling
And swollen lamps pick out with violet
Shadow the brows of famous poets, reeling
To waste the guerdon of art's blood-stained sweat.

My eye, turned inward, darkly can discern
This Hellish picture self-distorted thus,
The while I see in yonder taciturn
Corner myself, cold, mute – and envious.

Envying these creatures their tenacious lust,
These rattling skeletons their deadly mirth,
Envying all of those who gaily thrust
Honour or beauty to rot beneath the earth.

Envious, my heart! O dark and dreadful word!
When these with passion their bright destruction bless,
Who, drunk with the pulse of their own blood, preferred
Deep pain to death and Hell to nothingness.[19]

Baudelaire's vision of the gaming room and of the gambling table – musty and dingy, crepuscular, with a noted sense of decline – is a predictable representation coming from the master of decadent poetry. What is illuminating about the poem, and why it is useful to include it here, is the way that the gambling hall in the poem, as drab as it is, nonetheless serves as a location of extremely passionate action on the part of the players. While François Blanc's "temples" of modern gambling bear little physical resemblance to Baudelaire's gambling den, he was able to express – and even to celebrate – the self-destructive passions that gambling unleashed in the nineteenth century.

Other people visiting casinos around the time that Baudelaire wrote the poems that came together as *The Flowers of Evil* described the gaming tables in less-florid language, and in one case focus on the mechanical regularity of the games. Describing the gaming tables, Sala writes that "There is one table. Long, covered with green baize, tightly stretched as on a billiard-field. Lighted ... not so much by the gorgeous lustres as by

[19] C. Baudelaire, *The Flowers of Evil* (New Directions Publishing, 1989), 121–22.

bright oil-lamps, their glare shaded."[20] Having set the stage, Sala moves into a description of the roulette device itself. His didactic account focuses on a kind of global vision of the game:

> Oh! but you must be able to see every number on the wheel's compart-
> ments, every piece of money that is staked on the board, when gambling is
> your intent. In the midst of the table there is a circular pit, coved inwards,
> but not bottomless, and containing the roulette-wheel; a revolving disc,
> turning with an accurate momentum on a brass pillar, and divided at its
> outer edge into thirty-seven narrow and shallow pigeon-hole compart-
> ments, coloured alternately red and black, and numbered – not consecu-
> tively – up to thirty-six. The last is a blank, and stands for Zero, number
> Nothing. Round the upper edge, too, run a series of little brass hoops, or
> bridges, to cause the ball to hop and skip, and not fall at once into the
> nearest compartment. This is the regimen of roulette: the banker sits before
> the wheel – a croupier, or payer-out of winnings to and raker-in of losses
> from the players, on either side.[21]

Not only teaching visitors to Bad Homburg what to expect when they entered the gambling rooms, Sala also provides a clear description of the game and how it operated. The educational quality of the work, as dull as it is to read now, should be understood in a nineteenth-century context of not only travel guides like the ones published by Karl Baedeker but also how-to manuals that were presented in other genres. Sala's book, which was quoted at length in later texts like Andrew Steinmetz's two-volume 1870 publication *The Gaming Table*, provided an effective way both to publicize the casino at Bad Homburg and to teach prospective gamblers how the games worked.

John Addington Symonds, writing about Monte Carlo in March 1866, also noted the business-like and mechanical qualities of the gambling table. "Inside the gaming-house play was going forward like a business," Symonds wrote. "[The] tables were crowded. Little could be heard but the monotonous voice of the croupiers, the rattle of gold under their wooden shovels, and the clicking of the ball that spun round for *roulette*. Imperturbable gravity sat on the faces of men who lost or won. Several stern-faced, middle-aged women were making small stakes, and accurately pricking all the chances of the game on cards. A low buzz ran through the room."[22] Unlike Symonds's earlier description of the casino as forming a complete sensory experience, his take on the game alone focuses mainly on

[20] Sala, *Make Your Game*, 178–79.   [21] Sala, *Make Your Game*, 179.
[22] Symonds and Brown, *John Addington Symonds*, 203.

its auditory qualities, summoning a soundscape that remains relatively flat and, to use Symonds's own word, monotonal.

The descriptions of the gaming tables, which focus attention on the mechanical, the regular, the industrial, stand in contrast to the larger depictions of the resort casino that were anchored in descriptions of their monumentality, their volume, and their neo-sacral characters. Steinmetz gives a didactic description of the roulette table at Baden-Baden in 1870. Visitors to that casino would see a table covered in green cloth, at the center of which sits "a large polished wooden basin with a moveable rim, and around it are small compartments, numbered to a certain extent, namely 38, alternately red and black in irregular order, numbered from one to 36, a nought or zero in a red, and a double zero upon the black, making up the 38, and each capable of holding a marble."[23] Sala also offers a description of the "spin" in such a way as to highlight the mechanics of the game for those unfamiliar with its rules:

> Crying in a voice calmly sonorous, *"Faites le jeu, Messieurs"* "Make your game, gentlemen!" the banker gives the wheel a dexterous twirl, and ere it has made one revolution, casts into its maelstrom of black and red an ivory ball. The interval between this and the ball finding a home is one of breathless anxiety. Stakes are eagerly laid, but at a certain period of the revolution the banker calls out, *"Le jeu est fait. Rien ne va plus,"* and after that intimation it is useless to lay down money. Then the banker, in the same calm and impassible voice, declares the result.[24]

This is a world ruled by the banker, not the nobleman. Numbers are more significant than relationships. Sala describes roulette as a game that is inherently honest, although he uses curiously gendered language to make this point. "There are more chances, or rather subdivisions of chances, to entice the player to back the *numbers*, for though the stations of the ball are as capricious as womankind, it is of course extremely rare that a player will fix on the particular number that happens to turn up."[25] Like Sala, Steinmetz offers a description of the mechanics of roulette, and how the physics of the game ensure its honesty. "The moveable rim is set in motion by the hand," Steinmetz writes,

> and as it revolves horizontally from east to west round its axis, the marble is caused by a jerk of the finger and thumb to fly off in a contrary movement. The public therefore conclude that no calculation can foretell where the marble will fall, and ... in as much as the bank plays a certain and sure

[23] Quoted in Steinmetz, *The Gaming Table*, vol. 1, 162.   [24] Sala, *Make Your Game*, 179.
[25] Sala, *Make Your Game*, 181.

game, however deep, runs no risk of loss, and consequently has no necessity for superfluously cheating or deluding the public.[26]

Like Sala's book, the effect of Steinmetz's text is to inform his readers about the various casino games in a way that would allow neophytes to understand the game, and it therefore takes a very descriptive tone. And significantly, the language used to describe the casino and its games is drawn from science, mathematics, observation, and the calculatory. It was also in the interest of the casino to publicize the rules of the various games and to familiarize visitors with the basic conventions of play. To this end, the casino at Monte Carlo produced and distributed small cards that provided quick tutorials on roulette and Trente et Quarante (see Figures 3.16 and 3.17). While Symonds's description of gambling at Monte Carlo was written for his own edification – it was included in his journal – Sala and Steinmetz had different audiences in mind. And yet one thing that united these writers was the desire to describe the people in the casino, a task that attracted writers of all sorts in the nineteenth century.

Nineteenth-century casinos – while recalling and transforming other spaces – were anchored in attempts to form and encourage certain types of middle-class sociability. One aspect of casino literature, then, was to provide a visual dictionary of the social types and social behaviors that one might encounter at the casino. "The Game Season at Spürt," an 1854 essay included in *Household Words*, a publication edited by Charles Dickens, depicts a mid-nineteenth-century Rhenish spa casino, and like Sala's or Steinmetz's texts, it was especially focused on describing the mechanics of the games, in this case the card game Trente et Quarante. The author describes the elaborate rituals about the presentation of the bank, the conduct of the banker, the appearance of the croupier, and so on. But the ultimate result is also a description of the people working in the casino. The croupiers, the author writes, "sit, like four black spiders in the middle of a large green web, quietly waiting for the flies to come to them."[27] The psychology of the situation is important to him, and his description of the players focuses on their lack of will: "hardly any of the players come to the table thus spread for them with anything like an air of determination to engage in play. They generally lounge towards it in a state of abstraction; and then, after staring vacantly about them for a few seconds, drop into a seat, as if with a complete unconsciousness of what

---

[26] Quoted in Steinmetz, *The Gaming Table*, vol. 1, 162.
[27] W. Crowe, "The Game Season at Spürt," *Household Words*, 240 (1854), 262–64, 263.

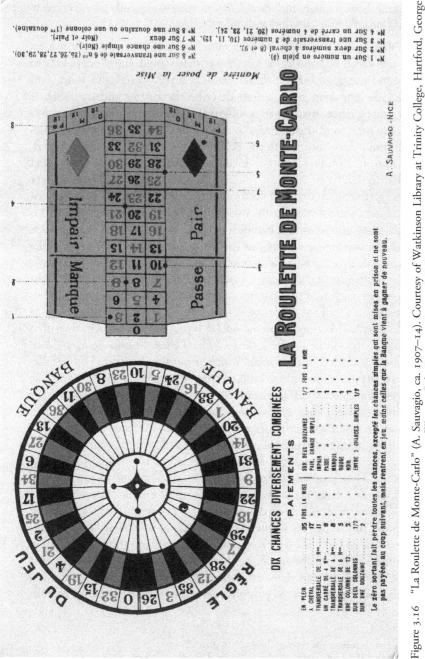

Figure 3.16 "La Roulette de Monte-Carlo" (A. Sauvagio, ca. 1907–14). Courtesy of Watkinson Library at Trinity College, Hartford, George Watson Cole European Postcard Collection.

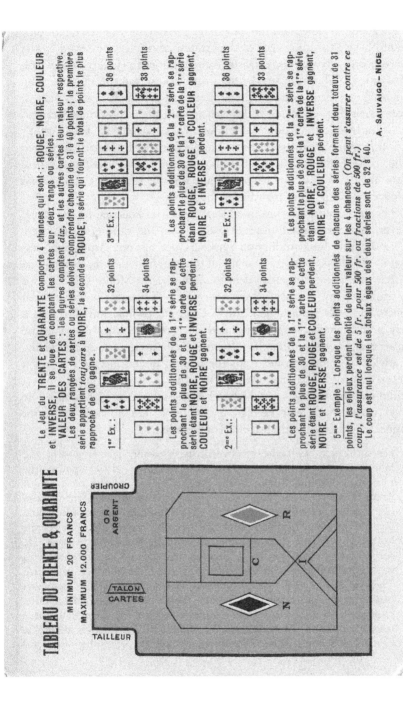

Figure 3.17 "Tableau du Trente & Quarante" (A. Sauvagio, ca. 1907–14). Courtesy of Watkinson Library at Trinity College, Hartford, George Watson Cole European Postcard Collection.

they are about."[28] The staff, too, play their parts in diffusing the emotional content of the situation: "One of the greatest advantages possessed by the bank over ordinary players, consists in the unmoved placidity with which it wins or loses. The croupiers, being simply paid servants of the company, and having very little or no personal interest in the result of each deal ... perform their duty of paying and receiving with the utmost unconcern; in fact, as nearly after the manner of automatons as possible."[29] The author's description of the gamblers is not unlike the one that Baudelaire produced in the "The Gaming Table." Tired and emotionally deadened, these players are drawn by the magnetic lure of the table, and the casino employees are little more than fleshy robots.

Other writers were more attuned to the passions liberated by the game, however, and their descriptions of gamblers in the gaming rooms were much more lush. John Addington Symonds, perhaps not surprisingly, was drawn to the physical beauty of many of the men in the room, although he too drew unsparing comparisons to the croupiers in Monte Carlo. "Two men attracted my interest," Symonds writes. "One was a terrier-faced Englishman, with reddish hair and a sanguine complexion. He staked largely, and laughed at his winnings and losings indifferently. A very astute man, who did not play himself, seemed to be backing him up and giving him advice." While Symonds finds the tableau interesting, he was much more excited by the second man. "The other," Symonds notes, "was a splendid-looking fellow – a tall, handsome, well-made Piedmontese he seemed to be – at least he had a favourable resemblance to Victor Emanuel." Symonds continues, clearly enamored:

> His small head, with crisp brown hair, fresh colour, light moustache and long imperial, cold bluish eyes, and steadfast frown, was set upon a little muscular neck, and that upon the body of a Hermes with most perfect hands. There was something innocent in his face; yet the whole man looked like a sleek panther. It would be easy to love him; the woman who should love him would be happy for some days, and then would most probably be broken. But strong determination and cool devilry sat in his face. He seemed once to lose everything. Then he went out and soon returned with bank notes, some of which he paid away and some of which he staked. Then he gained gold, bank notes and *rouleaux*, but he still continued playing with perfect *sangfroid*. When the *rouge et noir* stopped for a minute, he got up and made a large stake at *roulette*, and left a servingman to watch it for him when his favourite game began again. C. said he was like Rolla. Certainly when he is ruined he will shoot himself. At present he is fresh and

---

[28] Crowe, "Game Season at Spürt," 263.   [29] Crowe, "Game Season at Spürt," 263.

fair and charming to look at, his great physical and moral strength, though tempered wickedly, being a refreshing spectacle.[30]

Symonds's observation of the men playing, and his reflections on their physical perfection and animal natures – in these cases either a terrier, which is not especially flattering, or a "sleek panther," which is – generates a way of understanding the social space of the gambling hall that does not neglect the sexual frisson found in the location.

The passage continues, and Symonds pays special attention to the cool demeanor of his object of attention, whom he calls the "prince of gamblers" with "tigerish" nerves.

> We notice that almost all the gamesters had light blue eyes. No exhibition of despair was visible; yet I saw many very jaded young men, and nervous old men, blear-eyed fellows staking eagerly five-franc pieces. My young Rolla was the royal one – the prince of gamblers in that room – and but for him the place would have had no romance for me. It must be an odd life: lounging and smoking in the gardens, listening to Verdi in the music hall, gormandising in the *salle à manger*, and enjoying every beauty of southern spring, together with the fiery pleasures of that hazard.... I have not enough continuity of good spirits, of self-deception, and of resolution, to gamble. Under the influence of some kind of passion, I could fancy going into it for a moment, but the yoke would be to me most odious. How nerves can bear it I wonder. But my Rolla's nerves are tigerish, and like the tickling which would rend me to atoms. Perfect coolness and concentration of fever-producing calm marked this man. His whole soul was in the play.[31]

Symonds is clearly transfixed by this scene, and his thought experiment about how the emotional qualities of gambling might affect him (unlike "his Rolla") is an indication of the ways the gaming hall heightened and exploited emotional tension. Indeed, even observing the play, Symonds is hardly able to control his emotional responses; he wonders how "nerves can bear it." Writing just before George Miller Beard described "neurasthenia" as a medical pathology, Symonds recognized the symptoms in himself.[32]

Symonds also described the casino staff, again relying on the animal kingdom to supply the necessary archetypes. "The croupiers," Symonds explains, "are either fat, sensual cormorants, or sallow lean-cheeked vultures, or suspicious foxes. So I term them."[33] Symonds goes on to

[30] Symonds and Brown, *John Addington Symonds*, 204.
[31] Symonds and Brown, *John Addington Symonds*, 205.
[32] G. Beard, "Neurasthenia, or Nervous Exhaustion," *The Boston Medical and Surgical Journal*, 80/13 (1869), 217–21.
[33] Symonds and Brown, *John Addington Symonds*, 204.

comment on the ways that the staff's jobs have corrupted them, hardening them through their constant contact with misfortune and with the most "sordid" of financial transactions that also lack any hint of "honor."[34] Symonds writes, "[Y]et they [the croupiers] only look like wicked bankers' clerks, like men narrowed and made sordid by constant contact with money in a heartless trade, and corrupted by familiarity with turns of luck instead of honourable business rules.... [T]hese men of the gaming bank show every trace of a dissolute youth and a vile calling, of low sensuality and hardened avarice, upon their faces."[35] Symonds describes something important here: the ways in which the casino transformed human relationships and, perhaps more important, human sensations. We turn now to consider how the casino and the gaming hall generally, and the game specifically, generated a set of novel sensations in visitors. Understanding and analyzing how gambling changed how visitors experienced life is a key to understanding its broader popularity in nineteenth-century Europe.

We start with Symonds, in part because we have already noted the ways that he employed all of his senses in his first experience of the casino. He was direct in his assessment of what gambling did to sensory impression: "There is a passion which subdues all others, making music, sweet scents, and delicious food, the splash of the melodious waves, the evening air and freedom of the everlasting hills, subserve her own supremacy. When the fiend of play has entered into a man, what does he care for the beauties of nature or even for the pleasure of the sense?"[36] Indeed, gambling might imperil human interaction and sociability, culminating in what Symonds calls a "sober, sad reality."[37] Yet Monte Carlo never collapsed into such a condition; instead, it generated a suite of novel impressions, sensations, and experiences that together were unlike anything Symonds had experienced. He writes in his journal,

> I have seen it to-day with my own eyes. I have been inside the palace, and have breathed its air. In no other place could this riotous daughter of hell have set her throne so seducingly. Here are the Sirens and Calypso and Dame Venus of Tannhauser's dream. Almost every other scene of dissipation has disappointed me by its monotony and sordidness. But this inebriates; here nature is so lavish, so beautiful, so softly luxurious, that the

---

[34] H. Lempa argues in *Spaces of Honor: Making German Civil Society, 1700–1914* (University of Michigan Press, 2021) that spa towns were important locations for the navigation of honor codes. See pp. 90–114.
[35] Symonds and Brown, *John Addington Symonds*, 204–5.
[36] Symonds and Brown, *John Addington Symonds*, 202.
[37] Symonds and Brown, *John Addington Symonds*, 203.

harlot's cup is thrice more sweet to the taste, more stealing of the senses than elsewhere. I felt, while we listened to the music, strolled about the gardens, and lounged in the play rooms, as I have sometimes felt at the opera. All other pleasures, thoughts, and interests of life seemed to be far off and trivial for the time. I was beclouded, carried off my balance, lapped in strange forebodings of things infinite outside me in the human heart. Yet all was unreal; for the touch of reason, like the hand of Galahad, caused the boiling of this impure fountain to cease – the wizard's castle disappeared, and, as I drove homeward to Mentone, the solemn hills and skies and seas remained, and that house was, as it were, a mirage.[38]

Better than any reality, even a sad, sober one, the mirage of Monte Carlo and the combination of new pleasures that it made possible threw Symonds off balance and exposed him to some sort of the sublime: something he calls the "infinite outside me in the human heart."

Other observers of this phenomenon were perhaps more restrained. But in many accounts we see the argument that the casino produced an environment in which the emotions were unmoored, and new sensations attacked any previous emotional core that visitors possessed.[39] Unlike other spaces that channeled emotion – the cathedral or the court – the nineteenth-century casino did so in the service of play, pleasure, and financial gain. Margaret de Vere Stacpoole's 1913 novel provides one take on this issue. A central character, Jack, visits the casino, and as "they were ascending the Casino steps now . . . the spirit of the place had his mind in charge."[40] This "spirit" of the casino does important cultural work. Stacpoole writes, "On entering the rooms for the first time Jack Revell had experienced no other sensation than that of curiosity; the taste for gambling was the last vicious taste that he would have suspected in himself . . . and yet no gambler ever, perhaps, entered the rooms with a more burning desire for play than he to-day."[41] Other characters in Stacpoole's novel find the crowds dedicated to vice less appealing, strange, and even somewhat conflicted: "It was the first time that Julia [who is married to Jack Revell] had ever seen gambling on a big scale; and the sight . . . impressed her with an eerie sensation. . . . She felt that all these people were more or less on a bad business, engaged in what is recognized by society as a vice, and it was the commercial coldness and businesslike

[38] Symonds and Brown, *John Addington Symonds*, 203.
[39] See Y. B. Alaluf, *The Emotional Economy of Holidaymaking: Health, Pleasure, and Class in Britain, 1870–1918* (Oxford University Press, 2021), for the ways that emotions like pleasure and belonging shaped the experiences of leisure.
[40] M. de V. Stacpoole, *Monte Carlo: A Novel* (Dodd, Mead and Co., 1913), 99.
[41] Stacpoole, *Monte Carlo*, 100.

atmosphere of the place that gave her a little thrill."[42] Later historians of Monte Carlo note a similar emotional transformation. Egon Corti suggests the practice of gambling stems from the emotions liberated when a person enjoys a "good big run of luck and the mirage of boundless wealth that it creates."[43]

A common feature of writing on casinos in the nineteenth century was a focus on the issue of suicide, framing the practice as a novel reaction to the emotional stresses produced in the gambling hall. Unsurprisingly, casino staff were eager to avoid the scandal associated with suicide. Blanc's assistant Trittler declared that "in the neighbourhood of a casino like ours, from which so many depart in despair, anything that might make it easier for people to take their own lives when they have seen their last hopes destroyed should be removed. At such moments people are not in their sober senses, and are virtually madmen."[44] Manners, emotional display, and suicide were depicted in Bad Homburg, for instance, as a logical outgrowth of the inability of a particular type of person to manage the intense emotional strain of experiencing financial loss. In one especially dramatic account that was reproduced in multiple texts, a gambler commits suicide at the roulette table. The jarring event is handled, as Sala reports, calmly by the casino staff.

> People are too genteel at Hombourg-von-der-Höhe to scream, to yell, to fall into fainting fits, or go into convulsions, because they have lost four or five thousand francs or so on a single coup. I have heard of one gentleman, indeed, who, after a ruinous loss, put a pistol to his head, and discharging it, spattered his brains over the roulette-wheel. It was said that the banker, looking up calmly, called out "Triple zero" treble nothing, – a case as yet unheard-of in the tactics of roulette, but signifying annihilation, – and that a cloth being thrown over the ensanguined wheel, the bank at that particular table was declared to be closed for the day.[45]

Manners mattered, even in dire circumstances. But when the "genteel" could no longer withstand the stress, suicide remained an option. Suicide was a standard topic in reportage on Blanc's casinos, and his competitors would highlight this element of the industry as a way of underscoring his callously business-like nature. Indeed, rumors swirled that the bodies of suicide victims were collected before dawn each morning so that they would not disturb the experience of other gamblers; other reports claimed that all suicides were taken to Cannes and registered there. The practice of

[42] Stacpoole, *Monte Carlo*, 32–33.   [43] Corti, *The Wizard of Monte Carlo*, 98.
[44] Quoted in Corti, *The Wizard of Monte Carlo*, 103.   [45] Sala, *Make Your Game*, 185–86.

the "viatique," in which busted gamblers would be given a train ticket home by the casino, aimed to prevent suicide at the resort by despairing gamblers. And it was also suggested that suicides would appear in waves and that the dramatic evidence of one person's misfortune would stimulate suicide in others. Others, though, debunked this theory. Writing in 1890, W. Fraser Rae suggested that "Suicides and duels which end in death are not more common at Monte Carlo than at places where games of chance are never played in public."[46] The fact that the casinos were in the habit of paying broken gamblers to leave and return home alerts us to the fact that gambling in the nineteenth century was an increasingly transnational form of leisure. The nineteenth-century casino was produced by – and productive of – a certain form of bourgeois sociability characteristic of the time. Even the architects of modern gambling – François Blanc and Marie Hensel – indicate the transnational qualities of the activity. She was German (and a Huguenot), he was of course French (and twenty-seven years older).

We should focus on the fact that while the Hensel-Blanc marriage represents one typical of border regions like the Rhineland, gambling in the Blanc mode was a supremely transnational industry. The historical development of the casino in the nineteenth century, as we saw in Chapter 1, occurred first in Rhenish spa towns like Bad Homburg or Wiesbaden because they were long associated with leisure and health that appealed to a wide stratum of wealthy Europeans who were accustomed to traveling in order to pursue those things. As spa towns took on casino gambling, they were able to leverage those preexisting clientele. Reith argues that nineteenth-century casinos provide an especially compelling case study of the ways the "spheres of leisure and work" were finally severed from one another.[47] And in this sense too, spa towns like Bad Homburg, appealing both to aristocrats but also to wealthy bourgeois, represented a transnational and trans-class zone of privileged leisure.

Monte Carlo provided leisure space to a cosmopolitan group of wealthy Europeans but did so in ways that were represented in geographically convoluted forms. Stacpoole's novel explained that Monte Carlo is "an extension of Paris by way of Enghien, an entension of London, St. Petersburg, Berlin and New York by way of Paris – that is to say, an extension of their worst and most brilliant parts. Vice really magnificently

---

[46] W. F. Rae, "Play and Players on the Riviera," *The Nineteenth Century*, 27/February (1890), 240–57, 247.
[47] G. Reith, *The Age of Chance: Gambling in Western Culture* (Routledge, 1999), 74.

done: that is Monte Carlo."[48] Another character in the book, the Habsburg spy Carslake, describes the polyglot nature of Monte Carlo in casually racist ways typical of people at the time: "I've been counting Russians, Poles, Spaniards, Norwegians, Greeks, two Turks, a nigger, three Japanese."[49] Others who described the people flocking to the gaming rooms also focused on the national diversity of the crowd. Kingston explains that "it is always a very orderly crowd in the rooms. In the solemn cathedral-like hush which generally prevails the Babel of tongues is lost and the cosmopolitan crowd is reduced to the same consistency by the passion for gain. The language of the greater emotions is universal and money also speaks a language which everybody understands."[50] The desire for money, as Georg Simmel noted, dissolved national borders but also provided a universal language of desire.

Descriptions of Bad Homburg confirm these sentiments. One long passage from Sala's *Make Your Game*, which must be quoted in its entirety for the effect it produces, provides a fascinating description of the human diversity on display in the casino at Bad Homburg. "For *I* never," Sala writes,

> saw such a sweeping and raking together of people from all the five corners of the earth, and from the uttermost ends thereof, in my peaceful, but not altogether devoid of experience, days. Russian boyards, Wallachian way-wodes, and Moldavian hospodars; Servian kaimakans, Montenegrin proto-spathaires, Bulgarian Bey-oglous, Turkish pachas, effendis, naiks, and reis (strict fact, all in their national costume, consisting of ill-made European clothes, patent leather boots, white kids, and red fezes with blue tassels, which [the former] make them look like poppies in a field of corn); Tartar khans and Livonian Ritterschaft-Herren; North German counts and barons ad infinitum; Lubeck and Bremen burgomasters and ship-chandlers; Dantzic spruce merchants; Berlin glovers; stalwart Austrian and Prussian life- guardsmen; French marquises, viscounts, and chevaliers of industry and of idleness; New York stock brokers and dry goods importers (tremen-dous dandies these); New Orleans and South Carolina cotton and sugar planters (ineffable and haughty exquisites these, with exuberant coats of arms on their visiting cards and cigar-cases, claiming descent from ancient English families, indulging, not unfrequently, in covert sneers at republi-canism, and not caring to mix much with the men from the north); West Indian Creoles, shivering in the genial autumnal sunshine; swarthy Spanish dons, from old and new Spain, livid, as to their finger nails, with the *sangre azul,* and smoking paper cigars eternally; vivacious Swedes – the French

---

[48] Stacpoole, *Monte Carlo*, 32.   [49] Stacpoole, *Monte Carlo*, 38.
[50] Kingston, *The Romance of Monte Carlo*, 212.

men of the north, those blue-eyed, hospitable, courteous, much-bowing Swedes; sententious Danes; gesticulating Italians; silent and expectorating Dutch men; and Great British people![51]

Sala's unnamed narrator provides in the passage a long checklist of national types who have descended on the casino. Sala uses this opportunity to note the "universal character of the Hombourg visitors,"[52] and he reproduces a section of the *Fremdenblatt* (the "foreign news") that contained a list of prominent visitors and their hometowns. In Sala's assessment, the "universal" nature of leisure life in Bad Homburg was entirely due to the Blancs, whom he declared to "have metamorphosed a miserable mid-German townlet into a city of palaces."[53]

One argument about nineteenth-century gambling suggests that it proliferated in anti-democratic areas of Europe (visitors were required to hold entrance tickets and could be refused entry if they did not meet the visual standards set by the house; see Figure 3.18). In a different way, one may use the transnational leisure class that enjoyed resort living to argue that the spa towns and their casinos were in fact more democratic than other areas of Europe. Egon Corti, for instance, claims that gambling itself is a practice that promotes democratic exchanges among equals. In this sense, the nineteenth-century casino operated on a different footing than eighteenth-century courtly gaming. "Here [the casino at Monte Carlo] all ordinary standards were overthrown, and everyone was equal. The gaming table knew no distinctions of rank; the soldier of fortune in his elegant shabbiness sat next to the noble and the prince."[54] If gambling could be presented as a form of leisure activity that was pursued for the purpose of amusement, it could perform the important cultural work of bridging differences and creating a form of society and a manner of social interaction that aspired to universalism. As James Romain wrote in 1891, "Gaming is an amusement for many persons. Thousands enjoy the excitements of chance. It stimulates their spirits above the cares and drudgery of existence. Such men prefer a game to either book, piano or cigar. With them it is not a question of utility but of diversion. Is the value of entertainment to be measured in muscle or metal?"[55] Hiram Maxim, quoting extensively from Austrian Viktor Silberer, made a similar case for why Monte Carlo – and legalized gambling – was a good thing.

[51] Sala, *Make Your Game*, 162–63.   [52] Sala, *Make Your Game*, 163.
[53] Sala, *Make Your Game*, 168.   [54] Corti, *The Wizard of Monte Carlo*, 267–68.
[55] J. H. Romain, *Gambling: Or, Fortuna, Her Temple and Shrine. The True Philosophy and Ethics of Gambling* (Craig Press, 1891), 98–99.

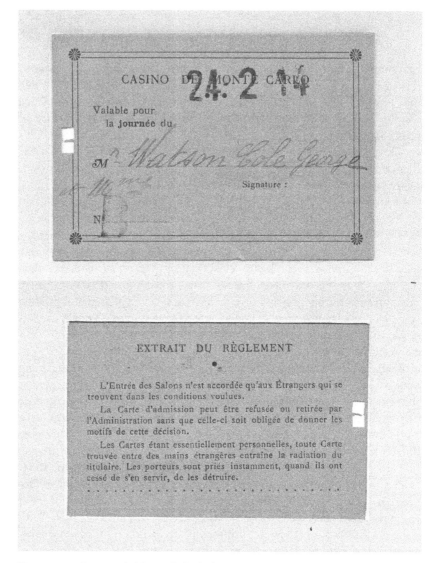

Figure 3.18   Entry card, Monte Carlo (unknown, ca. 1907–14). Courtesy of Watkinson Library at Trinity College, Hartford, George Watson Cole European Postcard Collection.

Transparency meant that players did not have to loan each other money; that debts were paid quickly; that winners and losers were not compelled to keep playing when they no longer wished to do so. Because the odds are something easy to calculate, roulette is actually fairer and more transparent than other games, especially horse racing. Money is a type of equalizer: "Without ready money, the Prince of Wales himself cannot play there."[56] However, as Silberer explains, "It is the unlimited capital of the Bank, with its always accessible gaming tables; in the constantly present possibility increasing winnings already made, or cancelling losses already incurred, it is in these characteristics, these *advantages*, that an *ever present irresistible temptation* lies, enticing men into the Casino day after day."[57] The social interactions that nineteenth-century casinos promoted and cultivated spoke to larger measures of modern life. Gambling could no longer be considered a vice, or even a sin, if in the course of modern living it was no longer possible to identify the victims. As one American anti-gambling advocate framed the issue in 1907, "Men used to know against whom they sinned, but in the complexity of modern life, it is simply against the public, and the public are so many and so indefinite that it does not count."[58]

Nineteenth-century casinos like Bad Homburg or Monte Carlo certainly attracted a transnational clientele, and they may have even promoted a certain porousness of class and status (at least the one dividing the aristocracy from wealthy commoners). Indeed, a mixture of social classes was one of the central plans that the Blancs executed in Bad Homburg. François Blanc "became the most successful gambling impresario of the nineteenth century because he so deftly adapted the older theatrical appeals of aristocratic gambling to suit the needs and tastes of the modern age."[59] But it is also important to recognize that the casinos included members of both genders. While we may be used to imagining these spaces as homosocial ones like the sex-segregated club or the imagined gambling dens of the western United States, it is worth reexamining the ways that the casino brought men and women together into the same space for the purpose of leisure or amusement. Figures 3.6, 3.13, 3.19, and 3.20 each depict the gaming room as a place of interaction between men and women. While some people in the casinos were sex workers, most were not. Written accounts from the time also indicate how the gaming room specifically but

[56] H. S. Maxim, *Monte Carlo: Facts and Fallacies* (Grant Richards, 1904), 241.
[57] Maxim, *Monte Carlo*, 245.
[58] C. G. Twombly, "The Evil of Gambling: Cancer on Moral Life of Community," *Pennsylvania School Journal*, 56 (1908), 284–87, 286.
[59] M. Braude, *Making Monte Carlo: A History of Speculation and Spectacle* (Simon & Schuster, 2016), 26.

Figure 3.19 *At the Gambling Table* (first plate) by Jean-Louis Forain, 1909. Courtesy National Gallery of Art, Washington.

Figure 3.20 *At the Gambling Table* (second plate) by Jean-Louis Forain, 1909. Courtesy National Gallery of Art, Washington.

the resort more generally provided a location of interaction and courtship in the nineteenth century. One of the extended subplots of Dostoyevsky's *The Gambler* revolves around the Gambler's pursuit of a woman with whom he has fallen in love. Stacpoole's *Monte Carlo* also indicates the ways that resort towns promoted cross-class and transnational love affairs.

But if the casino promoted certain class and gender norms, it also had the potential to throw gender into chaos: it could masculinize women by encouraging them to pursue activities like gambling too seriously; it could feminize men by making them too emotional. Andrew Steinmetz described the issue by first looking at the problem of female "games-tresses." "The passions of the two sexes are similar in the main; the distinctions between them result less from nature than from education. Often we meet with women, especially the literary sort, who seem veritable men, if not so, as the lawyers say, 'to all intents and purposes'; and often we meet with men, especially town-dandies, who can only be compared to very ordinary women."[60] Later critiques focused on the seedier qualities of casino life. Stacpoole describes one female character in a way that equates her moral decline to that of Monte Carlo as a whole:

> Those eyes, beady and restless as the eyes of a bird, that mouth sensuous yet characterless, that face good looking yet devoid of softness, sense, or any trace of kindliness, all these spoke of the negative and the evil of littleness, yet at a distance this woman, well dressed as she was, had about her the quality of attraction. Passing her you would have thought her good-looking; speaking to her you would have found her plain in all charms that constitute true womanhood. She was Monte Carlo incarnate.[61]

One way to discern the social nature of the casino is to focus on the ways that various gambling "types" were represented in descriptions of the gaming rooms. Corti describes Sophie Kisselev, a Russian princess who frequented Bad Homburg, and who was a dedicated gambler. Corti asserts that Kisselev would arrive at the tables in a completely weakened condition, but "the moment she heard the rattle of the fateful ball, she suddenly became rejuvenated, followed the course of the little ivory ball with glowing eyes and bated breath, and staked sums which often amounted to hundreds of thousands."[62] Kisselev is an important figure. Not only does she represent the ways that the Russian aristocracy enjoyed the mild Rhenish climate in the wintertime, but she was also used by Dostoevsky as the template for the character of the Grandmother in *The Gambler*. Aside from her somatic responses to the sounds of the gaming room, Kisselev was

---

[60] Steinmetz, *The Gaming Table*, vol. 1, 254.   [61] Stacpoole, *Monte Carlo*, 193.
[62] Corti, *The Wizard of Monte Carlo*, 55.

also very superstitious: "The old lady was so superstitious that she was always surrounded by hypnotists, spiritualists and inventors of systems who persuaded her that they could calculate in advance how the ivory ball would fall. These people were known as 'professors,' and they abused the old Countess's credulity till their failures became too gross and she drove them away in disgrace."[63] In this passage from Corti we see the fabrication of two well-known types: the rich, foreign, and superstitious female gambler, and the "professor" who claimed to have divined a "system" that could unfailingly beat the odds, but never did.

Professional gamblers were another group that was often singled out for description. One type of professional gambler is known as the "bank breaker," the person who travels from casino to casino attempting to "break the bank" by winning all the money and closing down the table. One such person is described in the "Game Season at Spürt": H. R. H, the Prince of Fatino, possesses a "bullying confidence in his own fortune" and who "with his massive head, massive person, and massive hands, clenched always upon the table before him, looks impregnable."[64] Those who do not attain the status of bank breaker are still regarded with suspicion, and professional gamblers are held in low opinion. They are "the dirtiest and shabbiest-looking members of the community" who sometimes sell "systems, or martingales, to new-comers, and will even play, themselves, for a consideration, with the capital of other men."[65] Such opinions were widely held, if not shared. Queen Victoria wrote in her diary after a visit to Monte Carlo that "One saw very nasty disreputable looking people walking about at Monte Carlo, though many respectable people go there also for their health. The harm this attractive gambling establishment does cannot be overestimated. The old Prince of Monaco derives his income from it and therefore does not wish to stop it, though efforts are being made to do so."[66] Inventor Hiram Maxim, who wrote a long debunking of the systematizers at Monte Carlo, was unsparing in his depiction of several "objectionable characters," he saw at the casino there. He noted, for instance a "human spider," a woman with a large hat: "Seated at the table with her hooked nose, claw-like hands, and peculiar hat, she looked curiously enough like a bird of prey, or, I might say, a human spider concealed under her web."[67] Maxim is particularly incensed that she often

[63] Corti, *The Wizard of Monte Carlo*, 60.   [64] Crowe, "Game Season at Spürt," 264.

[65] Crowe, "Game Season at Spürt," 264.

[66] Quoted in J. A. S. Hale, *The French Riviera: A Cultural History* (Oxford University Press, 2009), 40.

[67] Maxim, *Monte Carlo*, 209.

claims the winnings of other players, grabbing coins in the confusion between spins of the roulette wheel. Maxim reports that when such practices were noticed, and the alarm raised, the casino often preferred to pay both parties rather than risk a disturbance. "Everything goes on with regularity and mathematical precision. The small percentage in favour of the Bank is well known and recognised by all; the fairness of the play is above suspicion, and all stakes are paid after every 'coup,' no matter whether the amount is five francs or a hundred thousand!"[68] Exotic visitors to the casino also generated their share of descriptive passages. One, Mustapha Fazil Pasha, was described as a "Turkish grandee" who, while at Bad Homburg, sat in the casino "with imperturbable Oriental calm." The passage continues by explaining that "the Turk followed the course of play, only his gleaming eyes betraying his passionate excitement."[69]

Many observers were quick to argue that the casino management itself was dishonest. Indeed, Stacpoole contrasts the casino with the work of fishermen in Italy: "They were hauling in a seine net, and Julia watched them with interest; this honest bit of labour was the best thing she had seen on the Riviera, that paradise of parasites on society."[70] And yet one interesting thing about Monte Carlo is that it markets itself as the place to play honest games so that the gambler does not have to worry about being fleeced by unsavory sharpers, con artists, or crooked gambling instruments. Even Maxim describes the knock-on effects the casino has had on the Riviera, concluding that gambling has had many positive effects through-out the region, not the least of which was that the transparency and honesty of the casino had transformed social life within the region. The villain in Stacpoole's novel, Carslake, agrees:

> I've heard it said that the management rely upon bad air to help them in their business; people get hypnotised by the tables and lose control of themselves quicker when the air is bad. But that's all nonsense; I mean it's nonsense to say that the management conspire to poison people with bad air so as to get their money. They are perfectly honest; in fact, I should think that, as a business establishment, this is the most generous and honestly-conducted in the world. Why should it not be? It is a machine so constructed that it must win. It has no need of trickery.[71]

With this in mind, we turn next to an analysis of chance, luck, and probability in the nineteenth-century casino.

---

[68] Maxim, *Monte Carlo*, 295.   [69] Corti, *The Wizard of Monte Carlo*, 214.
[70] Stacpoole, *Monte Carlo*, 232.   [71] Stacpoole, *Monte Carlo*, 44–45.

CHAPTER 4

Probability and the Casino

The Blanc casinos were marketed through the cultivation of an impression of honesty and mechanical universality. The study of probability, which arose historically in relationship to the calculation of gambling odds, provided a way to measure the honesty of a casino.[1] Probability, as it was expressed in the context of nineteenth-century resort casinos, was the object of renewed interest among professional mathematicians and amateurs seeking to understand the logic of the games they played. There are three avenues through which this amplified interest in probability was expressed in the nineteenth century: the analysis of "runs" (a long sequence of identical results), the systems that gamblers developed for beating the odds, and the casino as an experimental space for mathematicians in the nineteenth century. Together, these developments suggest that the nineteenth-century casino provided a novel opportunity for inquiry into areas such as the nature of time, the limits of causation, and the science of probability.

It is important to remember that probability as a branch of knowledge was, even in its first moments, concerned with calculating the odds of incidence that could be applied to gambling.[2] Reith suggests that this appearance of chance and the development of an understanding of probability was situated historically between the seventeenth and nineteenth centuries – there was a fundamental reorganization of human thought on the issues of fate, luck, chance, and probability that forced a rethinking of causation and correlation as well. If we place these intellectual trends in the context of the collapse of the baroque order, the creation of the early eighteenth-century "consumer revolution," and the extension of European mercantile empires across the globe, we can see a broader

[1] D. G. Schwartz, *Roll the Bones: The History of Gambling* (Gotham Books, 2006), 73–91; T. M. Kavanagh, *Enlightenment and the Shadows of Chance: The Novel and the Culture of Gambling in Eighteenth-Century France* (The Johns Hopkins University Press, 1993), 9–28.
[2] See L. Daston's *Classical Probability in the Enlightenment* (Princeton University Press, 1995).

intellectual transformation taking place. The calculation of odds – whether that was done in the context of insuring shipping, of placing a bet at the gambling table, or of speculating on the nascent stock and financial markets – developed in tandem. And each calculation attempted to capture numerically the problem of probability.

Reith argues that the "paradox of probability" means that a set of ideas developed that lets us know what should happen, but not what will happen. The tendency toward abstraction is very powerful, but it also means that the general replaces the specific, the long-term replaces the instant, the "average" replaces the "individual," and, I would add, the theoretical replaces the real. Quantification in the nineteenth century transformed this intellectual mode, and one sees in the rise of statistics a new way to apprehend reality.[3] Reith argues that the shift from probability analysis to statistical analysis was one of the great epistemological transformations of the nineteenth century and helped shape a "new consciousness of the self" that appeared, as we have seen in relation to the social nature of the casino, in some form to be democratic in its orientation. Appeals to the norm and to the average meant that "an individual [was] in no way privileged above any other."[4]

***

There are a number of tales about a remarkable series of events that occurred at the roulette tables in European casinos. The stories are generally congruent, except for the date of the alleged miracle.

> [I]n the majority of cases, your capital is *not* strong enough to carry out the combination in the face of a heavy run against you – as when you are backing red, and black turns up eighteen, or, as it did once at Geneva, twenty-seven times; and you are broken and cleaned out – it may be, irremediably ruined, on the very eve of success.[5] (1860)

> Rouge has appeared twenty-eight times in succession at Monte Carlo.[6] (1892)

> [A]t the end of a run of twenty-six on red, there would be no greater likelihood of black's turning up next time, than there would be had black and red been alternating in the usual proportions.[7] (1899)

---

[3] See T. M. Porter, *The Rise of Statistical Thinking, 1820–1900* (Princeton University Press, 1986).

[4] G. Reith, *The Age of Chance: Gambling in Western Culture* (Routledge, 1999), 34.

[5] G. A. Sala, *Make Your Game, or, The Adventures of the Stout Gentleman, the Slim Gentleman, and the Man with the Iron Chest: A Narrative of the Rhine and Thereabouts* (Ward and Lock, 1860), 219.

[6] N. Young, "Systems of Gambling," *National Review*, 18/29 (1892), 449–60, 450.

[7] "The Science of Chance," *The Saturday Review of Politics, Literature, Science, and Art*, 88 (1899), 97–98, 97.

[There is the] recorded fact that red has turned up at Monte Carlo twenty-eight times running.[8] (1900)

What should we make of this event, one that been repeatedly described (although taking place in different years, in slightly different contexts, and with different reactions)?[9] Long "runs" of one color on the roulette table, or of one side in coin tosses, were understood in the 1860s as "curious instances of the irregularity of chance."[10] Yet even these occasions did little at the time to affect the emotional lives of gamblers. Runs, the same author reports, did not generate "distressing scenes ... the players win and lose with an absence of expressed emotion very marvelous."[11] Ever since Bernoulli's law of large numbers, gamblers have sought to understand runs and to imagine the ways that a long run required what was termed an "evening" of the odds over time. Bernoulli's law forms the basis for what people today recognize as the "gambler's fallacy," the idea that a long run had somehow thrown the occult logic of chance out of whack and that a reckoning was due.

It is important to recognize that Bernoulli's law and the gambler's fallacy project a certain understanding of time, causation, and historical change. That is, both understand that past events, while not directly influencing the present or the future, nonetheless give clues about what might happen later. In reality, of course, each toss of the coin or spin of the roulette wheel is fully independent of all others. In the nineteenth century, the divergence between a vision of events that were largely *dependent* on one another – the logic of evening – and a vision of events that were entirely *independent* of one another was played out on the floor of the casino. One of the implications of this debate was that mathematicians and probabalists began to see history in a new light as something that did not matter and should not be considered. As one logician framed the problem in the mid-twentieth century, "Most difficulties with probability lie in three areas: inequality of chances; small numbers of cases; and letting history creep

---

[8] J. H. Schooling, "Lotteries, Luck, Chance, and Gambling Systems. Part IV – Gambling Systems," *Pall Mall Magazine*, 20/81 (1900), 377–86, 385.

[9] There are many additional examples following this general form. See C. Kingston, *The Romance of Monte Carlo* (J. L. the Bodley Head, 1925), 208; M. Blume, *Côte d'Azur: Inventing the French Riviera* (Thames & Hudson, 1992), 58; D. Huff, *How to Take a Chance* (W. W. Norton, 1959), 28–29; S. Macknik and S. Martinez-Conde, *Sleights of Mind: What the Neuroscience of Magic Reveals about Our Brains* (Henry Holt, 2010), 196; H. Tijms, *Understanding Probability* (Cambridge University Press, 2012), 82–83.

[10] W. Crowe, "The Game Season at Spürt," *Household Words*, 240 (1854), 262–64, 264.

[11] Crowe, "Game Season at Spürt," 264.

in."[12] We see in the emerging science of probability and statistics an understanding of time and history peculiar to the industrial logic of the nineteenth century.

Writing in 1899, one writer claimed that the "doctrine of averages" as proposed by one Buckle correctly understood the connections between events. Buckle asserted that the number of suicides, fires, and blank envelopes mailed was constant in a particular population, and that therefore variability over time must equalize. This argument lead to a counter claim, not really believed by the author, about the maturity of chances: "Similar reasoning, if applied to the game of roulette, results in the conclusion that if one colour has turned up twenty-six times (and the annals of roulette, we believe, record no longer run) the reemergence of the other colour *cannot* be far off."[13] The author uses a language of religion to describe the gambler who buys into these ideas: "the gambler accepts the necessitarian doctrine of chances and averages as a sort of holy mystery (for the gambler's unreasoning faith would make the fortunes of a religious sect)."[14] While the use of occult means to understand the future is not limited to nineteenth-century casino-goers, other methods were also used. Applying the law of averages to the casino allowed for the proliferation of systems that could be used in ways that would allow a gambler to maximize profit. "Systematizers" sought to build foolproof ways to make money at the casino. The debates between the systematizers and those who ridiculed their efforts can tell us much about how people in the nineteenth century understood probability, chance, and luck.

Gambling systems were not a child of the nineteenth century, but there was a resurgence of interest in applying scientific or even mechanical knowledge to the problem of gambling in the period. With the precision of a train timetable, gambling systems purported to have uncovered the hidden mysteries of the roulette wheel. Mathematical, occult – and, to be sure, erroneous – gambling systems provided nineteenth-century casino-goers with a tool they could use when going into battle against the house. There were countless systems developed in the eighteenth and nineteenth centuries that promised to assist gamblers in the casino. Some were of an occult or superstitious nature, which we will discuss later; others were mechanical, asking bettors to order their wagers in a precise way and demanding no deviations. Generally speaking, this second method of gambling could be collectively termed a "martingale." Martingales came

[12] Huff, *How to Take a Chance*, 23.   [13] "The Science of Chance," 97.
[14] "The Science of Chance," 97.

in head-spinning diversity. One example – a relatively simple one, in this case – instructed gamblers to bet on one single color on the roulette wheel (either red or black). The odds of winning were 50:50. The rules of this particular martingale commanded that a gambler double their wager after each loss, and after a win to reset the wager to a baseline. By this logic, a gambler would recoup any losses and could in fact come out ahead.

Many observers of nineteenth-century casino gambling were skeptical of systems. Sala writes that "It is very curious, and very ludicrous, to think of the infinity of devices, half puerile, half shrewd, and sometimes wholly superstitious, by which gamesters endeavour to bind chance in bonds, to make a certainty of the odds, and to tempt fortune to their side of the *tapis vert*."[15] He notes the existence of a range of mysterious acts that could bend the odds in one's favor: cutting cards and betting on the color revealed, placing wagers based on the date or some other numerologically significant figure, wagering based on a dream or other vision, even using borrowed money because it was perceived to be luckier.[16] While these methods are more comfortably aligned with superstition or the occult, the ones that Sala describes in the book were derived from some exotic or esoteric source. The three players employ a range of systems, one of which was frankly orientalist.

> He had learnt it, he said, of a Polish Jew, who had it from a Russian Chamberlain, who had extracted it by torture from a Tartar horse-dealer, who had brought it from the Great Wall of China, where it was the means of replenishing the coffers of the Mandarins with many millions' worth of sycee silver per mensem.... To myself and the bystanders, it appeared chiefly to consist in accesses of raging madness, accompanied by extreme ferocity and hoarse mutterings in an unknown tongue, which he afterwards stated to be Romaic or Modern Greek, a dialect in which (although I have only his personal statement to prove it) he had been an adept in the sunny days of youth. I will say little of this strange man tearing his hair, clenching and unclenching his fists, beating diabolical tattoos with his feet, viciously rubbing that empurpled proboscis of his, and squinting horribly, because these were physical and facial peculiarities germane to him in his normal morose-imbecile state.[17]

One critical issue in Sala's description of Rhenish gambling and the systems at work before 1860 is to note the absence of explicitly mathematical systems. As mathematics was applied with greater urgency to the

[15] Sala, *Make Your Game*, 216.   [16] Sala, *Make Your Game*, 216–17.
[17] Sala, *Make Your Game*, 208–9.

fabrication of systems, the mathematicians began to attack the use of math in this area in increasingly public and vigorous ways.

In his 1866 book *The Logic of Chance*, John Venn – the probabilist and logician best known for representing coincidence visually in the form of a "Venn diagram" – addresses the issue of systems in a section of the book dedicated to fallacies.[18] Considering the creation of martingales, Venn writes that "Accordingly by mere persistency he [the gambler playing according to a martingale] may accumulate any sum of money he pleases, in apparent defiance of all that is meant by luck."[19] Not shy about displaying his thoughts on the issue, Venn continues, issuing a blistering critique of the illogic of the system in general. "What causes perplexity here," Venn writes, "is the supposed fact that in some mysterious way certainty has been conjured out of uncertainty; that in a game where the detailed events are utterly inscrutable, and where the average, by supposition, shows no preference for either side, one party is nevertheless succeeding somehow in steadily drawing the luck his own way."[20] When Venn comes to the topic of the gambler's fallacy and the maturity of chances, he is mystified at the habits of mind that would allow a person to believe that they had any occult influence over material objects. Using a coin toss as an example, Venn explains that the odds of a flip are still only 50:50 despite what has happened before: "Suppose we have had four heads in succession; people have tolerably realized by now that 'head the fifth time' is still an even chance."[21] While he believes that reasoning people can understand that concept, gamblers remained committed to a different set of principles. Anyone can see the logic of odds, he writes, "Except indeed the gambler. According to a gambling acquaintance whom Houdin, the conjurer, describes himself as having met at Spa, 'the oftener a particular combination has occurred the more certain it is that it will not be repeated at the next *coup*: this is the groundwork of all theories of probabilities and is termed the maturity of chances."[22]

The maturity of chances appeared to systematizers to legitimate a view of historical causation that generated adherence to the theoretical odds over time. Mathematicians, while agreeing that Bernoulli's theory was correct, refused to accept the idea that some events were dependent on others. Like John Venn, the mathematician and astronomer Richard

---

[18] J. Venn, *The Logic of Chance: An Essay on the Foundations and Province of the Theory of Probability, with Especial Reference to Its Application to Moral and Social Science* (Macmillan, 1866). I am quoting from the third edition of the text, issued in 1888.
[19] Venn, *The Logic of Chance*, 344.   [20] Venn, *The Logic of Chance*, 345.
[21] Venn, *The Logic of Chance*, 361.   [22] Quoted in Venn, *The Logic of Chance*, 361.

Proctor acknowledged that a central problem was that the predictive qualities of probability were extremely seductive. In his chapter "Gambler's Fallacies," Proctor writes that "The more familiar a man becomes with the multitude of such combinations, the more confidently he believes in the possibility of foretelling – not, indeed, any special event, but – the general run of several approaching events."[23] Proctor calls this outlook on the part of the gambler a "fatal confidence."[24] The maturity of chances is "the most mischievous of gambling superstitions."[25] Discussing the ruin of one gambler at roulette (he won £700 on the first day, basing his bets on the theory of evening, then lost nearly all of it on succeeding days), Proctor explains: "He took a very sound principle of probabilities as the supposed basis of his system, though in reality he entirely mistook the nature of the principle."[26] To Proctor, this insight meant that history and dependence must be segregated from any analysis of odds as they related to a specific event. "To suppose otherwise," according to Proctor,

> is utterly to ignore the relation between cause and effect. When anyone asserts that because such and such things have happened, therefore such and such other events will happen, he ought at least to be able to show that the past events have some direct influence on those which are thus said to be affected by them. But if I am going to toss a coin perfectly at random, in what possible way can the result of the experiment be affected by the circumstance that during ten or twelve minutes before, I tossed "head" only or "tail" only?[27]

Proctor notes the "paradox" that both the theory of evening and the independence of events are correct: "It may appear paradoxical to say that chance results right themselves – nay, that there is an absolute certainty that in the long run they will occur as often (in proportion) as their respective chances warrant, and at the same time to assert that it is utterly useless for any gambler to trust to this circumstance."[28] Proctor concludes by affirming the truth of each statement and demanding that the validity of each be recognized.

Even popularizers of gambling like Steinmetz subscribed to the arguments made by mathematicians like Venn and Proctor. Steinmetz notes that a "distinction must be made between games of skill and games of chance. The former require application, attention, and a certain degree of

[23] R. A. Proctor, *Chance and Luck*, 2nd ed. (Longmans, Green, and Company, 1887), 15.
[24] Proctor, *Chance and Luck*, 15.   [25] Proctor, *Chance and Luck*, 19.
[26] Proctor, *Chance and Luck*, 19.   [27] Proctor, *Chance and Luck*, 20–21.
[28] Proctor, *Chance and Luck*, 30.

ability to insure success in them; while the latter are devoid of all that is rational, and are equally within the reach of the highest and lowest capacity."[29] Noting that what he called the "Doctrine of Chances or Probabilities" was a "very learned science," Steinmetz believed that a study of probabilities could in fact assist gamblers, but only those who played games of skill. The science of probability "has been applied to gambling purposes; and in spite of the obvious abstruseness of the science, it is not impossible to give the general reader an idea of its processes and conclusions."[30] Steinmetz explains that probability is uniquely suited to give gamblers the critical information in what might be called a panoptic style – possibilities could be represented in global fashion or, as he puts, as a "unity." Probability is as much a form of representation as it is an encapsulation of possibility.

Mathematicians like Proctor and Venn were suspicious of martingales specifically and systems generally. It is valuable to note, however, that voices from the pro-gambling community disliked the theoretical principles of probability, favoring an experimental approach instead. Presenting a critique of statisticians and the theoretical range of possibilities against which practice and reality is judged, James Romain argues in his pro-gambling book that "the philosophy of supposition [is, by statisticians,] substituted for that of caprice. We are asked by the mathematician, at the very outset, to assume something he has not proved, and which is not susceptible of proof. We are required to take for granted the imaginary premises upon which his argument depends. Is this not the acme of intellectual audacity?... So much for the boasted 'Doctrine of Chances.'"[31] Romain continues in this vein, arguing that mathematicians sought to "demonstrate the inequalities of chance, hoping thus to dissuade humanity from its pursuit. Their efforts are idle.... These gentlemen have extended their conjectures to the risks of loss or gain in general commerce; the probable continuity of life and duration of marriage; the contingencies in political results and the verdicts of juries; the distributions of sex in births.... In fact, should their guesses be heeded by the world, enterprise and hope would depart."[32] Dismissing statisticians as moralizers, Romain seeks to discredit the intellectual foundation of theoretical probability,

[29] A. Steinmetz, *The Gaming Table: Its Votaries and Victims*, 2 vols. (Tinsley Brothers, 1870), vol. 2, 235.
[30] Steinmetz, *The Gaming Table*, 237.
[31] J. H. Romain, *Gambling: Or, Fortuna, Her Temple and Shrine. The True Philosophy and Ethics of Gambling* (Craig Press, 1891), 66.
[32] Romain, *Gambling*, 67.

replacing it instead with an appeal for continued "hope" that one could beat the odds. His larger attack on the use of statistics in public life and the growing application of data to all sorts of policy discussions seems hopelessly outdated, even in the 1890s.

When the philosopher Friedrich Nietzsche wrote in his 1889 book *The Twilight of the Idols*, "I mistrust all systematists and avoid them. The will to a system is a lack of integrity," it is unlikely that he was discussing the various systems developed to improve the odds at the casino.[33] That said, Nietzsche was not alone in his suspicions that "systematists" were unlikely to achieve their goals. An 1890 essay detailing "Play and Players on the Riviera" provides one contemporary critique of systems. W. Fraser Rae writes,

> Of all the delusions to which the human mind is liable none is more absurd than that which causes a man to think that any system of play can prevail over the "bank" at Monte Carlo. The most skilfully devised system may prolong the player's agony, and that is all. There is a large class which gains a livelihood by concocting systems and selling them, and in this case the buyers are the persons who, in slang phrase, are really sold. All system-makers hold out the inducement that, by following their counsel, the player "ceases to be a gamester and becomes a speculator," and they delight in repeating, what they maintain Bonaparte once said, that "the gaming-banks will be conquered by calculation." To continue making money by playing upon any system is as ridiculous as to form any combination of machinery and say that it will go on for ever by itself. Perpetual motion is the dream of an ill-regulated and unbalanced mind. An infallible system at play is the equivalent to perpetual motion.[34]

Rae's position was also an attack on superstition and the fallacious belief in "evening." He writes in another passage in the essay that "It will be asked, Why, then, should players continue a losing game? Because they are superstitious, or foolish, or both. The superstition and folly consist in arguing that because a number or colour turns up once it will do so again, or else that a number or colour which has turned up once will not turn up a second time."[35]

Others from the time issued similar attacks. In an 1892 *National Review* essay, "Systems of Gambling," Norwood Young tackled the issue of systems and the vision of historical causality embedded in them. "A

---

[33] F. Nietzsche, *Twilight of the Idols* (Oxford University Press, 2008), 8.
[34] W. F. Rae, "Play and Players on the Riviera," *The Nineteenth Century*, 277/February (1890), 240–57, 251.
[35] Rae, "Play and Players," 253.

'system' of gambling," Young argues, "presupposes the belief that in matters of chance the future is affected by the past, and that by watching the course of events, as they successively march into the past, deductions may be made tending to modify the normal uncertainty as to the future. This belief is a remarkable superstition. Superstitions, however, die hard."[36] His attack on systems, in other words, was partially an attack on historical thinking more broadly. Recalling the lore about long runs, Young addresses this issue by stating "that when twenty rouges have appeared in succession the twenty-first will probably show noire. Many a gambler has been ruined by this fancy. It is a sad commentary on the progress of human intelligence that the experience of centuries has done nothing to cure this absurd folly."[37] This leads Young to a different type of critique, one in which he attacks the common practice of publicizing the numbers *en retard* (i.e., the ones that have not appeared recently) in Italian and Austrian lotteries, which turns into a fascinating critique of the morality of advertising that attempts to sucker people into playing numbers that have no more or less probability of appearing than any other. Such a strategy on the part of state lotteries was widespread – by publicizing those numbers that had not appeared, they could in some sense persuade people that those numbers had some kind of historical duty to appear. Young is appalled at this misappropriation of historicity, writing that "The most curious aspect of the crazy belief in the influence of a past chance event over a future one is to be found in the words on roulette by standard teachers."[38] Most significant of those included a bizarre reversal of causality: "Discussing the opinion of those who disbelieve in any influence of the past over the future in matters chance, M. [M. Martin] Gall says: – '. . . I shall not undertake to establish the contention that the past has any influence upon the production of future results; but I shall say that *every future result has an incontestable influence upon past results.*'"[39] Young's attack on gambling systems proceeded from two interrelated arguments. First, the logic of historical causation had to be excised from any serious approach to gambling. Anything less was mere superstition. Second, Young cast doubt on those who attempted to apply history to gambling – such as those advertising previous results of state lotteries – as morally dubious.

A similar set of arguments may be seen in J. Holt Schooling's discussion of gambling systems published in 1899 in the *Pall Mall Magazine*. Part IV

---

[36] Young, "Systems of Gambling," 449.   [37] Young, "Systems of Gambling," 449.
[38] Young, "Systems of Gambling," 450.   [39] Young, "Systems of Gambling," 451.

of a series, this section of Schooling's text was dedicated to probing the ways that probability theory entered into public representations of gambling. Schooling, quoting mathematician W. Allen Whitworth, begins by arguing that risk is the key issue of which gamblers should be aware, and therefore insurance and gambling operated in similar but opposite directions. Schooling also provides quotes from several advertisements peddling fool-proof systems – mathematical and otherwise – that could be used to bend the odds at Monte Carlo. The problem leads Schooling to his analysis of the maturity of chances, a "wholly fallacious notion . . . at the bottom of many of the systems [that] inspires gamblers to persevere in losing their money."[40] The problem, as Schooling – like Young before him – saw it, is historical: "how can the past, whatever its nature, possibly affect in the slightest degree the result of the tossing of a coin yet to be decided?"[41] Indeed, one major issue with the fallacy of the maturity of chances, as Schooling notes, is imperfect historical knowledge. Attempting to bring chances into the parity by betting on apparent losers, the fallacious gambler lacks the knowledge of prior results. In other words, a run of odds may be making up for a longer run of evens that occurred at some point in the forgotten past.

Schooling's essays on gambling represented a popular intervention in larger debates about the degree to which numbers could accurately capture some element of the reality of life. Not surprisingly, this issue was of interest to people working in a wide range of disciplines. German sociologist Georg Simmel, for instance, was especially attuned to the ways that relations between people had increasingly been subjected to a type of quantification. "The mathematical character of money," Simmel argued in his *Philosophy of Money,*

> imbues the relationship of the elements of life with a precision, a reliability in the determination of parity and disparity, an unambiguousness in agreements and arrangements in the same way as the general use of pocket watches has brought about a similar effect in daily life. Like the determination of abstract value by money, the determination of abstract time by clocks provides a system for the most detailed and definite arrangements and measurements that imparts an otherwise unattainable transparency and calculability to the contents of life, at least as regards their practical management. The calculating intellectuality embodied in these forms may in its turn derive from them some of the energy through which intellectuality controls modern life.[42]

---

[40] Schooling, "Lotteries, Luck, Chance, and Gambling Systems. Part IV – Gambling Systems," 379.
[41] Schooling, "Lotteries, Luck, Chance, and Gambling Systems. Part IV – Gambling Systems," 379.
[42] G. Simmel, *The Philosophy of Money*, 3rd ed. (Routledge, 2004), 445–46.

To be clear, Simmel's concern with understanding how abstract forces and relationships could be represented materially was a product of elite German academic discourse. But his attempts to divine how numbers revealed the "energy through which intellectuality controls modern life" was arguably the central issue animating nineteenth-century debates about the proper constitution of society. And gambling, rather than being a mute diversion or merely pleasurable distraction, was at the heart of attempts to understand chance and to quantify it.

The concerns of academics like Proctor, Venn, and Simmel appeared at the same time as the efforts of the American inventor Hiram Maxim to debunk the pervasive myths that a system could break the bank at Monte Carlo appeared in popular form. Maxim, the inventor of the Maxim gun (a forerunner to the modern machine gun) as well as the curling iron, became a British subject and was knighted by Queen Victoria and Edward VII in 1901. Because of his stature as an inventor who could take complex engineering problems and create commercially viable products with a mass appeal, Maxim was the perfect spokesman to address the interplay between chance, Monte Carlo's roulette tables, and the systems that people employed to bend the odds in their favor. Maxim's book *Monte Carlo, Fact and Fallacy* (1904) consists of a letter from Maxim about gambling in Monte Carlo that was originally published in the *New York Herald*.[43] The letter was somewhat of a bombshell, and it generated a heavy correspondence that Maxim also reprinted, and to which he responded in detailed ways.

Maxim's first letter in the *New York Herald* was his critique of aleatory gambling in general, and Monte Carlo roulette in particular. He so disliked games of chance that he offered in his letter a critique both of systems like the various possibilities of martingales and of systemless play. "A system, although a bad one, is better than no system at all."[44] "Punting," or playing for small stakes without any direction or plan, was particularly ludicrous to Maxim because it frittered away the gambler's capital. He felt it was better by far to take one's whole stake and put it down in one single large bet on either black or red, because at 50-50 the odds were the best. Maxim especially hated martingales, which he argued were a particularly dumb form of punting. Like previous evaluations of systems, Maxim's attack on martingales was oriented around a critique of

---

[43] H. S. Maxim, *Monte Carlo: Facts and Fallacies* (Grant Richards, 1904).
[44] Maxim, *Monte Carlo*, 19.

the gambler's fallacy that was founded on the materiality of independent chance. "Each particular 'coup,'" Maxim explained in his letter,

> is governed altogether by the physical conditions existing at that particular instant. The ball spins round a great many times in a groove. When its momentum is used up, it comes in contact with several pieces of brass, and finally tumbles into a pocket in the wheel which is rotating in an opposite direction. It is a pure and unadulterated question of chance, and it is not influenced in the least by anything which has ever taken place before, or that will take place in the future.[45]

In other words, each spin of the wheel was completely unpredictable, random, and independent. Maxim counseled gamblers in Monte Carlo – given that they felt driven to bet – to place just one large wager with even odds. Anything else, especially if it was derived from some system, represented a gift to the casino.

Maxim's letter generated a host of responses. One, from the novelist Herbert Vivian (a coauthor of *The Green Bay Tree*), presented a defense of the theory of "evening" as it was generated by the maturity of chances. Vivian argues that with 37 million spins, one would expect 18 million red, 18 million black, and 1 million zero. And then he relates the old story about a long run in support of the idea that, over time, things even up. "During a long experience," Vivian relates, "I have never seen an even chance come more than twenty-eight consecutive times."[46] This prompts Vivian to conclude that "Facts, therefore, disprove the mathematical theory that each spin is utterly uninfluenced by its predecessors."[47] Maxim dryly replied: "I think I have discovered that 99 per cent. of the players have a blind spot in their intellects."[48]

Arguing that the "'evening up' theory is emphatically THE fallacy of Monte Carlo," Maxim reproduced a set of letters in support of his arguments.[49] T. P. O'Connor writes that Maxim "ultimately comes to the same conclusion as everybody does who has ever studied Monte Carlo – that there is but one safe principle to adopt, and that is, not to gamble at all. The Bank will get even with you in the end if you only play long enough."[50] Another correspondent, anonymous, argues that "there is no more fallacious theory than that the chances of a run's continuation grow less with every additional 'coup.'" A third noted the famous quip that "Rouge gagne quelquefois, Noir souvent, mais Blanc toujours" (Rouge

---

[45] Maxim, *Monte Carlo*, 14–15.   [46] Maxim, *Monte Carlo*, 34.   [47] Maxim, *Monte Carlo*, 34.
[48] Maxim, *Monte Carlo*, 36.   [49] Maxim, *Monte Carlo*, 46.   [50] Maxim, *Monte Carlo*, 57.

sometimes wins, Black often does; but [François] Blanc always).[51] Other writers noted that the "consensus of opinion, even at the most celebrated of all the shrines of the blind goddess, and where ninety-nine hundredths of those who sojourn are her votaries, to a greater or less extent, is in full accord with Sir Hiram's views."[52]

Yet doubts remained. Fitzroy S. Erskine disagreed with the critique of systems and concluded, "No, sir, the whole game is a lottery, with many winners and many losers; and I shall maintain that, with a fair capital, good nerve, and iron constitution, one can triumph over the much vaunted *refait de la Maison*."[53] Erskine was a resolute supporter of the D'Alembert system (also called the Rosslyn model, after its most famous supporter, Lord Rosslyn, who was Erskine's brother), which was based on what Rosslyn called the "laws of equality." The martingale required a large capital reserve. Playing steadily on both colors simultaneously and advancing bets (1, 3, 5), Rosslyn claimed success based on the theory of evening (one must play long enough for "the laws of equality for one colour to equalise an adverse run of the other").[54] But, Rosslyn notes, one needs certain character elements to succeed: "There is no doubt about it, that perseverance, strong nerve, and the constitution of a drayhorse are absolutely necessary to success."[55] Robber baron Jay Gould disagreed, reminding readers that the validity of a system was likely nothing more than a false consciousness based on positive results. "The punter who, by following a certain method of play, leaves the tables a winner, is likely to be convinced that Chance is a mathematical problem of which he has found the solution; while he who loses is just as apt to curse fortune as a jade and to scoff at the 'law of probabilities.'"[56] Gould suggests that the issue is not one of "mathematics, but of dynamics," and if one could "measure the degree of impulsion given to the wheel, the speed of the ball, and the friction exercised upon the ball by the divisions, it would be an easy matter to predict with absolute certainty the result of the 'coup.'"[57] Other correspondents charged systems as something contrary to logic and, perhaps worse, an expression of emotion: "the passion for the game knows no reason, and as science has no reply to dogma, it is best only to go there for fun and not to think that fickle fortune is going to make exception in our favour."[58] Others used the occasion to attack occult or superstitious thinking: "'Impossible' [the pen name of a letter writer] ... mentions

[51] Maxim, *Monte Carlo*, 60.　　[52] Maxim, *Monte Carlo*, 62.　　[53] Maxim, *Monte Carlo*, 65–66.
[54] Maxim, *Monte Carlo*, 69.　　[55] Maxim, *Monte Carlo*, 69.　　[56] Maxim, *Monte Carlo*, 70–71.
[57] Maxim, *Monte Carlo*, 71–72.　　[58] Maxim, *Monte Carlo*, 78.

eighteen occult and ghostly factors which he says I have left out of the equation. Two of these factors are 'nervousness' and 'vanity.' How unfortunate that 'Impossible' did not explain how all these ghostly factors happened to pull in the direction of the Bank! [W]hat is to prevent some one from performing incantations which would cause the influence to work in the other direction?"[59]

The flurry of interest and debate on the validity of systems that Maxim's letter in the *Herald* generated was remarkable. In a reply to the critics, Maxim reiterated his position, explaining again that "Each 'coup' is a completely independent act, depending on a great number of ill-defined factors, including an always varying personal factor. In a word, there are so many factors in the equation, especially as regards roulette, all of which are unknown and unknowable, that the result is a pure matter of chance."[60] And Maxim also reintroduced his system: reduce the likelihood of zero by making one single large bet. He also noted the public relations machine that could swing into action to promote feel-good stories about the Riviera. He claims that these stories were generated by everyone in the region in order to continually promote Monte Carlo (and then they will continue to reap the collateral benefits). "At least once a week one will find in these papers a remarkable article stating how some deserving person, generally a young lady in distress, had gone to Monte Carlo with only a five-franc piece, and had very soon won a small fortune which completely dissipated her financial troubles."[61]

Maxim's second letter on the issue generated a renewed flurry of activity across the *Herald*'s letters to the editor page. Maxim taunted Rosslyn, wondering why he had been unable to publicly display the validity of his system by winning vast sums of money at Monte Carlo. Rosslyn's self-diagnosis of the failure of his system takes us to the heart of the systematizer's dilemma: the fact that one's system never really seemed to work. "'The system worked all right,'" Rosslyn conceded, "'but the temptation was so great to bet on numbers that I lost the winnings of the system by staking on numbers. I lost because I did not stick strictly to the system.' Evidently the passion was so strong and unconquerable that he gambled away the winnings of his syndicate as fast as they came in, on the worst chances, because he was in such close proximity to the numbers that he could not resist the temptation."[62] Other contributors to the exchange were also attuned to the role played by excitement, but noted the

[59] Maxim, *Monte Carlo*, 84.   [60] Maxim, *Monte Carlo*, 98.   [61] Maxim, *Monte Carlo*, 117–18.
[62] Maxim, *Monte Carlo*, 309.

mechanical nature of roulette meant that the game itself – because it was passionless – did not respond to systems. "Mathematician," for instance, wrote that "Roulette is a problem in dynamics, and not a very difficult one either, but it is one of those problems in the higher mathematics that it is more difficult to put the question of than to find the answer to; there are many such."[63]

Other contributors exhibited transparent delight in the opportunity that Rosslyn's collapse provided to mock systematizers in general. One, "Johnny Doolittle," claimed that

> Players at Monte Carlo may be divided into two classes: Class A, ordinary fools; Class B, d—d fools. They are easily distinguished; those with cards and pins [used to keep track of runs and systems] and those making hurried calculations belong to Class B. The reason why the laws of probabilities are not understood by players is not on account of the non-existence of these laws or any lack of teachers.... The fault lies altogether in the brain of the player, and may result from a variety of causes, such, for example, as extraordinary thickness of the skull, small brain capacity, a lack of grey matter in the brain, or perhaps a deficiency in the number of convolutions in the brain. The most common fault, however, results from the adulteration of the brain with some cheap substitute, such as ordinary batter.[64]

Another wrote to complain about the innumeracy of gamblers, arguing that "I am well aware of the fact that everything that smacks, even in the least degree, of mathematical calculations or reasoning, is distasteful to the majority of mankind. They do not like it. It is too cold and unsympathetic for their aesthetic tastes."[65]

Books like those written by Proctor or Maxim represented a chance to take complex mathematical concepts and present them to a popular audience.[66] John Maynard Keynes recognized the value of these projects, writing that the "literature of gambling is very extensive, but, so far as I am acquainted with it, excessively lacking in variety, the maturity of the chances and the martingale continually recurring in one form or another."[67] Others who collected the popular lore surrounding Monte Carlo were faced with a similar dilemma: How should gambling – and its

---

[63] Maxim, *Monte Carlo*, 144.   [64] Maxim, *Monte Carlo*, 157–58.

[65] Maxim, *Monte Carlo*, 184.

[66] S. Kern, in *A Cultural History of Causality: Science, Murder Novels, and Systems of Thought* (Princeton University Press, 2004), explains that understandings of causality underwent dramatic change in the nineteenth century. Using murder mysteries as source material to bring these changes into view, Kern bridges the scientific and the literary to show the broad contours of this cultural history.

[67] J. M. Keynes, *A Treatise on Probability* (Macmillan and Company, 1921), 364.

odds – be represented to a public increasingly interested in resort gambling? Charles Kingston solved this problem by highlighting the point that systems always fail. Kingston tells his readers that the "consistent and unimpeded triumph of the bank at Monte Carlo since the sixties [1860s] has created suspicion in the minds of those who study the laws of chance and averages, but whether conducted honestly or dishonestly the casino must win."[68] Given that reality – that the casino is a business that must win to stay open, and which therefore has created games like roulette that ensure a small but significant percentage of the wagers flow back to the house – Kingston offers what should be read as a warning that mirrored the one presented by Maxim. "The bank wins," Kingston explains to his readers, "because it is not altogether dependent on the law of averages. It can survive the most extraordinary runs against, runs which would break the richest player. Most gamblers, by the way, have the most eccentric notions as to what the law of averages means, and it is because of this that all their systems eventually fail."[69] Kingston's idea that "systems eventually fail" – a principle that seems more at home at the end of the twentieth century – pointed toward an important proposition: mathematics demonstrates that one's use of a system did nothing to change the ratio of wins and losses.

One of the important contributions of gambling was to present an opportunity to test mathematical principles in a real-world environment. Casino gambling constituted an experimental space for mathematicians, and it provided data that could be used to test the theoretical foundations of probability.[70] Sala recognized that casino gambling was a way to make sense of luck and chance within a rigid system, and he concluded that both luck and a system were equally ridiculous ideas. "Thus act the men who speculate on chance, and mere chance, and who have their lucky and unlucky days – rigidly abstaining from play on the latter: – as when it rains, or when such and such a croupier is not present, or when they have had their nails cut."[71] Having mocked the ludicrous superstitions that

[68] Kingston, *The Romance of Monte Carlo*, 207.
[69] Kingston, *The Romance of Monte Carlo*, 207–8.
[70] In a volume dedicated to exploring the life cycle of scientific ideas, Lorraine Daston suggests that scientific materials can be apprehended through the genre of life writing. Like similar arguments posed by Bill Brown and Arjun Apparadai, this approach, when applied to the material culture of popular science – such as the roulette wheel – allows the material and the cultural to be usefully joined. See L. Daston, ed., *Biographies of Scientific Objects* (University of Chicago Press, 2000); A. Appadurai, ed., *The Social Life of Things: Commodities in Cultural Perspective* (Cambridge University Press, 1986); B. Brown, "Thing Theory," *Critical Inquiry* 28/1 (2001), 1–22; B. Brown, ed., *Things* (University of Chicago Press, 2004).
[71] Sala, *Make Your Game*, 217.

informed gamblers' search for luck, Sala also attacked the systematizers: "Then there are the gentlemen who delight in fantastic combinations."[72] Nowhere was the fantasy more ridiculous than those gamblers who only wagered that the ball would land on zero. Sala needled those who sought to make wealth literally out of nothing, "in the hope of this eventuality the disciples of Zeroaster will go on backing 'no thing,' which nonentity lies at the head of the number-table, close to the tire of the roulette wheel, with amazing patience and perseverance."[73]

Thirty years later, Norwood Young emphasized the fact that martingales, with their gesture toward systematic play, were in decline. He remarked on those for whom "the amount of the stake is increased or diminished according to the success or the failure of the past."[74] Young, like other mathematicians, was able to test the theoretical success or failure of various martingales against actual roulette results from Monte Carlo. Working out the results of martingales following traditional, the d'Alembert, and the Labouchere methods in light of data published in the newspaper *Le Monaco* (which recorded the result of every spin at every table in Monte Carlo), Young found no system that would have worked were it in use when the data were collected. Young concludes, in fact, that systems are terrible and never work. The author notes that "it may be suggested that, after all, the mass of the Monte Carlo moths are bent only upon amusement, and not upon the filthy business of money-gathering," and that therefore gambling represented a harmless diversion.[75] Nonetheless, Young warns, prepare to lose if you gamble.

No one used Monte Carlo as an experimental space more effectively than the mathematician, polymath, and eugenicist Karl Pearson. Pearson's *Chances of Death* presented his application of probability and statistics to a range of topics including life span and actuarialism as well as the honesty of the Monte Carlo tables. In his essay on life span, Pearson notes a historical shift from chance as something that represented chaos to chance as "obedience to law"[76] and he seeks in the essay a way to "resuscitate the mediaeval conception of the relation between Death and Chance and to express it in a more modern scientific form."[77] Pearson recognizes a complete historical break in the way that chance is understood between the medieval and the modern: "where we cannot predict, where we do not

[72] Sala, *Make Your Game*, 217.   [73] Sala, *Make Your Game*, 218.
[74] Young, "Systems of Gambling," 453.   [75] Young, "Systems of Gambling," 459–60.
[76] K. Pearson, *The Chances of Death, and Other Studies in Evolution* (E. Arnold, 1897), 2.
[77] Pearson, *The Chances of Death*, 8–11.

find order and regularity, there we should now assert (as in the case of the Monte Carlo roulette returns) that something else than chance is at work. What we are to understand by a chance distribution is one in accordance with law, and one the nature of which can for all practical purposes be closely predicted."[78] He used large sets of experiments to identify a curve – thousands of dice rolls and chip selections – but also notes that "when this distribution round the mode does not take place – as for example, at Monte Carlo – then we assert that some cause other than chance is at work. Our conception of chance is one of law and order in large numbers; it is not that idea of chaotic incidence which vexed the mediaeval mind."[79]

Casino gambling like that practiced at Monte Carlo represented to Pearson a fascinating case study that could be used to illuminate a range of issues related to probability and chance. In the essay titled "The Scientific Aspect of Monte Carlo Roulette" (first published in the *Fortnightly Review* in February 1894), Pearson suggests that "My object in the present essay is to show that chance in this sense, chance as it applies to the tossing of an unladed coin, has no application to Monte Carlo roulette."[80] Like Norwood Young, Pearson took advantage of the fact that the weekly *Le Monaco*, issued in Paris, provided easy access to the putatively random data generated by the roulette wheels at Monte Carlo. Pearson begins with the law of large numbers, explaining that in theory a chance of heads or of reds or of any other binary option should be 50 percent. In reality, demonstrated through a range of different experiments (roulette, coin tossing, lottery drawing, etc.), the results were very slightly different. Pearson's calculation of red/black roulette results came in at 50.15 percent (and he provides other examples showing similar results). The issue then becomes, how large a deviation from the theoretical norm may exist for a game still to be characterized as one of chance? Pearson puts the issue like this: "Is such a deviation [a number derived from one observer, de Whallay, who reported that red appeared 50.27 percent of the time] ... a probable or an improbable one?... How great must the deviation ... be in order to lead us to assert that we are not dealing with a game of chance? What are the odds against such a deviation?"[81] Pearson, in other words, realized that the actual data, based on thousands of trials, still did not conform to the theoretical expectations.

If, however, one were to repeat the experiment over and over to determine whether one particular experiment was an outlier, valuable

---

[78] Pearson, *The Chances of Death*, 11.   [79] Pearson, *The Chances of Death*, 15.
[80] Pearson, *The Chances of Death*, 42–43.   [81] Pearson, *The Chances of Death*, 49.

information would emerge. Pearson concludes that "as far as the average total numbers of *rouge* and *noir* results go, Monte Carlo roulette obeys the mathematical laws of chance."[82] The actual numbers were a different matter, however. Pearson found – based on the results published in *Le Monaco* – that the ball fell on numbers in ways that deviated from the expectation. Comparing those data with the ones obtained by de Whalley, Pearson concluded that the roulette tables at Monte Carlo were unexpectedly odd. As Pearson put it: "Monte Carlo roulette ... is from the scientific standpoint anything but a game of chance."[83] This was a stunning announcement, one that prompted Pearson to begin a larger analysis of runs. Pearson began his study of roulette permanencies by noting that the probability of a run rises geometrically: getting one red is 1:2; getting two in a row is 1:2 × 1:2, or 1:4; getting three in a row is 1:2 × 1:2 × 1:2, or 1:8, and so on. Pearson repeated the analysis with two other data sets that confirmed his suspicions: "Roulette as played at Monte Carlo is not a scientific game of chance."[84] The result, as Pearson notes, is an alarming one: "The reader cannot be too often reminded that what is popularly termed 'chance' may be chaos or it may be design, but it cannot be scientifically chance unless the improbable happens in its due proportions."[85] The key method here, as Pearson notes, is to determine the rate of "*fluctuations from the averages*," which constitute the "sole reliable test."[86] In Pearson's judgment, "Monte Carlo roulette ... is ... from the standpoint of exact science the most prodigious miracle of the nineteenth century ... we are forced to accept as an alternative that the random spinning of a roulette manufactured and daily readjusted with extraordinary care is not obedient to the laws of chance, but is chaotic in its manifestations. It is no exaggeration to say that such a conclusion is of the very highest moment for science."[87] What he saw, in other words, was chaos, not predictable chance. Pearson finishes the essay by asking if the theory should be adjusted to conform to the results, or if the results indicate a flawed system, and he concludes that the casino should be seized and the tables converted to a laboratory that could be used for the study of probability, "in particular, of the new branch of that study, the application of the theory of chance to the biological problem of evolution, which is likely to occupy so much of men's thoughts in the near future."[88]

---

[82] Pearson, *The Chances of Death*, 51.
[83] Pearson, *The Chances of Death*, 53.
[84] Pearson, *The Chances of Death*, 55.
[85] Pearson, *The Chances of Death*, 60–61.
[86] Pearson, *The Chances of Death*, 61.
[87] Pearson, *The Chances of Death*, 61.
[88] Pearson, *The Chances of Death*, 62.

Pearson's work was enormously influential. J. Holt Schooling, performing his own analysis of roulette results, drew on Pearson's essay, and Hiram Maxim also built upon the method, even reproducing six days of results from Monte Carlo so that readers could perform their own analyses.[89] John Maynard Keynes also used Monte Carlo roulette results published in *Le Monaco* in his *Treatise on Probability*. "Gamblers study these returns on account of the belief, which they usually hold, that as the number of cases is increased the *absolute* deviation from the most probable proportion becomes less, whereas at the best Bernoulli's Theorem shows that the proportionate deviation *decreases* while the absolute deviation *increases*."[90] Keynes found Karl Pearson's essay to be an especially valuable way of writing about complex ideas for the public. Keynes, like Pearson before him, was drawn to the ways that results from casinos could be used to produce new knowledge about probability and chance. However, Keynes remained critical of people whose work on probability exhibited what he considered evidence of a different type of fallacious thinking.

Keynes was especially skeptical of the German mathematician and linguist Karl Marbe, who had used the result of 80,000 spins of the wheel at Monte Carlo to question many of the bases of modern probability. Keynes writes that Marbe "arrived at exactly opposite conclusions; for he claims to have shown that long runs, so far from being in excess, were greatly in defect. Dr. Marbe introduces this experimental result in support of his thesis that the world is so constituted that long runs do not as a matter of fact occur in it. Not merely are long runs very improbable. They do not, according to him, occur at all."[91] In a scathing passage, Keynes writes that Marbe's work, discussed widely in Germany for what it suggested in terms of his experimental design, resulted in the fact that "Dr. Marbe has been given far more attention by his colleagues in Germany than he conceivably deserves."[92] What these passages demonstrate is that even in the first decades of the twentieth century, the casino still generated excitement as an experimental space. The fact that Keynes singled Marbe out for such blunt critique suggests how potent the field of probability remained.

The history of probability suggests a long trajectory of attempts to generate knowledge about degrees of certainty. Accurately determining the odds or being able to note correlations was a useful capability for those laying wagers. While a huge number of trials might over time correspond

---

[89] Maxim, *Monte Carlo*, 321–26.   [90] Keynes, *A Treatise on Probability*, 363–64.
[91] Keynes, *A Treatise on Probability*, 365.   [92] Keynes, *A Treatise on Probability*, 365.

to a theoretical probability, that endeavor was fraught with intellectual peril. One could easily slip from a calculation of odds in the future to an attempt to place future odds as a consideration of past events. Keynes, writing in the *Quarterly Journal of Economics* in 1937, commented on aspects of this problem, finally acknowledging that there were areas of human life that were governed by uncertainty, not chance. "By 'uncertain knowledge' . . . I do not mean to distinguish what is known for certain from what is only probable. The game of roulette is not subject, in this sense, to uncertainty.. . . The sense in which I am using this term is that in which the prospect of a European war is uncertain, or the price of copper and the rate of interest twenty years hence, or the obsolescence of a new invention.. . . About these matters, there is no scientific basis on which to form any calculable probability whatever. We simply do not know!"[93] Keynes's insight into the important differences between uncertainty and chance speaks to a larger human concern with understanding the flow of time and the likelihood of an event. We turn in Chapter 5 to an analysis of the ways that chance and luck were defined, understood, and represented in the nineteenth century.

[93] Quoted in T. J. J. Lears, *Something for Nothing: Luck in America* (Viking, 2003), 236.

Chance and Luck

Probability reflects the attempt to project a degree of certainty on a sequence of uncertain events. Chance – and the philosophy of chance created around the turn of the nineteenth century – was akin to probability, but it was fundamentally oriented around uncertainty and its effects. Chance was one way to understand the way the universe operated. Recognizing the limits of human knowledge and the barriers preventing pure observation of events, chance represented a dark zone of human intelligence. Chance, the scientists finally decided, might adhere to certain laws, but those laws still operated in ways that made it difficult to see or understand them. Luck, on the other hand, represented a far different proposition, with its gesture toward human agency and its winking acknowledgment that its possession was a short-lived and wondrous thing. Ever the trickster, luck came and went. People sought to lure luck to them, or to prevent its departure, but its existence represented a way to understand the world that emphasized human attempts to control their own lives. In "The Science of Chance," an essay published in 1899, readers were told,

> Chance comes into being only when nature and the action of a man combine to produce some results which the man does not intend or is not able to control.... Chance is merely a name for human ignorance; and apart from human ignorance it would not only not exist, it would not be even thinkable. Its home is entirely in the gap which our limited faculties constantly leave between what we do and our knowledge of what we are doing.... Chance is merely a name for the inability of human beings to apply a general law to the individual cases which illustrate it.[1]

Other accounts struck a different tone but made a similar argument: "Monte Carlo is their [gamblers'] natural environment and its gaieties

---

[1] "The Science of Chance," *The Saturday Review of Politics, Literature, Science, and Art*, 88 (1899), 97–98, 98.

and fascinating unrealities provide the make-believe world they are happiest in, even if their puny personalities and punier concerns are lost in the great crowd of worshippers of the goddess Chance."[2] Chance represented a black hole to people at a time when science and technology were able to offer increasingly precise ways to measure time and space. Writing specifically about novels (but I argue the point holds in a larger sense as well), historian Stephen Kern asserts that in the nineteenth century, "chance or coincidence was invariably a sign of some transcendent controlling destiny if not divine plan. In the modern novel, chance is more often evidence of life's fundamentally stochastic nature and the absence of any ultimate designing mind."[3] This shift in the nineteenth century from fate to chaos as the governing influence over our lives was, like the theory of probability, inflected by its relationship to gambling. We examine in this chapter the ways that gambling and chance were related and how the philosophy of chance intersected with casino gambling in ways that emphasized the pleasures of aleatory gaming.

Andrew Steinmetz distinguished between chance and luck, denying that the two terms were synonyms for one another and suggesting that a "doctrine of chances" had undermined any serious belief in the existence of luck. "The doctrine of chances," Steinmetz writes, "tends to explode the long-standing superstition that there is in play such a thing as *luck*, good or bad."[4] The casino, with its emphasis on aleatory games, was attuned to the idea that humans had little control, and it provided the opportunity to differentiate between chance and luck. Chance, of course, revolved around indeterminacy and uncertainty; luck represented a bending of the "laws of chance" in ways that generated a greater degree of determinacy and certainty. Luck increased probability; chance accepted it.

The casino provided a unique location to probe the logic of chance to those seeking to understand fortune and misfortune, causation and correlation. One pro-gambling voice from the early 1890s characterized gambling as a space of pure chance, and therefore one that should suffer no legal sanction. The ubiquity of chance was a key element of its legitimacy as a worldview. James Romain explained in 1891, "Chance is at present the great motive power of the world. It sustains hope, and stimulates endeavor. Through its operation men are enriched and nations aggrandized. That

---

[2] C. Kingston, *The Romance of Monte Carlo* (J. L. the Bodley Head, 1925), 213.
[3] S. Kern, *A Cultural History of Causality: Science, Murder Novels, and Systems of Thought* (Princeton University Press, 2004), 11.
[4] A. Steinmetz, *The Gaming Table: Its Votaries and Victims*, 2 vols. (Tinsley Brothers, 1870), vol. 2, 242.

some meet with disaster and encounter misfortune does not prove that appeals to chance are criminal in their nature.... Consistently, therefore, gambling cannot be forbidden because in its pursuit some persons are foolhardy and others unfortunate."[5] Chance, found everywhere, could not be considered morally dubious, and those who sought to label games of chance as a forum for sinful activity missed this critical element. "Where, in the old or new testament, is a similar transaction denounced as a sin? But, it may be said, perhaps, the foregoing definition does not suffice for moral consideration: it ignores the element of chance, which enters more or less into all games."[6] The author, noting chance's universal qualities and its value-free status, suggests that games of chance should not be attacked. Indeed, chance's absolutely amoral qualities meant that it could express an inherent democracy that treated all as equals under its law.

Chance has an old pedigree. Even some of the earliest stories in the Western tradition center on the role of chance in determining basic aspects of our lives or, indeed, even the question of life. The origin of the term "scapegoat," for instance, is anchored in a narrative about chance. The term comes from Leviticus 16:8, in which Aaron drew lots to select a sacrificial victim who would expurgate his sins. One goat was selected by chance to sacrifice; the other was the so-called scape-goat who was sent as a representative of all the sins of a community not expunged through sacrifice into exile. Seventeenth-century texts recalled the older trope of the wheel of fortune that distributed rewards and punishments randomly. One of the issues informing our understanding of chance and luck, in other words, is how that experience could be used to translate our place in the world into larger theological or cosmological frameworks. How did luck fit into God's plan?

The issue of providence remained important to nineteenth-century observers of gambling. E. T. A. Hoffmann described chance as the outward display of divine will. Writing in his 1819 story "Gambler's Luck," Hoffmann describes two sorts of players who differ in their relationship to chance – and, by extension, to God – as it was framed in the context of the gaming table.

> For many the game itself as a game, irrespective of gain, affords an indescribably, mysterious pleasure. The singular effects of chance work themselves out in the strangest concatenations, the rule of the higher power

---

[5] J. H. Romain, *Gambling: Or, Fortuna, Her Temple and Shrine. The True Philosophy and Ethics of Gambling* (Craig Press, 1891), 224.
[6] Romain, *Gambling*, 55.

emerges more clearly, and it is just this that stimulates our spirit to stir its wings and try whether it cannot soar in the dark kingdom, into the fateful workshop of that higher power, and eavesdrop on its workings.[7]

Later novelists recalled these earlier forms of chance when they wrote about happenstance or accident. The relationship between chance and older concepts of fortune and divine will surfaced as well. One description of a gambler's experiences at the tables illustrates how chance continued to be related to conceptions of human passivity: "The tide of chance into which luck had been diving so valiantly had suddenly vanished, dried, cut off at its source, leaving only mud and potsherds, tin kettles and dead cats to the gazer on the bank."[8] Chance is related to disaster, misfortune, and the inability of humans to exercise control.

Rather than witnessing the working-out of chance as evidence of a larger state of disorder, other observers of chance in the gaming room saw proof of the opposite. Chance – related in this regard to theories of evening stemming from the doctrine of the maturity of chances – helped generate predictability. In his novella *The Gambler*, Dostoyevsky saw that chance demonstrated a larger order: "although there is no system in the course of random chance, there really does appear to be some sort of order, which, of course, is very peculiar."[9] For Dostoyevsky, this order could take the form of permanencies on the roulette table. "The very next day or next evening, red comes up time after time; and this might happen, for example, more than twenty-two times in a row and will certainly continue like this for some time, for instance, during a whole day."[10] Nearly a century later, mathematicians examining the logic of systems concluded that gambling and chance remained areas in which to find evidence for unseen processes:

> This conception of a force controlling chance so as to produce a stated average is at the bottom of many a gambler's "system." In fact it is a nice question whether the gambler is not to be defined as a person who does *not* believe in pure chance.... Perhaps, then, there is something to be said for the gambler's disbelief in "pure chance" and the view that previous events do have an influence over subsequent trials.[11]

In both accounts, the innate order of a particular system was expressed in chance. In this way chance was implicated in a larger debate about the

---

[7] E. T. A. Hoffmann, *The Tales of Hoffmann* (Frederick Ungar Publishing Co., 1963), 223.
[8] M. de V. Stacpoole, *Monte Carlo: A Novel* (Dodd, Mead and Co., 1913), 175.
[9] F. Dostoyevsky, *The Gambler and Other Stories* (Penguin, 2010), 144.
[10] Dostoyevsky, *The Gambler and Other Stories*, 145.
[11] "Gambling," *The Mathematical Gazette*, 15/212 (1931), 347–58, 355.

constitution of the universe as being a system that was by nature either inherently disorderly or ordered. One way around this duality was to envision chance in a new light as something that generated novelty, diversity, and variety. And in this way, chance begins to look like a computational system. J. Holt Schooling advocated for the increased reliance on chance to produce novelties. The essay, part of a larger series on luck, gambling, and chance, concludes with a description of what Schooling called the "Idea-Machine," a computational system that would – through the random selection of cards with various plot elements – allow writers to produce new fictional settings with ease. Schooling's emphasis on computational attempts to produce artistic objects connects with the work of others, such as Karl Pearson, who advocated for the use of the casino as a computational tool that could be used for research into other areas.

The French mathematician Henri Poincaré developed a similar argument in his discussion of how card shuffling and permutation theory were related. "The probability of a particular permutation ... depends on the player's habits. But if this player shuffles the cards long enough, there will be a great number of successive permutations, and the resulting final order will no longer be governed by aught but chance."[12] Poincaré wrestled with this issue, debating whether or not chance generated diversity or uniformity, and his answer in some ways reverts back to Bernoulli's law of large numbers. Time helps chance generate uniformity. Poincaré writes that "since the beginning of the ages, there have always been complex causes ceaselessly acting in the same way and making the world tend toward uniformity without ever being able to turn back."[13] This insight led him to celebrate the unique contributions of the historian, who had a special capability to make meaning while at the same time acknowledge how gaps in the historical record tend later to contribute to a weak analysis of events due to the vagaries of chance. Poincaré writes,

> It is just the same in the moral sciences and particularly in history. The historian is obliged to make a choice among the events of the epoch he studies; he recounts only those which seem to him the most important. He therefore contents himself with relating the most momentous events of the sixteenth century for example, as likewise the most remarkable facts of the seventeenth century. If the first suffices to explain the second, we say these conform to the laws of history. But if a great event of the seventeenth century should have for cause a small fact of the sixteenth century which no

---

[12] H. Poincaré, "Chance," *The Monist*, 22/1 (1912), 31–52, 39.   [13] Poincaré, "Chance," 47–48.

history reports, which all the world has neglected, then we say this event is due to chance. This word has therefore the same sense as in the physical sciences; it means that slight causes have produced great effects.[14]

Henri Poincaré was, with Albert Einstein, one of the great theoreticians of time and space working in the late nineteenth and early twentieth centuries.[15] His essay on chance, published just before his death in 1912, was his last. Poincaré's fascination with chance placed him alongside a suite of other thinkers around the turn of the century who sought to understand what chance was, and how it operated on us as humans.

Gamblers, who had long been called by the "voice of Fate," represented a unique way to probe the meaning of chance around the turn of the century.[16] Earlier participant-observers in gambling, like Dostoyevsky, described situations in which his characters felt as if fate controlled the situation, attaching itself to them in ways impervious to logic. Dostoyevsky writes of one character that it was

> as if fate were urging me on. This time, as if on purpose, a circumstance occurred that, however, happens rather frequently in gambling. Chance becomes attached, say, to red and doesn't drop it for ten times, even fifteen times in a row. The day before yesterday I had heard that the previous week red came up twenty times in a row; nobody could even recall that happening in roulette and it was talked about with amazement. It goes without saying, everybody immediately drops red, and after the tenth time, say, almost nobody risks placing a stake on it. But none of the experienced gamblers stakes on black, the opposite of red, either. The experienced gambler knows what the "caprice of chance" means. For example, it would seem that after coming up red sixteen times the seventeenth time without fail will come up black. And all the novices rush forward in crowds to double and triple their stakes, and lose terribly.[17]

Fate remained an important cultural motif for Europeans in the fin-de-siècle, one that was expressed in fields as divergent as Wagner's operas, new spiritualist movements like theosophy, and the budding field of eugenics. The basic issue confronting people who sought to understand fate revolved around the degree to which humans could influence destiny. While this was an old problem, it took on new urgency in the late nineteenth century when the forces of modernity cracked open the old traditional ways and offered a range of newly transformative practices. Fate and chance, in other

---

[14] Poincaré, "Chance," 49.
[15] P. Galison, *Einstein's Clocks and Poincaré's Maps: Empires of Time* (W. W. Norton, 2003).
[16] Stacpoole, *Monte Carlo*, 33.   [17] Dostoyevsky, *The Gambler and Other Stories*, 241–42.

words, no longer looked quite the same after the Declaration of the Rights of Man and Citizen, capitalism, and the railroad eroded old traditions. If fate was the language in which the "idiocy of rural life" was spoken, how could the concept operate in the new system?

One way to investigate the issue is to consider how superstition was analyzed in relation to casino gambling. There was no shortage of superstitions employed by gamblers to redirect fate or to bend chance, and commentators delighted in recounting the ones they considered most ridiculous. Even in the 1880s, superstition was examined as part of an unreflective belief in "obscure forces" that shaped human experience. One review of Richard Proctor's *Chance and Luck* published in *Science* explained the situation by commenting on the persistence of old cultural forms in the changed context of modernity.

> The persistency of a superstition can generally be referred to the subtleness and persuasiveness of the logic upon which it is founded or to the fact that it appeals to a strong instinct in human nature. Doubtless both of these influences have been at work in keeping alive, among those in whom the hazarding instinct is at all strong, a fondness towards a belief in their own favoritism, in the obscure forces which control luck, and in the sundry other agencies which go to make of chance something which is more than chance.[18]

Another way to investigate this topic was to imagine how one might steer clear of a superstition. "It is somewhat singular," Proctor writes, "that attempts to correct even the more degrading forms of superstition have often been as unsuccessful as those attempts which may perhaps not unfairly be called tempting fate."[19] Superstition, instinctual but also subtly logical, managed to exert a strong influence over the ways in which people perceived the world and then behaved in relation to it. Chance, in other words, was something that still defied explanation, and when people resorted to occult or hermetic justifications for their actions, they were not acting in ways that were completely illogical.[20]

---

[18] "Review of Chance and Luck: A Discussion of the Laws of Luck, Coincidences, Wagers, Lotteries, and the Fallacies of Gambling; With Notes on Poker and Martingales," *Science*, 10/233 (1887), 43–44, 43.

[19] R. A. Proctor, *Chance and Luck*, 2nd ed. (Longmans, Green, and Company, 1887), 95.

[20] The incorporation of putatively premodern cultural forms – occultism, superstition, magic, and so on – into modern life has been explored in a variety of formats, but it is useful to remember that modernity is only weakly rational. The basic contours of this argument were proposed in T. W. Adorno, *The Stars Down to Earth and Other Essays on the Irrational in Culture* (Routledge, 2002). Anthropologists have also built on this thesis in useful ways; see P. Geschiere, *The Modernity of Witchcraft: Politics and the Occult in Postcolonial Africa* (University Press of Virginia, 1997).

In his 1891 pro-gambling treatise James Romain suggests that there should be a "philosophy of gaming" that would allow gambling to be subjected to the same type of critical and dispassionate analysis that other areas of human interaction enjoyed. Romain initiated his discussion with a defining question: "As a gamester, I sought the philosophy of gaming. What is chance? How far does it influence all mankind and circumscribe their efforts? What is gambling, in the broadest sense of the term? Is gaming wrong per se: i.e., absolutely vicious?"[21] Romain's answers to these questions are easy to determine, but they were expressed in the context of a larger intellectual system that was wrestling at exactly the same time with a basic issue raised in the text: What is chance?

For philosopher William James, chance provided an opportunity to contemplate the creation of better worlds and to produce a way to found faith on the basis of reason.[22] In that way, chance can be seen doing a range of important cultural work in that a discussion of chance was never just a discussion of odds, probability, or certainty. The sociologist Georg Simmel brought a similar insight about the malleability of money as a cultural sign in his *Philosophy of Money*.[23] The sections of the work that most concern us here focus on how Simmel used gambling and risk as a forum to discuss the larger dimensions of chance and uncertainty. Simmel viewed gambling as a relationship to money that was unlike any other. "All money outlays for the purposes of acquisition fall into two categories – with risk and without risk. Viewed abstractly, both forms exist in every single outlay if one excludes gambling."[24] Gambling represented more than just a calculation of odds. Because money was involved, it also was complicit in a highly emotional process in the midst of which a person could lose track of rationality. "A personal factor must also be considered. In every economic situation," Simmel writes, "a certain fraction of one's possessions should not be risked at all, regardless of how large and how probable the chances of profit might be. The desperate risk of the final gamble, which is usually justified by the statement that one 'has nothing more to lose,' indicates by this very argument that any vestige of rationality

Historians of early modern Europe have also benefited from this insight, refreshingly explored in J. P. Coy, *The Devil's Art: Divination and Discipline in Early Modern Germany* (University of Virginia Press, 2020).

[21] Romain, *Gambling*, 11.
[22] W. James, *The Will to Believe: And Other Essays in Popular Philosophy* (Longmans, Green, and Company, 1911).
[23] G. Simmel, *The Philosophy of Money*, 3rd ed. (Routledge, 2004).
[24] Simmel, *The Philosophy of Money*, 260.

has been deliberately abandoned here."[25] In the heat of the wager, chance overwhelmed the senses, and money's ability to dissolve and reconstitute social relations was diminished in favor of pure emotion that clouded one's assessment of risk.

Writing on risk and rational economic behavior, Simmel noted that money made it impossible to objectively measure risk through some kind of alchemical dissolution of any real notion of value. The miscalculation of chance was crucial to the psychic processes at work. "The money form of values easily tempts one to misjudge this economic dictate [not to stupidly throw money into investments known to be bad] because it subdivides values into very small portions and so tempts the person with slender means to take a risk that, in principle, he ought to avoid."[26] To illustrate this point, Simmel uses the example of penny stocks in mining companies (low value; small chance of high profit) and state lotteries:

> A similar state of affairs is created in the Italian lottery. However, in many countries, modern legislation relating to shares attempts to counteract this danger to the welfare of the people by establishing a fairly high minimum for the nominal value of any share offered.... The tragedy in all this is that people whose income provides only the minimum level of existence, and who therefore should not risk anything at all, are most strongly subjected to such temptations.[27]

For Simmel, risk was a coded way of understanding the operation of chance in the modern money economy. Even in low stakes settings, chance presented an irresistible lure. And to those who were least able to afford risk, the presence of chance offered – as it perhaps did for William James as well – the dream of a better world.

Georg Simmel was not the only turn-of-the-century social scientist interested in understanding how risk and chance operated in the minds of people at the time. American lawyer Clemens J. France, in a remarkable essay published in the *American Journal of Psychology* in 1902, offered an analysis of what he labeled the "Gambling Impulse."[28] While the essay is not focused narrowly on casino gambling and is informed by a trans-Atlantic academic ethos, France describes what he calls a "psychology of uncertainty" that was evaluated by questionnaire.[29] His experimental sample included 70 men, 340 women, and 33 who remained "unstated."

---

[25] Simmel, *The Philosophy of Money*, 260.   [26] Simmel, *The Philosophy of Money*, 261.
[27] Simmel, *The Philosophy of Money*, 261.
[28] C. J. France, "The Gambling Impulse," *The American Journal of Psychology*, 13/3 (1902), 364–407.
[29] France, "The Gambling Impulse," 377.

France asserts that the data demonstrate the existence of three general groups of people. Roughly 18 percent of his respondents "have frequent and strong impulses to break away from their daily routine and enter on some venturesome habit."[30] Twelve percent, he determined, were risk averse: "subjects are extremely cautious and feel strongly averse to taking any risk."[31] He noted the presence of a third group with "no marked inclination or disinclination to run risks."[32] The survey included questions on topics like "are there times when you desire to risk something?"; "Do you like to know far ahead what you are going to do or what is going to happen?"; and "Are there days when you get up in the morn and feel: To-day I will be lucky?"[33] Respondents reported engaging in common risks like going to class unprepared, smoking, bicycle riding, skating on thin ice, exposure to cold, jumping from high trees, and cutting out a dress without a pattern. They also reported taking chances in ways that are now unfamiliar or seem so incredibly dangerous that they do not qualify as common: jumping from a fast moving train; crossing a high, long railroad bridge; attempting to stop a runaway team hitched to a bindery in a way that required the person to run in front of the knives; and jumping off and on moving cars.[34] France also reports a gender difference in the ways people approach risk, and a gendered divergence becomes increasingly visible with puberty. A chart demonstrates a kind of gendered risk curve showing a major split occurring around age seventeen, which France interprets in biological ways:

> The fact that the boys' curve rises, as the ages approach those of maturity, we believe to be in line with the general biological thesis of the male being the more iconoclastic, exploiting and venturesome element, while the fact, that the curve of the girls' falls, is, on the other hand, in line with the biological thesis, that woman is the conservative and cautious element.[35]

While France's conclusions seem to confirm little more than the existence of certain cultural conventions about gender from the turn of the century, the project remains a fascinating description of the psychology of chance and risk from the time. Observing France's results from the standpoint of historical analysis we see how social-scientific methodologies were applied to the study of abstract qualities like chance. The conclusions that France

---

[30] France, "The Gambling Impulse," 378. [31] France, "The Gambling Impulse," 378.
[32] France, "The Gambling Impulse," 378. [33] France, "The Gambling Impulse," 377.
[34] France, "The Gambling Impulse," 379. Horse-drawn reapers, mowers, and binders like those invented by Cyrus McCormick revolutionized agricultural production beginning in the mid-nineteenth century.
[35] France, "The Gambling Impulse," 380.

drew – that the willingness to embrace chance was conditioned by gender and age – are not especially surprising; what is helpful is his assumption that chance was a legitimate object of scientific study.

We have already considered aspects of Henri Poincaré's 1912 essay "Chance." We need to take it up now in greater detail because it provides clear examples of how chance was being explored in the natural sciences in the period just before World War I. Poincaré is best remembered for his answer to the "three body problem" in physics, which probed the ways that three entities would interact with one another while in orbit. Poincaré's great insight was that the three bodies would interact in unanticipated and unreproducible ways. A forerunner to chaos theory, Poincaré's work on this issue is oriented around chance and indeterminacy.

Poincaré opens the essay in a provocative way, taking issue with Joseph Bertrand's position that law and chance were antithetical to one another. Quoting a passage from Bertrand's *Calcul des Probabilités* ("How dare we speak of the laws of chance? Is not chance the antithesis of all law?"), Poincaré strongly asserts the opposite case: "Chance is only the measure of our ignorance. Fortuitous phenomena are, by definition, those whose laws we do not know."[36] This definition of chance as something that follows laws, but which is also made real only by the limits of human intelligence and observation, prompts Poincaré to imagine the role of history and of historical thinking in our ability to judge accurately the connections between events. Poincaré writes, "Some years ago a philosopher said that the future is determined by the past, but not the past by the future; or, in other words, from knowledge of the present we could deduce the future, but not the past; because, said he, a cause can have only one effect, while the same effect might be produced by several different causes."[37] This is not an especially controversial topic, but in taking up the work of Nicolas Camille Flammarion, the French astronomer, paranormal researcher, and science-fiction novelist, Poincaré addresses the ways that the flow of time might be reversed. "Flammarion once imagined an observer going away from the earth with a velocity greater than that of light; for him time would have changed sign." Poincaré continues, "History would be turned about, and Waterloo would precede Austerlitz. Well, for this observer, effects and causes would be inverted; unstable equilibrium would no longer be the exception. Because of the universal irreversibility all would seem to him to come out of a sort of chaos in unstable equilibrium. All

---

[36] Poincaré, "Chance," 31–32.   [37] Poincaré, "Chance," 36.

nature would appear to him delivered over to chance."[38] If all of nature were turned over to chance, chaos would reign. Poincaré was in some ways the anti-Flammarion. He found the argument ludicrous, but he still sought to understand what chance was and how it operated.

Poincaré sought to uncover, unlike Joseph Bertrand, the laws of chance. Poincaré bluntly stated that chance "obeys laws."[39] Tellingly, the evidence for this argument comes not from science fiction but from the gambling hall. Poincaré first turns to roulette and focuses on the issue of the spin of the wheel: "The datum of the question is the analytic function representing the probability of a particular initial push. But the theorem remains true whatever be this datum, since it depends upon a property common to all analytic functions. From this it follows finally that we no longer need the datum."[40] Poincaré explains that a similar logic could apply to the orbits of planets or to the shuffling of cards: "the great number of shuffles, that is to say the complexity of the causes, has produced uniformity."[41] Chance, the random, the stochastic, the chaotic, ultimately generates its own regularity. Like the spinning fractal patterns that cohere into recognizable shapes, Poincaré's chance – while appearing chaotic – ultimately conformed. The world might be buffeted by forces we do not understand, but in the end law generates patterns.

Chance was arguably a centerpiece of fin-de-siècle European thought. Few ideas, whether appearing under the name fate, destiny, or chance, represented quite the same threat to enlightened Europeans of the nineteenth and early twentieth centuries, only in part because it suggested a lack of control and an inability to know. If chance represented a destabilizing force to Europeans, luck might provide the antidote. Luck offered a way to bend the rules and to minimize the effects of chance. Gambling – and the vagaries of fortune as it applied to the gambling table – provided the perfect vehicle for Europeans to assess the meaning and value of luck.

Reith provides a useful description of luck as it relates to what she calls the "magical-religious worldview." "The outcome of a game," Reith argues, "is governed by chance and is therefore immutable, but it is luck that determines how gamblers will bet on a game, inducing them to make the right choice. Luck is therefore a force which provides the gambler with foreknowledge of the outcome of a game.... [L]uck is essentially an order of knowledge and implies a reversal of causation in time."[42] The definition of luck that Reith produces here is a valuable indication of the type of cultural

[38] Poincaré, "Chance," 37.   [39] Poincaré, "Chance," 41.   [40] Poincaré, "Chance," 41.
[41] Poincaré, "Chance," 43.
[42] G. Reith, *The Age of Chance: Gambling in Western Culture* (Routledge, 1999), 167.

work that luck was imagined to perform. That said, it is also important to recognize that because luck was a force strong enough to bend the field of chances or to modify the probability curve, it was also manufactured by humans. The dream of creating luck at will and through human agency permitted the application of magical, occult, or hermetic powers to the generation of wealth. Reith hints at just such a theory of luck when she suggests that luck may be seen as a force akin to magic. One method of understanding luck, she argues, "likens the gambler's state of mind to that of the magician: 'The modern gambler behaves as though he . . . can control or contradict the laws of probability by certain types of thought or action. He is not unlike the sorcerer who has similar ceremony and paraphernalia.'"[43]

Other scholars of luck argue for alternate understandings of the concept. Jackson Lears, for instance, suggests that over the course of the development of colonial society in North America, luck – in the Protestant tradition so important to the historical development of colonial North America – was absorbed into a language of Grace that indicated the working out of a Providential plan, thus subsuming luck into Protestant worldviews that spoke to larger issues of will and human freedom.[44] But it is important to Lears that we accept that the Puritans were just one set of players among many. He explains that the planter class in the mid-Atlantic and Southern colonies also saw a role for fortune. Lears asserts that the cultural element binding both of these religious types together was a willingness to include African religious traditions in a larger understanding of fortune or providence. The story of luck in the American colonies was also the story of religious syncretism characteristic of the Atlantic world. Magic, as he puts it, was "blackened" and "reddened" through the inclusion of African and indigenous beliefs.[45] After the colonial period, Lears argues, luck was incorporated into a growing commercial and political culture that promoted certain aspects of the sporting life as the hallmark of American masculinity. Lears writes that there were structural similarities in the social spaces that gambling and business occupied: "A commercial ethic of fortune flourished amid the glitter of a Gilded Age. Successful gamblers and stock speculators jointly fostered a nouveau riche style. It was on display in the opulent palaces (casinos, hotels, resorts) where paunchy bejeweled sybarites could flash their ill-gotten gains – ill gotten, at least,

---

[43] Reith, *The Age of Chance*, 167.
[44] T. J. J. Lears, *Something for Nothing: Luck in America* (Viking, 2003), 33–35.
[45] Lears, *Something for Nothing*, 50–53.

from the perspective of the Protestant ethic of mastery."[46] In both arenas – it is important to note – one was expected to make one's own luck.

Of course, luck has an ancient pedigree. In the classical period, Fortune was represented "standing on a ball, or holding a wheel, symbolizing the changeableness of all existing things, and expressing the incalculable and transitory nature of human destiny" (see Figure 5.1 for a more recent example of this method of representing luck).[47] The medieval Wheel of Fortune reproduced these ideas, and in the opinion of one writer, it "appeared rather as a symbol of the eternal ups and downs and vicissitudes of fortune in life and at the gaming table. The goddess of chance turns the wheel, to the rim of which cling human forms, which rise to the top and then sink into the depths again as it turns."[48] One could see, in this description, a corollary in peasant carnival that inverted power hierarchies in order to demonstrate the cyclical nature both of time and of social relations.[49]

We may argue that three visions of fortune were advanced in the early modern period. Paracelsus, writing in the early sixteenth century from the standpoint of hermetic mysticism, argued that fortune was the product of human toil, intelligence, and discipline. Michel de Montaigne, writing fifty years later but as an example of Renaissance learning, reinscribed Fortune in the mode of an allegory that nonetheless exerted an unpredictable but powerful pull over human affairs. Ninety years after Montaigne's essays were written, Antoine Arnauld's *Logic, or the Art of Thinking* appeared, in which we see a version of luck that is produced within human relations. When we shift to consider evidence from the nineteenth century, a different picture of luck emerges, one that is confined within mathematical proof, exhibited in various systems designed to generate wins at the gambling table, to lure a person through any number of bizarre superstitions, and that is made the object of social scientific inquiry. Despite these new contexts within which luck emerged, we still see gestures to the old images of the wheel of fortune, with a bare-breasted Fortuna standing astride its hub distributing her shares unequally (see Figure 5.1). Juxtaposed against a photograph of the casino at Monte Carlo we see temporal and aesthetic disjunction, the (imagined) old and the new rubbing up against one another. A similar example of fortune's excess splashed across an image of the gaming table at Monte Carlo may be seen in Figure 5.2, titled "Monte-Carlo – Salle

[46] Lears, *Something for Nothing*, 148–49.
[47] E. C. Corti, *The Wizard of Monte Carlo* (E. P. Dutton, 1935), 28.
[48] Corti, *The Wizard of Monte Carlo*, 28.
[49] M. M. Bakhtin, *Rabelais and His World* (Indiana University Press, 1984).

Figure 5.1 "La Fortune Monte Carlo" (unknown, ca. 1907–14). Courtesy of Watkinson Library at Trinity College, Hartford, George Watson Cole European Postcard Collection.

821. MONTE-CARLO – Salle de Jeu (Veine et Déveine)

Edition GILETTA

Figure 5.2 "Monte-Carlo – Salle de Jeu (Veine et Déveine)" (Giletta Frere, ca 1907–14). Courtesy of Watkinson Library at Trinity College, Hartford, George Watson Cole European Postcard Collection.

de Jeu (Veine et Déveine)" (Monte-Carlo – Gambling Hall [Good and Bad Luck]). One fortunate gambler waves a fistful of bank notes, his upturned moustache a visual indicator of his rising fortunes. His unlucky counterpart, hair disheveled with an unwaxed and droopy moustache to match, clenches his empty fist with a distraught look on his face. The images, available as postcards in the early twentieth century, provided a visual index of fortune that was used at the same time to advertise the resort at Monte Carlo.

The nineteenth century was the age of industry, and this logic applied as much to the manufacturing of luck as it did to the manufacturing of iron. Nineteenth-century mathematicians like Richard Proctor described luck as something that existed outside law. Proctor wrote, "In the operations of nature and in the actions of men, in commercial transactions and in chance games, the great majority of men recognise the prevalence of something outside law – the good fortune or the bad fortune of men or of nations, the luckiness or unluckiness of special times and seasons – in fine ..., the influence of something extranatural if not supernatural."[50] This characterization of luck as an external force that did not conform to any rational set of expectations was a characteristic element of late nineteenth-century thought. In another passage, Proctor argues that luck provides an unnatural compulsion to continue playing. Looking closely at the psychodynamics of "evening," Proctor employs a language of faith to describe the unbalanced reasoning of the gambler. "[N]o gambler was ever yet content to stay his hand when winning, or to give up when he began to lose again. The fatal faith in eventual good luck is the source of all bad luck.... Every gambler has this faith, and no gambler who holds to it is likely long to escape ruin."[51] Arguably aligned with the growth of psychical research as a field of inquiry that excited a wide range of European thinkers at the time, attempts to understand luck and how it could be manufactured, cultivated, or channeled remained a topic of wide interest.

J. Holt Schooling tackled the issue of luck in essays from 1900. Schooling really believed in luck, and he correlates luck with gambling in dramatic ways: "it is rare to find a gambler who does not believe in his own luck: a gambler who believes he is essentially unlucky, and who still continues to tempt Fortune, combines a maximum of unreason with his gambling which renders argument addressed to him as futile as it would be if spoken to one of Madame Tussaud's wax-figures."[52] Basing his

---

[50] Proctor, *Chance and Luck*, 1.   [51] Proctor, *Chance and Luck*, 14.
[52] J. H. Schooling, "Lotteries, Luck, Chance, and Gambling Systems. Part II – Luck," *Pall Mall Magazine*, 20/81 (1900), 84–93, 85.

argument about the existence of luck on the natural variability of a population, Schooling argues that "in any community or society one selects, there must be persons who are constantly lucky, whatever be the nature of their ventures, and that conversely there must be persons who are constantly unlucky."[53] The upshot, he claims, is that "luck, luck of all shades, is a substantial reality."[54] He demonstrates this argument through a thought experiment: a series of state lotteries in which half the participants win and half lose. Once one has lost, participation in subsequent lotteries is halted. After twenty-five years, Schooling claims, there will be one person who has won every single lottery and who could be legitimately described as lucky. The existence of a singularly unlucky person also could be determined. The thought experiment is extended in ways that allow him to assert that

> we may expect ... that some persons will be constantly lucky through life, while others will be constantly unlucky throughout life – and that there will be all shades of good and bad luck between these two extremes of luck ... we may now realise ... not only that some persons are actually more lucky than others to a very high degree, but also we may infer quite logically that for every person's luck to be equal would necessitate a condition of things in actual life as extraordinary and as inconceivable.[55]

Schooling imagines an economy of luck, distributed unequally, and operating independently of privilege, education, intelligence, skill, and hard work. He concedes in one passage that "people often ascribe to good luck results which have nothing to do with luck, but which are the outcomes of the energy, skill or foresight of the so-called lucky person."[56] Nonetheless, he was more attuned to the idea that fortune and misfortune operate, importantly, as things "beyond our control," thus hinting at a larger conception of fate that channels our opportunities and ambitions.[57] Schooling is quick, however, to argue that he does not advocate "reliance upon luck, either good or bad," because it is "impossible for any person to know if he or she be destined to receive good luck or bad luck, and it is also impossible for any person to know for how long an existing run of luck will continue."[58] In fact, Schooling asserts – in a nod toward a secular formulation of predestination – that "nothing we can do can possibly affect our

[53] Schooling, "Lotteries, Luck, Chance, and Gambling Systems. Part II – Luck," 85–86.
[54] Schooling, "Lotteries, Luck, Chance, and Gambling Systems. Part II – Luck," 86.
[55] Schooling, "Lotteries, Luck, Chance, and Gambling Systems. Part II – Luck," 92.
[56] Schooling, "Lotteries, Luck, Chance, and Gambling Systems. Part II – Luck," 93.
[57] Schooling, "Lotteries, Luck, Chance, and Gambling Systems. Part II – Luck," 91.
[58] Schooling, "Lotteries, Luck, Chance, and Gambling Systems. Part II – Luck," 92–93.

future experience of this curious and important factor of life, which has given rise to so much foolish superstition and also a shortsighted disbelief in luck."[59] We see in these essays from Schooling a strange combination of ideas. Luck is real, an external force that shapes our destinies and governs our options. Yet luck is also scientifically quantifiable – we could conduct experiments that would identify (at least in Schooling's mind) those individuals uniquely lucky or unlucky. And at the same time, luck remains unknowable, existing outside the ken of human intelligibility.

Schooling's description of luck, to be sure, was meant for a popular audience and does not rise to the level of what we might consider elite intellectual life. That should not diminish its importance as an indication of how luck was popularly conceived at the turn of the century. Attempts to cultivate luck, or to lure it to one's possession, remained a hallmark of nineteenth-century conceptions of the category. More than a feeling, luck was something that people could generate, manufacture, cultivate, or capture. This element of human agency found in the attempts to channel luck or prevent its dissipation speaks to a way of imagining the world that promoted the basic ideas of human power and control while also acknowledging their limits. Gambling systems and superstitions, especially when they did not rest on the foundation of the "maturity of chances," were at their heart modern attempts to bend luck to one's side.

George Sala noted that "there is no end to the silly little devices by which the votaries of play endeavour to propitiate that goddess, who, so far from being blind, as she is usually represented, strikes me as being, so far as Hombourg is concerned, the farthest-seeing and clearest-sighted deity in all Olympus."[60] Setting his use of the language of pagan sacrifice aside, Sala's observation is helpful in laying out the ways that gamblers in the nineteenth century referred back to older traditions of luck associated – perhaps – with the classical past. Dostoyevsky echoes those ideas, suggesting that luck could be cultivated or tainted depending on the actions of the gambler. The titular character of *The Gambler* remarks: "It was an extraordinarily unpleasant sensation, and I wanted to have done with it as soon as possible. I kept thinking that by playing for Polina I was undermining my own luck. Is it really impossible to come into contact with the gaming table without at once becoming infected with superstition?"[61] Andrew

---

[59] Schooling, "Lotteries, Luck, Chance, and Gambling Systems. Part II – Luck," 93.
[60] G. A. Sala, *Make Your Game, or, The Adventures of the Stout Gentleman, the Slim Gentleman, and the Man with the Iron Chest: A Narrative of the Rhine and Thereabouts* (Ward and Lock, 1860), 217.
[61] Dostoyevsky, *The Gambler and Other Stories*, 137.

Steinmetz also provided readers with examples of what he called the "gambling superstitions" that could be observed at Bad Homburg or Monte Carlo. In fact, Steinmetz produced an entire set of prescriptions for those seeking to win – a kind of road map to success at the gambling table. Basing his system on one produced by the magician Jean Eugène Robert-Houdin, Steinmetz counseled his readers to follow these rules if one wanted to win. First, one should play roulette, because one can bet in a number of different ways. Second, Steinmetz was adamant that players should remain calm in the heat of the game: "if he gets into a passion, it is all over with prudence, all over with good luck – for the demon of bad luck invariably pursues a passionate player."[62] Third, players must remember that by playing they ran the risk of losing. Finally, a player should perform some test to determine if they are "in vein" – that is, lucky – or not, and "in all doubt, you should abstain."[63] Steinmetz also suggests that the unlucky should never play, that stubbornness is a road to ruin, and that "Fortune does not like people to be overjoyed at her favours, and that she prepares bitter deceptions for the imprudent, who are intoxicated by success."[64] Steinmetz is less prescriptive than we might expect about how to attract luck. His suggestion that players merely interrogate their own luckiness does not provide a lot of information about how they might go about doing so.

Other observers found the idea of luck to be preposterous. Richard Proctor sought to demonstrate the unlikely possibility of luck with a thought experiment that was remarkably similar to the one proposed by J. Holt Schooling discussed above. Proctor pictured an experiment with 20 million players who would be subdivided into winners and losers. An experiment dividing the group in half would be carried out twenty times, resulting in twenty who had won every time and twenty who had lost on each occasion. These two groups – the putatively lucky and the unlucky – then carried a certain reputation with them. Proctor is quick to point out, however, that luck is the wrong label to use. "But it should hardly be necessary to say that that which must happen cannot be regarded as due to luck."[65] In this way, Proctor's model contradicts the one appearing later in *Pall Mall Magazine*. The upshot of Proctor's argument is to suggest that a belief in luck is fundamentally superstitious:

> This form of belief in luck is not only akin to superstition, it is superstition. Like all superstition, it is mischievous. It is, indeed, the very essence of the gambling spirit, a spirit so demoralising that it blinds men to the innate

[62] Steinmetz, *The Gaming Table*, vol. 2, 255–56. [63] Steinmetz, *The Gaming Table*, vol. 2, 256.
[64] Steinmetz, *The Gaming Table*, vol. 2, 257. [65] Proctor, *Chance and Luck*, 6.

immorality of gambling. It is this belief in luck, as something which can be relied on, or propitiated, or influenced by such and such practices, which is shown, by reasoning and experience alike, to be entirely inconsistent not only with facts but with possibility.[66]

Following on this argument, Proctor goes on to assert that a belief in luck, aside from its fallacious nature, is also correlated to a set of beliefs held by colonized non-Christians whose beliefs Proctor describes as "absurd." "Such practices are like the absurd invocation of Indian 'medicine men'; there is a sort of vague hope that something good may come of them, no real faith in their efficacy."[67] Luck was part of a prerational belief system, a way of interacting with the world that is foreign to Proctor's worldview and, perhaps most illuminating, not very effective anyway. The magical reasoning that underlies a belief in luck was also a condition of its diminished status.

Systems – when they were applied to the problem of gambling – worked in a similarly magical way, and they generated a similar set of reactions. One respondent to Hiram Maxim's exposé of Monte Carlo, writing under the name "Deacon Uriah Perkins," suggested that Lord Rosslyn's martingale system was merely a cloaked version of luck. "Perkins" explained that the "class headed by Lord Rosslyn, invents so-called systems and appears to believe that chance is blind, [and that] it may be confused and put off the scent, providing a sufficiently intricate and complex system can be found."[68] Seeming to equate chance and luck, anthropomorphizing each, Perkins goes on, "I assert, and am prepared to prove, that it is not a question of finding a confusing and complicated system to fool blind chance, and that mathematics has no more to do with gambling than it has to do with catching fish. No, it is none of these, but purely and simply a question of LUCK."[69] Perkins concludes bluntly that "it is invariably the lucky players that win, and always the unlucky ones that lose."[70] Such arguments were infuriating to those who sought to depict systematizers – like those subscribing to superstition more generally – as people whose capability for logic suffered. As one writer put it in 1925, "No system can guarantee success, but some have the advantage of enabling the player to reduce the odds against him. When all is said and done, however, every system is dependent on luck. The most curious thing about them all is that they invariably begin well and end badly."[71]

[66] Proctor, *Chance and Luck*, 9.   [67] Proctor, *Chance and Luck*, 9.
[68] H. S. Maxim, *Monte Carlo: Facts and Fallacies* (Grant Richards, 1904), 195.
[69] Maxim, *Monte Carlo*, 196.   [70] Maxim, *Monte Carlo*, 199.
[71] Kingston, *The Romance of Monte Carlo*, 209.

Superstitions were equally contentious. While superstitious practices and gambling have a long history and were considered evidence of dishonor at best and witchcraft at worst in the early modern period (one example from 1586, for instance, revolves around a man who cut off the toe of an executed criminal because he thought the fetish would bring him luck at the gambling table), by the nineteenth century superstition was more likely to be taken as evidence of a primitive worldview.[72] Proctor describes some of the strange ways that people change their luck, such as turning around in one's chair three times before resuming a game. Superstition, in Proctor's mind, was related to passion, and passion led to bad luck. Quoting the same passage from Houdin as Steinmetz would later, Proctor explains that

> "the demon of bad luck invariably pursues a passionate player." At a game of pure chance good temper makes the player careless under ill-fortune, but it cannot secure him against it. In like manner, passion may excite the attention of others to the player's losses, and in any case causes himself to suffer more keenly under them, but it is only in this sense that passion is unlucky for him.[73]

After complimenting Americans on their invention of poker ("The existence and still more the flourishing condition of such a game as poker, outside mere gambling-dens, is one of the most portentous phenomena of American civilization"[74]), Proctor opened up a further discussion of luck and confidence, explaining that "As a result of confidence in luck ... poker-players often trust in hands of far less value than such as would give a fair chance of winning. It never seems to occur to them that the possession of a bad hand should in itself be regarded ... as an evidence that at the moment they were not in the vein."[75] In this way, Proctor hints at a useful understanding of luck that emerges from the way a player responds not only to their hands but also to the larger social context of play. Luck – as Proctor uses the term here – does more than just assist a particular player; instead, gamblers must be astute enough to recognize its presence or absence and then respond accordingly.

If Proctor sought to some degree to discredit luck as a category, other nineteenth-century observers of casino gambling were much more excited by the prospect of cataloging the various superstitions that people brought

---

[72] K. Stuart, *Defiled Trades and Social Outcasts: Honor and Ritual Pollution in Early Modern Germany* (Cambridge University Press, 1999), 124.
[73] Proctor, *Chance and Luck*, 34.   [74] Proctor, *Chance and Luck*, 111.
[75] Proctor, *Chance and Luck*, 113.

to tables with them. Maxim, describing what he called "Luck and Occult Influences," includes descriptions of what was called a "jumpy" table, that is, one in which the runs on a color were minimal and gamblers could anticipate frequent shifts from red to black that went against any notion of random chance. He also notes the practice of people who "follow" tables, attempting to locate a roulette table they consider especially lucky at a particular moment. "It is surprising how many players imagine that one's success at the tables depends upon luck; many of them believe that certain persons are surrounded by a halo of occult influence that somehow or other gets hold of the little ball and pitches it into the pocket that they happen to be betting on at the time."[76] Maxim also drily notes the ineffectiveness of all of these occult interventions: "Suppose, for instance, that the play at Monte Carlo should be swayed to the extent of one percent. in favour of the players, by incantations, sentiment, good luck, fetiches, or ghostly influence, the Bank's percentage would be completely wiped out, and the fairest spot on the Mediterranean would, in a few years, resemble a Western mining camp where the diggings had given out."[77] Maxim's use of the word "occult" to describe these practices is significant and follows on previous analyses of gambling superstition that focus on the close connections between gambling, superstition, and divination.

Those writing after the turn of the century invoked a similar language of the occult to describe the inner workings of luck. Clemens J. France suggests that luck functions as a kind of inner voice that perhaps guides the gambler to make certain decisions. As France explains,

> We have two important factors, one – the very essence of the belief in luck – and especially that phase of the belief represented by guardian angels, etc., – a semi-conscious feeling of a guiding power which gives one a cue to the result; second, we have an exaggerated feeling of one's own skill. Both of these are closely allied, both have their basis in a feeling of self-confidence, and both are common to men playing games of chance or entering on chance adventures. These inner feelings or premonitions are very strong in gamblers – the "hunch" as it is called and, like the inner voice of Socrates, it is followed most religiously.[78]

The gambler's imagination, especially when it appears in the form of a guiding interior monologue that suggests and confirms a player's instinct, is also a key element in the psychological attraction of gambling. France writes that the "player hears in roulette the ball rolling, sees it fall and

---

[76] Maxim, *Monte Carlo*, 191–92.   [77] Maxim, *Monte Carlo*, 185.
[78] France, "The Gambling Impulse," 396.

beholds himself a winner – 'not as though it were a hope but as a living reality, does he perceive it with the inner eye and ear of the imagination.'"[79]

Similar descriptions of luck appear in literary accounts from the time as well. Stacpoole comments in one passage that "One is driven to say that there is positively such a thing as luck, let scientific men sneer as they will. This thing we call luck has nothing to do with the thing we call chance. The thing we call chance is producing runs of colours … at Monte Carlo.… Luck is the imp who sits in the sub-conscious mind and tells the conscious mind what chance is about to do, and the conscious mind … has a run of luck."[80] The language of the subconscious that appears in Stacpoole's description of luck is not unlike the secret voice of Socrates that France employs to personify luck in his article. Stacpoole addresses the inner workings of luck in another passage, comparing luck to a dog hunting in the deep pool of the unconscious and retrieving useful information. Stacpoole writes,

> How luck plunges into the next moment like a diving dog and brings up in his teeth the thing that is going to happen I cannot say, an excusable ignorance in a world where all philosophy is based on two grand illusions, Time and Space; but the thing does happen – of that I am certain. As certain as I am of the folly of those who try to find out what chance is going to do by means of a system formulated by their conscious brains and based on a record of what chance has done. All gamblers will bear me out when I say that there comes to the player at times an *estro*, during which he feels himself borne along on a propitious tide. He feels that he can't do wrong, and he is right; he wins, and wins, and wins, whilst the fools who sit around pricking cards and fumbling with ghastly formulae wonder at his luck. You should not play unless you are in the vein. That is the only system worth considering at all; if you add to it the corollary – leave off when luck gets tired. Give the diving dog a chance, for he soon gets tired, and presently he will begin to bring up wrong numbers and colours in his mouth.[81]

Like Proctor's poker player who recognizes when luck has moved on and thus stops gambling, Stacpoole's player must not overtax the skill of their canine homunculus.

The climax of the action in Stacpoole's novel – recreating in some way a similar turning point in Dostoyevsky's *The Gambler* – comes when Jack, dejected at the thought that his wife Julia has left him, makes one final trip

[79] France, "The Gambling Impulse," 397. The quote comes from a text titled *Reize des Spiels* by M. Lazarus, published in Berlin in 1883.
[80] Stacpoole, *Monte Carlo*, 172–73.   [81] Stacpoole, *Monte Carlo*, 173–74.

to the casino, where he loses everything. Then he finds a gold coin on the ground and after some debate, returns to the casino and begins to win; he leaves his stake on the table and wins again. "Luck had taken him by the hand and led him to the throne and crowned him. He felt as though he were sitting in a strong blaze of light. Light that brought vitality with it.. . . With the most absolute daring, playing with the conviction of success, he continued; the *estro* had come."[82] Jack ends up winning more than £4,000 before the tables close for the night, and he finds that he has broken the bank. He and Julia are reunited, and all their misunderstandings are cleared up after he explains how much he has won. To be clear, Stacpoole's book was not mistaken for great literature. Nonetheless, she does give a range of useful ways to see how luck was personified, embodied, and conceptualized in popular ways in the period before World War I. Luck, as these passages from Stacpoole's novel show, could do a lot of different types of cultural work: it floated, mysterious and unseen, until it guided a person in just the right way at just the right time. And at that point, a furious self-confidence could explode.

We are used to hearing that nothing succeeds like success; Stacpoole reconfigured that, orienting it around luck instead. The upshot, as another early twentieth-century commentator put it, was that "Fortune is ever mutable and capricious, and the wise gambler is ever on the look out for reverses. He knows that roulette and its fellows are irresistibly alluring and that they demand more than they give."[83] The author of that passage was Charles Kingston, writer of a popular analysis of gambling titled *The Romance of Monte Carlo*, a title that surely clued readers in to the premise of the book. Nonetheless, Kingston's take on luck as it related to institutionalized gambling in its modern form includes a fundamental element of the analysis of luck performed by social scientists at the time: that casino gambling in fact generated a type of belief in players that fundamentally shaped who they were as people. As one reviewer of Proctor's *Chance and Luck* put it, "The wide-spread belief in luck is in many ways easy to account for, and even to defend. There is an element of chance that enters in the lives of every one of us; and it is but natural that where this chance favors the success of our projects . . . this should have a decided influence in the shaping of our character."[84]

Thorstein Veblen has much to say about luck and gambling (some of which we will consider in later chapters). He makes one argument in

---

[82] Stacpoole, *Monte Carlo*, 289–90. [83] Kingston, *The Romance of Monte Carlo*, 177.
[84] "Review of Chance and Luck," 43.

relation to animism and a pious outlook on life that resonates with those descriptions of luck that located its basis in the occult or in superstition. Veblen suggested that gambling was a way of making the unreal real:

> The basis of his gambling activity is, in great measure, simply an instinctive sense of the presence of a pervasive extraphysical and arbitrary force or propensity in things or situations, which is scarcely recognised as a personal agent. The betting man is not infrequently both a believer in luck, in this naive sense, and at the same time a pretty staunch adherent of some form of accepted creed. He is especially prone to accept so much of the creed as concerns the inscrutable power and the arbitrary habits of the divinity which has won his confidence.[85]

Other social scientists saw similar actions at work when they investigated gambling and luck. France, for instance, defined luck in the following way: "A feature closely allied with that of the state of tension, and largely influential in increasing it, pervades and permeates the whole fabric of the gambling impulse – that of luck."[86] France went on to locate luck as an element of lawlessness – unlike chance, which conformed to law – thus ensuring its ability to generate absolute chaos. France writes that despite its stochastic potential, luck is inherently soothing; it generates some form of rescue from the psychic distress caused by an awareness of overwhelming chance and indeterminacy. Chance, truly destabilizing to the enlightenment self, could be neutered by luck. France writes that for some players "Lawlessness is put aside for fate, law or will. This is the very meaning of luck, the substitution of a conscious, determining force or will, for an indeterminable, precarious, headless chance, – law in place of lawlessness."[87]

France saw in luck a somewhat desperate affirmation of agency on the part of a player. Seeking to disrupt the relentlessness of chance, luck provided a welcome antidote, thus securing a deeply satisfying psychological connection to the idea that one had choices in life and that those choices could be inflected in some way by forces beyond one's own self. This was an astute observation of the psychology of luck (about which we will learn more in Chapter 8), but luck remained something that could be confirmed only in certain localized circumstances: victory. The loser does not possess luck, only the winner. Recognizing this simple fact, Georg Simmel sought to determine how luck and skill interacted with one

---

[85] T. Veblen, *The Theory of the Leisure Class: An Economic Study of Institutions* (Macmillan and Company, 1912), 296.
[86] France, "The Gambling Impulse," 388.   [87] France, "The Gambling Impulse," 398.

another. In his 1908 essay "Conflict," Simmel notes the ways in which a prize was never especially significant to the players. Far more important was the ability to demonstrate through victory that one's skill (on one hand) or luck (on the other) confirmed one's social status. Simmel writes that the

> purely sociological attraction of becoming master over the adversary, of asserting oneself against him, is combined here, in the case of games of skill, with the purely individual enjoyment of the most appropriate and successful movement; and in the case of games of luck, with favor by fate which blesses us with a mystical, harmonious relation to powers beyond the realm of the individual and social. At any rate, in its *sociological motivation*, the antagonistic game contains absolutely nothing except fight itself. The worthless chip which is often contested as passionately as is a gold piece suggests the formal nature of this impulse, which even in the quarrel over gold often greatly exceeds any material interest.[88]

Winning, Simmel recognized, was everything. Whether that victory was achieved through skill or luck was generally unimportant. But luck could be equated with skill, and the person who enjoyed, as they say, being lucky rather than being good had immense social capital. The fact that skill and luck might be combined did not escape Simmel. Writing in his 1911 essay "The Adventurer," Simmel suggested that the social type of the adventurer (which seems to be related to the gambler) was able through some alchemy to fuse the two attributes: "The adventurer relies to some extent on his own strength, but above all on his own luck; more properly, on a peculiarly undifferentiated unity of the two. Strength, of which he is certain, and luck, of which he is uncertain, subjectively combine into a sense of certainty."[89]

Georg Simmel was one of the savviest observers produced by his society. His insight that luck and skill – welded together in one's psychological outlook and then demonstrated again and again through a relentless display of masterful capability – remains a bold depiction of the uses of luck to generate social status. We have considered a range of topics related to luck – the way it was conceptualized, the early modern contexts within which luck emerged in the nineteenth century, its relation to the self, how a person was lured to it, and how it was categorized and classified by social scientists around the turn of the century. Luck, especially when it appeared

[88] G. Simmel, *On Individuality and Social Forms* (University of Chicago Press, 1971), 83.
[89] Simmel, *On Individuality and Social Forms*, 194.

at the gambling table, was never just a fantasy. Players sought to cultivate it, and when they felt its presence they sought to absorb it into their bodies. We turn in the next chapter to a closer analysis of two related issues: How did gambling affect the body in the nineteenth century, and, maybe more basic, how did gamblers feel when playing?

CHAPTER 6

Gambling and the Body

Luck and chance were two ways that people in the nineteenth century wrestled with larger questions about fate, agency, and will. We saw that gambling as it was experienced in the casino was one area around which people could discuss these abstract concepts in ways that made the arguments more pointed and direct. We turn now to the ways in which the body was integrated into discussions of gambling, looking, for example, at luck as a tangible thing that the body could experience. We focus in this chapter on two issues. We look first at the somatic effects of gambling and the ways that gambling marked the body in profound ways, considering too the ways that gambling could disrupt bodily boundaries or throw them into confusion. We also consider the ways that luck, chance, and gambling were thought to have left their historical imprint on the human species, looking in particular at the ways that social Darwinist and evolutionary thought wrestled with gambling and sought to understand its evolutionary meaning. In all these ways, we consider how gambling could be understood as an intensely physical activity, rooted in the actions of the body.

Observers of gambling prior to the nineteenth century were attuned to the seductions of game-playing, both physical and mental. Thomas Kavanagh describes the intersection in ancien régime France between games of chance and the drama of seduction.[1] British critiques from the late eighteenth century fixated on gambling as a source of physical malady. Richard Hey notes in a 1784 text that the "Employment which Gaming gives to the Mind, is peculiarly detrimental to Health. Anxiety and other perturbations, besides the immediate pain of them, do moreover, through the certain though inexplicable connexion of body and mind, consume insensibly our corporeal vigour; and, not improbably, introduce direct

---

[1] T. M. Kavanagh, *Enlightenment and the Shadows of Chance: The Novel and the Culture of Gambling in Eighteenth-Century France* (The Johns Hopkins University Press, 1993), 9.

attacks of disease."[2] While Hey indicated that the most direct attacks on health that stemmed from gambling were launched at a person's mind, these nonetheless had debilitating effects on a person's physical health. Of course, in the nineteenth century, a stay at a casino could be represented as a perfectly healthful antidote to the stress of modern living, but in the first decades of the nineteenth century, that way of understanding the gambling resort was still in the future. The clear message of Hey's writings, which by 1812 linked gambling, dueling, and suicide as three social problems, was that gambling made people ill.

Gambling, in Hey's estimation, could have other profound physical effects as well. He was particularly concerned about what gambling might do to female players, but his text gives voice to a profound concern about gender disarray caused by the "pernicious effects" of gambling on men and women alike. Considering the ways that gambling transformed femininity, Hey asked his readers to "Conceive, on the one hand, the delicacy, the sensibility, the prompt benevolence, the sympathizing timidity, the susceptibility of every tender and affectionate emotion, – in youth the cheerful and unsuspecting innocence which attracts and exhilarates, in riper years the soft and placid mildness which conciliates and consoles: – conceive all these qualities such as we attribute them to Females of the first excellence, the examples of their sex."[3] Hey's is a depiction of idealized femininity, to be sure, but it is also one that conforms in predictable ways to gender codes. The passage continues, however, painting an image of the terrible toll that gambling might take on this idealized femininity. "Conceive, on the other hand, the harsh, the rigid, the chilling, and austere character, which appears, in some sort, as a qualification necessary to a serious and earnest pursuit of Gaming: conceive the gradual consequences to be dreaded from a perseverance in deep Play, – the habits of suspicion, peevishness, avarice, and dishonesty, the selfish and uncommiserating heart."[4] The comparison could not be clearer, and the charge that gambling was both physically and morally transformative formed the basis of Hey's critique of the practice.

Others writing in the early nineteenth century were less concerned about gender confusion or physical decline, but nonetheless found gambling the occasion to comment on other physical responses to the game.

---

[2] R. Hey, *Three Dissertations; on the Pernicious Effects of Gaming, on Duelling and on Suicide* (J. Smith, 1812), 19. Hey's text was first published in 1786; later iterations grew to include essays on dueling and suicide.
[3] Hey, *Three Dissertations*, 47.   [4] Hey, *Three Dissertations*, 47.

E. T. A. Hoffmann, for instance, describes one gambler as being "excited by the gambling."[5] Others, writing after the advent of Blanc-style casino gambling, also commented on the physical toll that gambling took on players. George Sala describes the somatic consequences of one person's time at the gambling tables. One particularly illuminating passage indicates how playing affected a person's physical state. Sala writes,

> By dinner time his hands were black as negro's by continually fingering of dross, and greasy notes of the Landgravate or de Banque de France, which to his great distaste he was sometimes compelled to take when the tables had been hit unusually hard. His hair, never very elegantly disposed, became hideously dishevelled; his eyes glared; hectic spots appeared on his dun cheeks; his tongue lapped thirstily from his mouth; and the regular habitues of the gaming table, who were ruined or enriched every day in the week, always with the same imperturbable quietude and nonchalance, looked with amazement, not unmingled with alarm, upon this wild man of the Kursaal, who played so fiercely, and gave utterance to such strange noises.[6]

Casino gambling, at least in Sala's depiction of the practice here, had asymmetrical impact. Some players were affected more strongly than others. Even those who lose and feel nothing but nonchalance look with horror and wonder at this character, whose physical appearance has been so radically altered in the course of play.

In other ways, however, the casino presented an opportunity for all sorts of different physical interactions. And in this way nineteenth-century gambling should be understood as an intensely physical and material practice. Sala, for instance, writes about the opportunities that casino gambling presented for physical interactions with members of another sex, and it is worth recalling here that one important element of Blanc's casino was its heterosocial nature.[7] Describing the women in the gambling room, Sala writes,

> Sometimes, on ball nights, these ravishing creatures wander in from the adjacent ball and concert rooms, in full evening dress, their white shoulders struggling like imprisoned doves in the meshes of lace and tulle; flowers rustling, the little *clinquants* of the *cachepeignes* (I don't know their English

---

[5] E. T. A. Hoffmann, *The Tales of Hoffmann* (Frederick Ungar Publishing Co., 1963), 216.

[6] G. A. Sala, *Make Your Game, or, The Adventures of the Stout Gentleman, the Slim Gentleman, and the Man with the Iron Chest: A Narrative of the Rhine and Thereabouts* (Ward and Lock, 1860), 210.

[7] Not all gambling was configured in this way, of course. S. Morton describes the connections between "bachelor masculinity" and gambling in *At Odds: Gambling and Canadians, 1919–1969* (University of Toronto Press, 2003), 69–88.

names) jingling. They lean over the players, and brush their hot faces with
their pendulous curls – the blondes are, for the most part, in ringlets; they
ask in the prettiest voices what number has last turned up; their little hands
venture between the burly, broad-clothed arms of the croupiers. They win,
and allow their stakes to remain and remain accumulating, till they lose all,
principal and interest. Then they make a provoking moue, utter some
sparkling little objurgation of unkind Fortune – risk more, double, treble
their stakes, lose again, sometimes all they have.[8]

Losing and winning was no longer the only point of gambling when one
visited a casino. Instead, the casino presented an opportunity to enjoy the
physicality of other people, to absorb their human presence, and perhaps
to take advantage of the social opportunities occasioned by the presence of
both men and women in the casino.

Indeed, the casino offered more than just an opportunity for
matchmaking. Unlike Hey and his concern about a type of gender chaos
that developed from play, Sala made an opposite point. The casino
environment, at least by 1860, reified sexual difference; it made gender
more obvious rather than less. Indeed, gambling was a practice that could
sharpen gender distinctions and in one case was represented – somewhat
comically – as a practice that amplified a form of robust masculinity. One
of Sala's characters proclaims that "playing at roulette, as a manly and
invigorating exercise, beat billiards, quoits, pulling against tide, and jumping in sacks; and quite threw partridge-shooting and the dumb-bells into
the shade."[9] These descriptions of bodily transformation and masculine
intensification accomplished through gambling – especially when they
took place by playing an aleatory game like roulette – gave voice to a
new way of understanding how leisure activities might affect gender
displays. Luxury, of course, had long been associated, negatively to be
sure, with femininity. And yet we see something of a reversal in these
descriptions of gender complimentary in the social environment of
the casino.

Later observers also commented on the ways that gender could be
transformed through casino gambling. W. Fraser Ray was especially concerned about the effects of gambling on the female body. In one passage
from his essay "Play and Players on the Riviera," Rae states his "belief that
the mischiefs and consequent miseries of gaming are intensified when
women follow the bad example of men. A man who has given way to
the degrading vice of drunkenness may be cured, but a woman who has

---

[8] Sala, *Make Your Game*, 197–98.   [9] Sala, *Make Your Game*, 207–8.

acquired a liking for intoxicants is irreclaimable. A female gamester is as sad a spectacle as a female drunkard."[10] Beyond redemption, the woman gambler is unable to accept the reality of continued losses at the tables. Rae explains that a "female gamester has too much imagination to accept the hard saying that she cannot win in the long run. Even if she admits one day that no system can lead to fortune, she will begin on another her pursuit after the unattainable, losing her money, and it may be something still more precious, in the chase."[11] The result of the situation was nothing short of catastrophic. "The moral and even the physical mischief is wrought when gaming and drinking become habits, and it is because this danger is greater in the cases of women than men that women should be hindered, as far as possible, from entering the broad road leading to either vice."[12]

A critical element of the social dynamic at work in the casino was the intensity of observation that took place. Everyone was on display, and everyone was being watched. While the ocular qualities of gambling also informed descriptions of gambling before the nineteenth century, the development of casino gambling raised the stakes. Descriptions of the process of observation and evaluation focus in important ways on the self-presentation of the gambler's body. One example can be seen in Dostoyevsky's 1866 *The Gambler*. In one passage the grandmother, an elderly Russian aristocrat enjoying the tables at "Roullotenburg," closely observes not only the play at her table, but more importantly one particular player. Dostoyevsky writes that "She particularly liked a certain very young fellow at the end of the table who was playing for very big stakes.... He was pale; his eyes sparkled and his hands were shaking; he was placing his bets now without even counting, by the handful, and meanwhile he kept winning and winning, and raking in more and more.... He had become visibly flustered."[13] An 1892 text includes a similarly detailed observation of a person who comes from that class of systematizers known as "professors" for the intricate and precise nature of their bank-breaking calculations. The author, Norwood Young, describes their physiognomy:

> Even the physique of the gambler is affected by his transports. The "professor," who may be taken as the type of the broken-down gambler, has a lean and hungry look. His furrowed features and attenuated frame, his

[10] W. F. Rae, "Play and Players on the Riviera," *The Nineteenth Century*, 27/February (1890), 240–57, 254.
[11] Rae, "Play and Players." 255.   [12] Rae, "Play and Players," 255.
[13] F. Dostoyevsky, *The Gambler and Other Stories* (Penguin, 2010), 196–97.

belief in systems, and the impossibility of rousing in him any of the generous emotions, are evidences of fearful degradation in mind, body, and soul.[14]

In both of these examples, much like John Addington Symonds's descriptions of other players, we see how character traits and bodily habitus were each transformed through the experience of the casino.

Other writers were more concerned with noting what might be called the interior somatic effects of gambling on the player's body. Dostoyevsky's gambler, for instance, recounts the bodily effects of anticipation and excitement when he thinks about a visit to the casino: "I set off for the roulette table. Oh, how my heart pounded! No, it was not the money that was dear to me!"[15] In another passage, he enjoys a remarkable series of wins that produce a torrent of somatic effects in his body. Dostoyevsky's gambler tells readers,

> Feeling as though I had a fever, I moved this entire pile of money on to red – and suddenly I came to my senses! And only this once during the whole of the evening, during all the time that I was playing, did fear course through me like a chill and cause my arms and legs to tremble. I sensed with horror and for an instant realized: what it would mean for me to lose now! My whole life was at stake![16]

In another instance, the gambler hears the croupier's call, and the sound triggers a wave of sensation throughout his body: "'*Rouge!*' the croupier cried – and I took a deep breath, fiery pins and needles ran up and down my body."[17] We should distinguish, however, between the setting of the action and the action itself. While this text is silent on the issue, we will see in other cases that the casino had a particularly intensifying effect on the ways that gambling was felt by the body.

Winning generates both amnesia and emotional satisfaction in Dostoyevsky's characters. Dostoyevsky writes, "I don't remember though what I was thinking about as I made my way [back to his hotel with his won fortune]; I had no thoughts about anything. I felt some sort of terrible delight at my good fortune, victory, power – I don't know how to express it."[18] Not surprisingly, loss also generated bodily responses. One story of a German count from 1925 illustrates the sad corporeal effects of loss.

---

[14] N. Young, "Systems of Gambling," *National Review*, 18/29 (1892), 449–60, 460.
[15] Dostoyevsky, *The Gambler and Other Stories*, 264.
[16] Dostoyevsky, *The Gambler and Other Stories*, 239.
[17] Dostoyevsky, *The Gambler and Other Stories*, 239.
[18] Dostoyevsky, *The Gambler and Other Stories*, 243.

When he entered the casino for the last time he was wild-eyed and haggard and he played with his few remaining gold pieces as if he was stricken with the palsy. He seemed to have grown very old, and he gambled with the despair of the man who knows that it is useless hoping for a miracle. When the croupier had gathered in the final coins the count drove back to his hotel at Mentone and took a dose of poison.[19]

In each of these situations, players experience the game in a visceral and embodied way, one in which the setting of the casino played a central role. By offering more than just a chance to observe closely other players or to rub up against them at the gaming table, gambling helped forge a new relationship between a player and their body. The nerves tingled, the heart pounded, the eyes might bug in alarm. Blood flushed the body, generating the feeling of feverishness. The arms and legs trembled, or were no longer capable of steadiness. One's memory was affected. Importantly, these descriptions of what now might be called an "acute stress response" coincided with the development of academic endocrinology: adrenaline was isolated in the 1890s and Walter Bradford Cannon first used the term "fight or flight" in 1915.

Observations of the effects of gambling on the body like the ones included above were one way to work through how the body was integrated into modern systems of work and leisure. But gambling – like luck and chance – also presented nineteenth-century observers with the opportunity to consider the deeply historical nature of gambling by investigating the ways gambling had perhaps marked the human species as a whole. Thinking about the evolution of gambling and the inclusion of luck or fortune into the development of the human species was a task carried out by a range of social scientists beginning in the 1880s. Gambling – as it was assumed by critics in the nineteenth and early twentieth centuries – might provide an evolutionary explanation for all sorts of racial and morphological differences between groups of people. Gambling and the evolution of luck were incorporated into evolutionary, social Darwinian, and eugenicist discourse. In this way it could be said that gambling left its mark not just on individuals but on the species as a whole. In order to investigate this issue, we widen our analysis beyond a study of how the casino structured gambling and the body to consider a different set of issues that revolve around the intersection of luck, gambling, and human biological and cultural change.

---

[19] C. Kingston, *The Romance of Monte Carlo* (J. L. the Bodley Head, 1925), 115–16.

We begin our analysis of this issue by looking at Richard Proctor's *Chance and Luck*, published in 1887. Proctor identified what he called the "savage mind" that was especially prone to gambling and false beliefs. He writes in the preface to the volume that "I wish I could hope that it would serve the higher purpose of showing that all forms of gambling and speculation are essentially immoral, and that, though many who gamble are not consciously wrong-doers, their very unconsciousness of evil indicates an uncultured, semi-savage mind."[20] Proctor then identified what might be called an "inheritance model" of gambling, imagining that the cumulative effects of the "influence of chance in moulding the minds and characters of our ancestors during countless generations, should have produced a very marked effect on human nature."[21] While Proctor is more interested in human nature or in character traits than he is in the effects of gambling on the human body, he remains conscious of the ways that gambling has shaped what he calls the human "spirit" over long spans of time. It is worth recalling that Proctor rejects the existence of luck, and yet he discusses the ways that humans have cultivated a belief in luck by encouraging the taking of chances and what he calls the "gambling spirit." Proctor engages in an extended thought experiment in which he considers the range of behaviors in the past that would have benefited from a gambling spirit, and which he assumes would have been passed down from generation to generation through the typical patterns of human inheritance. Contemplating how chance affected the fortunes of a "savage," Proctor sought to connect past to present, asserting commonalities across time. While not equating the world of hominids to that of Monte Carlo, there were congruencies. Proctor writes,

> An immense number of those from whom I . . . inherit descent, must in the old savage days have depended almost wholly on chance for the very means of subsistence. When "wild in wood" the savage (very far, usually, from being noble) ran, he ran on speculation. He might or might not be lucky enough to earn his living on any day by a successful chase, or by finding such fruits of the earth as would supply him with a satisfactory amount of food. He might have as much depending on chances which he could not avoid risking, as the gambler of to-day has when he "sees red" and stakes his whole fortune on a throw of the dice or a turn of the cards. We cannot be doubtful about the effects of such chance influences on even the individual character. Repeated generation after generation they must have tended to fill men with a gambling spirit, only to be corrected by many generations of steady labour; and unfortunately, even in the steadiest work the element of

---

[20] Proctor, *Chance and Luck*, preface.   [21] Proctor, *Chance and Luck*, 80.

chance enters largely enough to render the corrective influence of such work on the character of the race (as distinguished from the individual) much slower than it might otherwise be.[22]

In this remarkable passage, Proctor connects gambling to physical inheritance and evolutionary change over time. Casino gambling, as we will see in Chapter 9, is just an ersatz form of a deeply significant element of the human heritage. Evolution helped nurture gambling and chance-taking because – at least in Proctor's estimation – it helped members of the species survive. The gambling spirit, now depicted as a core element of the human experience, but one that is confined to the casino, was ideally replaced by what Proctor calls the "corrective" of "steady labour." Proctor helped solidify an idea in the popular mind that gambling was an outcome of evolutionary change. In 1891, one observer wrote that "Gambling, in some form, is a propensity of the general mind: an inclination now hereditary in the race."[23]

Fifteen years after Proctor's book was published, the idea of natural selection and its relationship to luck and gambling appeared in the work of American observers as well. Clemens France's "The Gambling Impulse" noted the ubiquity of gambling across cultures and across historical periods. But he also indicated his belief that gambling was something that was racially expressed, writing that the "passion for gambling is nowhere so strong as among savage and barbarous races."[24] He too suggested that humans had been conditioned by evolution to enjoy chance, and this also was inflected by race. "The race has been evolved," France explains,

> in an environment of uncertainty, and it may be that such an environment has thus become indispensable. It cannot be doubted that the state of mental tension, of being on the alert with ears pricked and nose in the air, is a factor of high selective value. We have reason to believe that this state of expectation not only links together and sets in a condition of unstable equilibrium motor centers, but also that in the higher association centers there is a preparatory condition produced. Not only reflex action and muscular co-ordination, but also memory, imagination, and judgment times would be quickened.[25]

---

[22] Proctor, *Chance and Luck*, 80–81.
[23] J. H. Romain, *Gambling: Or, Fortuna, Her Temple and Shrine. The True Philosophy and Ethics of Gambling* (Craig Press, 1891), 132.
[24] C. J. France, "The Gambling Impulse," *The American Journal of Psychology*, 13/3 (1902), 364–407, 373.
[25] France, "The Gambling Impulse," 385.

The body is the site of an intense drama – alert to danger and in a state of high tension – and it experiences chance and uncertainty in directly physical ways. But taking pleasure in these physical sensations, unlike merely using them to increase one's safety, is a different issue. France explains that the Chinese in particular, who have experienced what he calls an "arrested development," use gambling in order to perpetuate that mental state of uncertainty. France writes,

> Is it not thus that a condition of uncertainty holds the mind in a tonic and unrelaxed condition? As evidence that, as we approximate a dead level certainty, we tend to lose in mental efficiency, we have the case of the arrested development of the Chinese. It is significant in the case of the Chinese that the passion for uncertainty, having no exercise in the serious side of life, shows itself in the form of play – they being the greatest gamblers in the world. It is then this need of mental tension, this "either-or" state, which is one of the chief factors in chance games and gambling.[26]

In short, France proposes that the evolution of senses capable of heightened awareness of uncertainty is a condition of race and of racial characteristics.

An awareness of uncertainty and of an employment of forms of play that represented a mental state with what France calls a "high selective value" also was oriented around the evolution of other qualities, namely, luck. France writes that the "term luck is used here in a large sense to include a group of phenomena very significant in the study of chance. It is this group of phenomena which it is the purpose of the present section to attempt to explain in its biological origin and values."[27] He goes on to propose that luck evolved as a consequence of natural selection. Unlucky individuals simply did not factor into larger processes of inheritance to the same degree as lucky individuals have. "I would like to lay especial emphasis on the implications of natural selection in respect to the presence of long existing and strongly tenacious psychic manifestations – to wit, that such manifestations are based upon the psychic variations which must have been of use in the biological economy and thus have been of high selective value."[28] France's position is an important reminder of the ways that early twentieth-century social scientists conflated racial and characterological qualities. The fact that France saw that a heightened awareness of uncertain situations could be understood as a factor in natural selection and at the same time suggests that the pleasurable reconstruction of those

---

[26] France, "The Gambling Impulse," 385–86.   [27] France, "The Gambling Impulse," 388.
[28] France, "The Gambling Impulse," 388.

sensations in the form of gambling represented a form of degeneration is surely indicative of the cultural and intellectual worlds inhabited by scientists at the time.

France proposed that luck was a direct factor in evolution that could be explicitly tied to the biological. He writes,

> This conviction of safety, expressing itself in the more or less definite objective forms of luck, guardian angels, etc., is a definite biological product. Its effectiveness as a force in evolution in the increasing of actions, is enormous. It is, we believe, an instinct-feeling as well defined as fear, its direct opposite, and like other similar psychoses, is a result of natural selection. We must remember that the state of doubt, bred by fear is ever and anon present in force – but still the opposite feeling holds its own, and must be in the ascendant at the moment of action. These two states so strongly counteracting each other are intermittent; now one is focal in consciousness, now the other.[29]

An individual's belief in luck generates a type of self-assuredness that then translates to riskier behavior that in France's estimation can generate a virtuous reward cycle and thus an increased contribution to human inheritance. Luck "is the natural result in a race which has been evolved in an environment where to succeed and survive ventures and risks were necessary, and where those who did survive had been successful in their risks."[30] This long historical and evolutionary process culminates in the creation of a new type of self. France argues that

> Men with such a characteristic [faith in self] would in consequence be inclined to take greater risks, and those of them that were successful would be much favored in survival through their newly acquired knowledge. Thus the exploiting type of man with great interest in the unknown, with a feeling immuneness from harm, with a strong feeling of coming success, was developed.[31]

The remaining question, however, was how a highly developed sense of self-regard intersected with what France considered a degenerate passion for gambling. He addressed this issue by suggesting that

> With the savage . . . gambling and religion are almost identical. . . . Thus it is the savage is [*sic*] so desperate a gambler, regarding his whole fortune . . . even his wives and children as insignificant. . . . So also in a less intense degree is it with the modern believer in luck. This explains much of the

---

[29] France, "The Gambling Impulse," 398. [30] France, "The Gambling Impulse," 399.
[31] France, "The Gambling Impulse," 400.

almost inaccountable states of emotional frenzy gamblers display, and their tenacity in play.[32]

Gambling in European and North American societies, in other words, could be read as an atavistic practice, a form of leisure that places the European or American on the same cultural, intellectual, and emotional plane as a "savage." France, not surprisingly, was not the only one making such claims; as art historian Hal Foster argues, intellectuals as different as Sigmund Freud, Adolf Loos, and the European avant-garde advanced a theory of cultural evolution in which the adoption of "primitive" cultural displays or emotional states by Europeans indicated the presence of an atavism at the heart of the society.[33]

While never adopting the racialist positions that characterized France's work, Thorstein Veblen proposed a similar argument about gambling that projected it as evidence of what he called a "barbarian temperament." Veblen considers the problem of play and gambling, suggesting that the "gambling propensity is another subsidiary trait of the barbarian temperament. It is a concomitant variation of character of almost universal prevalence among sporting men and among men given to warlike and emulative activities generally. This trait also has a direct economic value."[34] Gambling and a belief in luck are related to what Veblen labels the "predatory type" that also projected a type of atavism.

> The gambling proclivity is doubtfully to be classed as a feature belonging exclusively to the predatory type of human nature. The chief factor in the gambling habit is the belief in luck; and this belief is apparently traceable, at least in its elements, to a stage in human evolution antedating the predatory culture. It may well have been under the predatory culture that the belief in luck was developed into the form in which it is present, as the chief element of the gambling proclivity, in the sporting temperament. It probably owes the specific form under which it occurs in the modern culture to the predatory discipline.[35]

Luck was directly tied to the creation and development of a character predating modern social relations. Veblen writes that the "belief is, in its elements, an archaic habit which belongs substantially to early, undifferentiated human nature; but when this belief is helped out by the predatory emulative impulse, and so is differentiated into the specific form of the

---

[32] France, "The Gambling Impulse," 401.   [33] H. Foster, *Prosthetic Gods* (MIT Press, 2004).
[34] T. Veblen, *The Theory of the Leisure Class: An Economic Study of Institutions* (Macmillan and Company, 1912), 276.
[35] Veblen, *The Theory of the Leisure Class*, 276.

gambling habit, it is, in this higher-developed and specific form, to be classed as a trait of the barbarian character."[36] Significantly, a belief in luck and a passion for gambling remained connected to animistic religious beliefs. "Those modern representatives," Veblen argued, "of the predaceous barbarian temper that make up the sporting element are commonly believers in luck; at least they have a strong sense of an animistic propensity in things, by force of which they are given to gambling."[37] To be clear, Veblen did not suggest a racialized expression of savagery, barbarian habitus, or atavistic passion for gambling. But he did see gambling as a form of social interaction that was inherently – if weakly – violent. Gambling and a belief in luck were not wholly modern activities. Instead, they represented in modified form aspects of a prior human condition.

Other writers at the time accepted Veblen's premise, but also enthusiastically racialized the trajectory of development gambling was thought to embody. One doctor, the Harvard professor and psychologist Hugo Münsterberg, produced a description of gambling that was explicitly racialist. Münsterberg was raised in Danzig, and earned a doctorate under Wilhelm Wundt while a student at the University of Leipzig (he also earned a medical degree from Heidelberg). "Some races," he writes in his 1914 book *Psychology and Social Sanity*,

> in which the gambling instinct is strong, are yet afraid of high risks, and the pleasure in seeking dangerous situations may prevail without any longing for the rewards of the gambler. It seems doubtful whether this adventurous longing for unusual risks belongs to the Anglo-Saxon mind. At least those vocations which most often involve such a mental trend are much more favoured by the Irish. It is claimed that they, for instance, are prominent among the railroad men, and that the excessive number of accidents in the railroad service results from just this reckless disposition of the Irishmen.[38]

The presence of the Irish in the United States, in Münsterberg's view, revealed deeper flaws in American culture. "Yet neither gambling and taking risks, nor suggestibility and imitation, are the whole of the story. We must not forget the superficiality of thinking, the uncritical, loose, and flabby use of the reasoning power which shows itself in so many spheres of American mass life."[39] While Münsterberg's last statement remains a valid critique of the United States, his suggestion that propensity for mindless risk-taking could be racially expressed and that certain vocations that drew

---

[36] Veblen, *The Theory of the Leisure Class*, 278.   [37] Veblen, *The Theory of the Leisure Class*, 290.
[38] H. Münsterberg, *Psychology and Social Sanity* (Doubleday, Page & Co., 1914), 258.
[39] Münsterberg, *Psychology and Social Sanity*, 264.

distinct ethnic groups were therefore more dangerous than those preferred by the "Anglo-Saxon" population remains, in a word, bizarre.

Gambling affected the body in myriad ways. Gamblers in the nineteenth century could be accused of gender instability; their bodies might be sickened by the stress of the gambling table. Gambling also induced people to closely observe the bodies of other gamblers, not only in the course of a game, but more generally too. The casino facilitated the mixing of men and women from a certain social status, and the body was at the center of that culture of mixing. But the gambler's body was also implicated in the course of play – gambling was an activity that was experienced in and on the body, and descriptions of the flood of somatic reactions to play were typical of nineteenth-century depictions of the practice. Gambling also represented something deeper to many observers from the time. It was evidence of physical, emotional, and cultural evolution, and when people sought to understand the mechanics of natural selection by focusing on the development of luck that was expressed asymmetrically across racial lines, they made gambling evidence of either racial superiority or racial decline.

CHAPTER 7

Gambling and the History of Emotions

We saw in the previous chapter that gambling was an intensely physical practice, one that generated sweeping effects in and on the body, yet gambling – as we have seen but not yet analyzed – was understood in the nineteenth century as a practice through which emotions and emotional control were central to the experience.[1] Seventeenth- and eighteenth-century discourse on gambling describes a cascade of emotions that were experienced sequentially in the heat of the game. The simple act of play unleashes a torrent of emotions that follow in predictable patterns but never find resolution. The young were thought to be particularly prone to the passions unleashed by gambling, and it was imagined that gambling was so emotionally enticing that young people were unable to resist the lure of play or to turn their minds to the more important demands of work. Gambling was also critiqued for providing illicit gains; wealth obtained through play – rather than through work – was illegitimate, and the emotional satisfactions of gambling represented a system of emotions that orbited around the dark sun of greed.[2] Some emotions – greed most significantly – could be intensified through play. The emotional context produced by gambling was one in which a base and greedy

---

[1] The history of emotions is now a well-established field, one that crosses disciplinary boundaries and temporal fields. See P. N. Stearns and C. Z. Stearns, "Emotionology: Clarifying the History of Emotions and Emotional Standards," *The American Historical Review* 90/4 (October 1985): 813–36; W. Reddy, *The Navigation of Feeling: A Framework for the History of Emotions* (Cambridge University Press, 2001); B. H. Rosenwein, "Worrying about Emotions in History," *The American Historical Review* 107/3 (June 2002), 821–45; U. Frevert, "Was haben Gefühle in der Geschichte zu suchen? (What Has History Got to Do with Emotions?)," *Geschichte und Gesellschaft* 35/2 (April 1, 2009), 183–208; M. Scheer, "Are Emotions a Kind of Practice (and Is That What Makes Them Have a History)? A Bourdieuian Approach to Understanding Emotion," *History and Theory* 51/2 (May 1, 2012), 193–220; H. Lempa, *Spaces of Honor: Making German Civil Society, 1700–1914* (University of Michigan Press, 2021); Y. Alaluf, *The Emotional Economy of Holidaymaking: Health, Pleasure, and Class in Britain, 1870–1918* (Oxford University Press, 2021).
[2] See J. Poley, *The Devil's Riches: A Modern History of Greed* (Berghahn Books, 2016), for a longer discussion of these issues.

desire set the stage for all sorts of other emotions to flood the player. And part of the problem for critical observers was that greed blinded gamblers to the essential distinction between work and play that it was assumed God had established. Entire social and cultural systems were upended by the worrisome prospect that one might gain through play rather than the "sweat of thy face," and the issue of virtuous wealth went right to the heart of the logic of early modern economic exchange.

Early modern critics of gaming commented on the ways gambling, emotional intensity, and reason interacted. Gambling was a pursuit that took a player's emotions and heightened them to a degree that one's reason was undermined, and this flood of passion left a person unable to govern themself. The "bundle of passions" experienced during a game destroyed a capacity for reason, for work, and for grace. By the late eighteenth century, gambling not only was depicted as having a particularly acute effect on one's emotions but also was imagined in new ways as a type of social problem that could be addressed by identifying its "pernicious effects."[3] Hey first addresses the degree to which gambling is a form of pleasure. Determining that it may be for some, he issues what might be called a provisional but utilitarian defense of gambling that positions play as a way of maximizing happiness. Happiness is in fact an organizing principle when players attempt to calculate probability in the course of a game. Money might make one happy, but it also exposed one to avarice. For critics like Hey, money won at the gambling table represented more than just additional means; it was also a vector for the emotion and imagination of the player – thus enabling its dangerous qualities. The gambler, drawn to the emotional intensity of the game, is unable to find emotional resolution, and therefore continues playing in a futile search for stability. Hey's astute observation of the mental and emotional drama of gambling hints at a type of behavioralism in which the repetition of certain practices was a key to understanding why a person kept returning to the table. We see in this scenario a description of loss that, while moralizing, still serves as a useful indicator of the way in which gambling set the stage for a remarkable emotional drama, one that drew its power from the way in which emotional abstraction could be made real, and the anguish of loss put on exhibition.

The cascade of feelings is perhaps linked in some broader way to utilitarian theories of emotion. One of the major problems that Hey

[3] R. Hey, *Three Dissertations; on the Pernicious Effects of Gaming, on Duelling and on Suicide* (J. Smith, 1812).

identified with gambling was that it was an antisocial practice, one that encouraged selfishness rather than communitarianism. In this manner, Hey depicted gambling as a practice that was broadly destructive to human relationships, and in this way gambling was a type of rejection of the usual arguments for capitalist self-interest. Hey's descriptions of gambling and the emotional states that gambling helped generate in a player allow us to consider gambling as a practice that also served as a mechanism of self-production. The behaviors, emotions, and practices that gambling generated proved to be quite useful in the creation of a certain type of person who cultivated self-interest, read social cues and reacted accordingly, masked or embellished certain outer expressions of emotion, and generally learned a suite of behaviors related to money, society, and self that, in hindsight, certainly seem characteristic of the bourgeois century. Given the importance that a culture of honor and self-presentation exerted in nineteenth-century Europe, the degree to which shame could be deployed as a tool of social control remained significant. Hey presented the issue as it related to gambling in terms of the presence or absence of a sense of shame on the part of a player. When a player lost their sense of shame, and correlated collapse of reputation, a host of problems developed. To Hey's mind, the moral collapse engendered by gambling hastened the appearance of a suite of other repulsive qualities. Hey explains that dishonesty follows avarice, then envy, and then revenge. Each of these emotions is characterized by its antisocial nature; not one of the vices lubricates the gears of a civil society.

Whatever one thinks of Hey's conclusions, he recognized that gambling was a highly emotional activity, one that could shape the player in profound ways. There are several points in Hoffmann's "Gambler's Luck" important to this discussion of emotion and gambling. One passage describes Siegfried's first foray to the gambling rooms, and it indicates how the game attracted him, not so much for the lure of money but for the pleasures of playing. Most important, the game absorbs his attention, keeping him playing through a series of rewards. Hoffmann writes that "the game gripped [Siegfried's] interest and held him fast for whole nights on end, so that, since it was not the gain but very definitely the game that drew him, he was forced to believe in the special magic of which his friends spoke and which he had by no means wished to confirm."[4] The pleasures of play only intensify, and as the rewards compound, new emotions – perhaps most important, avarice – take over his emotional life and

---

[4] E. T. A. Hoffmann, *The Tales of Hoffmann* (Frederick Ungar Publishing Co., 1963), 215–16.

fundamentally change who Siegfried is as a person. Readers learn in a different passage that "when he remembered what had happened, when he ran his hands through the gold pieces, when he complacently counted them and re-counted them, delight in filthy lucre passed for the first time through his whole being like a noxious, poisonous breath; it was all up with the purity of mind he had so long preserved."[5]

Siegfried's emotional trajectory in the story is shaped by his experiences at the gaming tables. Describing the way that gambling changed the Chevalier, Hoffmann writes, "As was inevitable after the Chevalier had been thus inwardly comforted, all the charm he has possessed before the mad, pernicious passion overwhelmed him was revived."[6] Other passages confirm this idea that one's confrontation with the pleasures of gambling reconfigure the player's emotional economy. Siegfried is warned: "In a word – you are in the process of becoming an impassioned gambler and ruining yourself."[7] And perhaps most alarming to Hoffmann, gambling and the passions that it unleashed might do lasting damage to the ability to feel emotions at all. The intensity of the player's emotional life could reach a breaking point. Readers are told that "all human emotion is alien" to Vertua, another character in the story.[8] Another passage explains that "all human emotions become foreign to the gambler."[9] One way to read the story is to see the ways that gambling heightens and then deadens a player's emotions. The dramatic intensity of the gambling tables, and the addictive qualities of play, could damage a person's emotional life in unforeseen ways. While "Gambler's Luck" is set in a time before the advent of Blanc-style casino gambling, Hoffman notes how the physical locations in which gambling took place contributed to its emotional power.[10]

Early observers of casino gambling like George Sala were alert to the emotional dynamics of gambling in that context. Sala, for instance, wrote about Bad Homburg as a place where the casino functioned as a machine that could systematically wear down players through emotional distress. Sala writes that "the bank [is] *always* at it, always gambling, whereas you can only devote a certain number of hours per diem to making your game; in the bank, in its *personale* of dealers and croupiers, being always calm, collected, sober, and indifferent as to gain or loss, whereas you, the player, are generally nervous and excited, never indifferent, and frequently . . .

---

[5] Hoffmann, *The Tales of Hoffmann*, 222.   [6] Hoffmann, *The Tales of Hoffmann*, 234.
[7] Hoffmann, *The Tales of Hoffmann*, 219.   [8] Hoffmann, *The Tales of Hoffmann*, 225.
[9] Hoffmann, *The Tales of Hoffmann*, 228.   [10] Hoffmann, *The Tales of Hoffmann*, 213.

considerably flushed with champagne."[11] As we will see, the player's emotions were often turned against them, weaponized by the casino, which was typically described as passionless. This way of understanding the emotional contexts of casino gambling remained a way to understand the dynamics of the casino by focusing on the emotional disequilibrium generated at the table.

Sala recognized an important fact about the casino: that passionlessness could be a key tool in the player's workshop. Earlier observers of gambling like Hey and Hoffmann also saw that the heightening and deadening of a player's emotions were outcomes of the process. Dostoyevsky offers a deeper analysis of the dynamic effects of emotion in the casino.[12] Dostoyevsky, who wrote *The Gambler* in twenty-six days in order to avoid the seizure of his publishing rights by his publisher, was similar to the title character and had a great deal of experience in the gambling halls along the Rhine in the mid-1860s. Dostoyevsky was also a keen observer of the emotional impact of gambling on a player. He acknowledges the pleasures of gambling in one passage:

> There are two types of gambling: one is gentlemanly; the other is plebeian, greedy, the gambling for all sorts of riff-raff. The sharp distinction is strictly observed here and – how vile, in essence, is this distinction! A gentleman, for instance, may stake 5 or 10 louis d'or, rarely more than that; however, he may also stake a thousand francs if he is very rich, but simply for the sake of the game itself, simply for the sake of amusement, simply to observe the process of winning or losing; he must on no account show any interest in his winnings. When he wins he may, for instance, laugh out loud, or make a remark to one of the onlookers, and he may even stake again and then double it, but only out of curiosity, in order to observe the workings of chance, to calculate, but not for the plebeian desire to win.[13]

As we see in the passage, Dostoyevsky notes the different effects of gambling on the emotions that were dictated in some ways by social class. One type of player is emotionally indifferent to how their wins and losses affected the bank account; the other could not sever their emotional commitment to money. This idea was articulated more pointedly by Dostoyevsky when he writes, "A true gentleman, even if he loses his entire fortune, must not show emotion. Money is supposed to be so far beneath a gentleman that it's almost not worth thinking about."[14]

[11] G. A. Sala, *Make Your Game, or, The Adventures of the Stout Gentleman, the Slim Gentleman, and the Man with the Iron Chest: A Narrative of the Rhine and Thereabouts* (Ward and Lock, 1860), 219–20.
[12] F. Dostoyevsky, *The Gambler and Other Stories* (Penguin, 2010).
[13] Dostoyevsky, *The Gambler and Other Stories*, 135.
[14] Dostoyevsky, *The Gambler and Other Stories*, 136.

Dostoyevsky's gambler describes a kind of deadening of emotion that was supposedly characteristic of an aristocratic response to money more generally. But the gambler also experiences a dramatic swerving of emotional intensity. At one point, the gambler remarks, "I was overcome by an unusual and strange sensation, which I found so unbearable that I decided to leave."[15] In another passage he comments on the pleasurable sensations aroused by contemplating a win: "Strange as it may seem, I still hadn't won, but I was acting, feeling and thinking like a wealthy man, and I couldn't imagine myself any other way."[16] The gambler experiences a "strange sensation," he "feels" rich, and then relishes a "terrible delight." His emotional reactions to gambling could be seen as contradictory in some way. In a final passage, we see the broken gambler, now emotionally deadened except for what he calls a feeling of "constant anxiety" that has settled over him now that he has dedicated his entire existence to gambling: "I live in constant anxiety, I play for the smallest stakes and wait for something; I make calculations, I stand for days on end by the gaming table and *observe* the play, I even see them playing in my sleep, but all that notwithstanding I seem to have become numb, as it were, as if I'd become mired in some sort of mud."[17] These depictions of emotional drama included in Dostoyevsky's text resemble the author's own experiences. He described his method of play in a letter written in August 1863, in which he claims, "I know the secret of how not to lose, but to win. I really do know the secret: it is terribly stupid and simple and consists of restraining oneself at every moment, no matter at what phase of the game, and of not losing one's head."[18] In a letter he sent from Bad Homburg in May 1867, Dostoyevsky writes that "if one is prudent, that is, if one is as though made of marble, cold, and *inhumanly* cautious, then definitely, *without any doubt*, one can win *as much as one wishes*. There is a Jew here: he has been playing for several days now, with horrible, *inhuman* composure and calculation."[19] In another letter from the same period, Dostoyevsky remarks on the connections between his system – such as it was – and emotion: "About twenty times now, on approaching the gambling table, I've made an experiment: if you play coolly, *calmly*, and with calculation, there's *no chance of losing!* I swear to you, there's not even a chance!"[20] In an earlier letter, he writes, "[M]y nerves are horribly tired

[15] Dostoyevsky, *The Gambler and Other Stories*, 138.
[16] Dostoyevsky, *The Gambler and Other Stories*, 166.
[17] Dostoyevsky, *The Gambler and Other Stories*, 265.
[18] F. Dostoyevsky, *Complete Letters* (Ardis, 1988), vol. 2, 57–58.
[19] Dostoyevsky, *Complete Letters*, 232.   [20] Dostoyevsky, *Complete Letters*, 239.

out, I've become more impatient, I'm more anxious to get a result, I hurry, I take risks, and of that comes a loss.... My nerves are on edge, and get tired (sitting in one place)."[21] The gambler, having subjected his emotions to intense swings of feeling, seems no longer able to recalibrate them. The emotional pendulum oscillates so quickly that he can only describe the response in terms of a diffuse anxiety.

Dostoyevsky wrote roughly twenty-five years after the casino at Bad Homburg opened, and yet his observations about the emotional toll of gambling strike the reader as a novelty. Observers at the time articulated similar arguments. Andrew Steinmetz suggests that gambling and its passions were a recent historical development. Quoting the Lord Chief Justice, Steinmetz notes, "'There can be no doubt ... that a spirit of speculation and gambling has taken hold of the minds of large classes of the population.'"[22] We see evidence of a dual movement: the casino heightened emotion as a way of bringing people to the tables; it also encouraged a certain deadening of their emotional responses so that gamblers continued to play despite reason. Lynn Hunt argues in *Inventing Human Rights* that novels and a culture of reading performed the important cultural work not only of introducing readers to a new language of emotion in the form of the novel but also of cultivating emotional qualities like empathy in the reading public.[23] It seems clear that the projection of emotional didacticism was not limited to the literary form of the novel but also was carried in a range of other texts, and books about gambling and gamblers were arguably one of the most significant areas in which this trend could be seen. Authors like Steinmetz invited readers to imagine their own emotional reactions to and participation in games. For instance, writing about the emotions unleashed in an attempt to break the bank, he uses a series of military metaphors:

> It is a melancholy amusement to any rational being not infatuated by the blind rage of gold, to witness the incredible excitement so repeatedly made to take the bank by storm, sometimes by surprise, anon by stealth, and not rarely by digging a mine, laying intrenchments and opening a fire of field-pieces, heavy ordnance, and flying artillery; but the fortress, proud and conscious of its superior strength, built on a rock of adamant, laughs at the fiery attacks of its foes, nay, itself invites the storm.[24]

[21] Dostoyevsky, *Complete Letters*, 233.
[22] A. Steinmetz, *The Gaming Table: Its Votaries and Victims*, 2 vols. (Tinsley Brothers, 1870), vol. 1, viii.
[23] L. Hunt, *Inventing Human Rights: A History* (W. W. Norton & Co., 2008), 35–69.
[24] Steinmetz, *The Gaming Table*, vol. 1, 164–65.

Steinmetz was more explicit about the emotional life of gambling – and of the gambling table as the primary educational field for the emotions – in other sections of the book. He writes, "'Sensation' is the very life of humanity; it is the motion – the reverse of 'death' – which we all abhor."[25] Steinmetz suggests that the casino holds a special importance as a place to explore, cultivate, and experience a range of emotions that speak directly to our humanity. Steinmetz provided a very direct account of what he called the "terrible drama" unfolding in people around the gaming table:

> But it is to the gaming room that we must go to behold the progress of the terrible drama – the ebb and flow of opposite movements – the shocks of alternate hope and fear, infinitely varied in the countenance, not only of the actors, but also of the spectators. What is visible, however, is nothing in comparison to the secret agony. It is in his heart that the tempest roars most fiercely.... It is only at play that we can observe, from moment to moment, all the phases of despair; from time to time there occur new ones – strange, eccentric, or terrible. After having lost quietly, and even with serenity, half his fortune, the father of a family staked the remainder, and lost it without a murmur.... He was literally a weeping statue. The spectators were seized with fright, and, although gamesters, they melted into pity.[26]

The sequence of emotions that Steinmetz lays out here – hope, fear, agony, despair, serenity, fright, and pity – that players and observers alike experience tells us something important about what the emotional phases unbound while "at play." His emphasis on the alternating qualities of emotions, the "ebb and flow of opposite movements," bears kinship to the torrents of emotion suddenly undammed in the descriptions of gambling from earlier periods. The constant fluctuation of emotional extremes – often associated with modernity in general – is here evidence of how a person could be driven to the edge of sanity.

Indeed, Steinmetz turns his attention in following sections to the emotional madness that accompanies gambling. Emotion, passion, and sanity were connected in the social space of the gambling hall. "What a 'sensation,'" Steinmetz writes, "it must be to lose one's *all*."[27] Naturally, Steinmetz turned his attention to suicide, but located it as the outcome of an emotional torrent that could not be contained. Importantly, he recognized that winning could also be source of emotional instability, writing that "sudden prosperity has deranged more heads and killed more people than reverses and grief; either because it takes a longer time to get

[25] Steinmetz, *The Gaming Table: Its Votaries and Victims*, vol. 2, 48–49.
[26] Steinmetz, *The Gaming Table*, vol. 2, 51–52.   [27] Steinmetz, *The Gaming Table*, vol. 2, 57.

convinced of utter ruin than great good fortune, or because the instinct of self-preservation compels us to seek, in adversity, for resources to mitigate despair; whereas, in the assault of excessive joy, the soul's spring is distended and broken when it is suddenly compressed by too many thoughts and too many sensations."[28] As we saw in earlier examples, emotional overstimulation, or the idea that the machinery of emotion could wear out through overuse, meant that an emotional deadness could set in. And ultimately, death was the most worrisome outcome of this emotional trajectory: "Many fine intellects among players have been brutified by loses [*sic*]; others, in greater number, have been so by their winnings. Some in the course of their prosperity perish from idleness, get deranged, and ruin themselves after ruining others."[29]

Steinmetz's conclusions about the ways gaming and play provided the context within which emotions unfolded and were experienced indicate an important way to think about the meanings of gambling in the late nineteenth century. Gambling, it was recognized, encouraged a deeply emotional relationship to the material world and to other people.[30] Sometimes that emotionality culminated in a deadening of the emotions; at other times it led to an overwhelming of the subject that only ended in insanity or suicide. Attempts to understand the microdynamics of this emotionality surfaced in gambling-oriented texts produced in the nineteenth century in a variety of ways, but together they mapped the emotional trajectory of the gambler. One example from 1873 traces these issues in relation specifically to loss. One player writes

> I was distinctly conscious of partially attributing to some defect or stupidity in my own mind every venture on an issue that proved a failure; that I groped about within me for something in me like an anticipation or warning (which of course was not to be found) of what the next event was to be, and generally hit upon some vague impulse in my own mind which determined me; that whenever I succeeded, I raked up any gains with a half-impression that I had been a clever fellow, and had made a judicious stake, just as if I have really moved a skillful move at chess; and that when I failed, I thought to myself, "Ah I knew all the time I was going wrong in selecting that number, and yet I was fool enough to stick to it," which of

---

[28] Steinmetz, *The Gaming Table*, vol. 2, 57–58.   [29] Steinmetz, *The Gaming Table*, vol. 2, 58.

[30] The connections between things and feelings has been theorized most extensively by Bill Brown and Arjun Appadurai. B. Brown, "Thing Theory," *Critical Inquiry* 28/1 (2001), 1–22; B. Brown, ed., *Things* (University of Chicago Press, 2004); A. Appadurai, ed., *The Social Life of Things: Commodities in Cultural Perspective* (Cambridge University Press, 1986). See also my "Gambling and Emotion," in D. Hillard, H. Lempa, and R. Spinney, eds., *Feelings Materialized: Emotions, Bodies, and Things in Germany, 1500–1950* (Berghahn Books, 2020).

course was a pure illusion, for all that I did really know was that the chance was even or much more than even, against me.[31]

The psychological mechanisms used to handle emotions of loss – in this case self-talk aimed at convincing oneself that fanciful connections between various unconnected elements truly existed – meant that there was a recognition that loss at the gaming table held some deeper meaning. If the game was truly random and did not respond to human intervention, skill, or intellect, it would suggest that no psychic or emotional wound would occur; the fact that this writer invested so much into convincing himself that his actions mattered – even when they did not – is surely evidence for a wistful form of agency at work in the nineteenth century.

We should not forget, despite these declarations of emotional turmoil culminating in loss, grief, mourning, madness, or death, that gambling was fun. Indeed, the pleasures of gambling were widely recognized and even included in the form of exam questions given to university students. One test prompt from 1874 given to honors students sitting their BA exams in London asked students to "Examine the grounds of the love of Gambling, and the nature and legitimacy of the ethical objections to it."[32] Cambridge students sitting for the tripos in 1882 were asked to "Analyse the pleasure of gambling."[33] Both questions were included in later test banks that students could use as study guides. One way to understand this deep interest in emotion and its relationship to gambling in the late nineteenth century is to investigate the ways that gambling seemed to confirm larger theories about the economy of emotion. Quoting Herbert Spencer, Richard Proctor considered these issues in his 1887 text, commenting on the back and forth between winners and losers. "'Benefit received does not imply effort put forth, and the happiness of the winner involves the misery of the loser: this kind of action is therefore essentially anti-social; it sears the sympathies, cultivates a hard egoism, and so produces a general deterioration of character and conduct.'"[34] This critique of gambling – that it produced hard people who were antisocial and devoid of feeling – was a common one at the time, and the way the critique aligned with larger discussions of, and anxieties about, the relations between individuals and

[31] G. A Sala,. "Saxon-les-bains: A Study in the Psychology of Gambling" (1873), 1242–43.

[32] F. Ryland, *Questions on Psychology, Metaphysics, and Ethics* (S. Sonnenschein, Lowrey & Company, 1887), 50.

[33] Ryland, *Questions on Psychology, Metaphysics, and Ethics*, 50.

[34] R. A. Proctor, *Chance and Luck*, 2nd ed. (Longmans, Green, and Company, 1887), 49–50.

society meant that gambling was perfectly situated as a forum for thought experiments on the issue.

Other critics picked up on Proctor's argument about the antisocial consequences of gambling, and they formulated the issue in terms of dependence. The nineteenth-century Czech educator Gustav Adolf Lindner, writing in his text *The Manual of Empirical Psychology as an Inductive Science* (first published in 1858), suggests that "Passion is blind and deaf to all opposing concepts of insight."[35] The passage goes on to argue that the "gambler can not leave his play, although his friends or his best friend, and his own reason, prove to him beyond a shadow of a doubt that he will ruin himself and his family by gambling. The passionate man is neither rational nor free in his action, because he conducts himself in opposition to his better judgment and his own ego."[36] Later observers made similar arguments about the violent passions operating during the game, concluding that the games are responsible for a rash individuality and dismissive attitude toward society. Norwood Young explains that the

> wild surge of passion which every gambler feels, would soon dispel the notion that roulette is a quiet, amusing game, at which to while away a few idle hours. The visitor to the gambling saloon is struck, immediately on his entry, by the astonishing silence: by the absorbed attention of the knot of from twenty to fifty ladies and gentlemen who stand or sit round, a long oblong table, watching the piles of notes and gold appearing and disappearing. Some of them present a spectacle of passion and tragedy such as seldom appears in ordinary life.[37]

These intense scenarios enact real violence on people, and Young concludes with a description of the "violence of this passion," explaining that the "passion of love itself is less absorbing, less enduring, less universal. As a vice, gambling is enthralling and debasing. It is easy to understand how an otherwise honourable man may, when trembling under the sway of this fiercest of fevers, completely forget himself."[38]

These writers focused on the ways that the emotional qualities that arose the context of gambling promoted individualism and undermined communal feeling. Others picked up on this aspect of the emotional residues of gambling, noting in particular the ways that personal enmity developed naturally out of the tides of the game. *The Green Bay Tree*, published in

---

[35] G. A. Lindner, *Manual of Empirical Psychology as an Inductive Science: A Text-Book for High Schools and Colleges* (D. C. Heath & Company, 1889), 230.
[36] Lindner, *Manual of Empirical Psychology as an Inductive Science*, 230.
[37] N. Young, "Systems of Gambling," *National Review*, 18/29 (1892), 449–60, 460.
[38] Young, "Systems of Gambling," 460.

1894, made this explicit. One passage traces the shifting fortunes of a game and comments on the hatred players feel and the recklessness that develops as a result.

> A blight seemed to have come over him and smothered all the joyousness of the good humour that had buoyed him up; it had taken all the sweetness even out of the incomparable pleasure of a run of luck. It was now fast turning into an avalanche of disaster, this run of luck. Sally's malevolent gaze was upon him and seemed to cast a spell, so that he could do nothing right. Nobody but a gambler can have any idea how rapidly a big pile of big bank notes will vanish, if only you have lost your head and are playing recklessly.[39]

Hatred, enmity, and recklessness come about in the charged emotional context of the game. Authors Wilkins and Vivian, like other commentators who focus on the way in which games intensify emotions, project a view of the game in which otherwise normal and rational people experience a heightening of emotion, a feedback process that continues until one has lost control.

The vision of the casino as a machine for intensifying emotion beyond any capacity for a human to bear was only one way that nineteenth-century commentators viewed the connection between gambling and emotion. Others focused on emotional disconnection instead, looking at the ways that gambling generated boredom or culminated in what the sociologist Georg Simmel called the "blasé attitude." One character in *The Green Bay Tree* exhibits this position. He "had long ago come to the conclusion that nobody but a millionaire can win against the bank at Monte Carlo, and he never played save with an ulterior object ... At the end of an hour and a half he was three louis to the good and announced that he had had enough of it, and that it was not worth all those emotions to win such a small sum."[40] Simmel describes the "blasé attitude" toward money characteristic of the rich gambler who loses vast sums but affects an attitude of carelessness. "The blasé person," Simmel writes, "has completely lost the feeling for value differences. He experiences all things as being of an equally dull and grey hue, as not worth getting excited about, particularly where the will is concerned.... As a rule, the blasé attitude is rightly attributed to satiated enjoyment because too strong a stimulus destroys the nervous ability to respond to it."[41] This type of

---

[39] W. H. Wilkins and H. Vivian, *The Green Bay Tree: A Tale of To-day* (Hutchinson & Company, 1894), 40–41.
[40] Wilkins and Vivian, *The Green Bay Tree*, 39.
[41] G. Simmel, *The Philosophy of Money*, 3rd ed. (Routledge, 2004), 256.

gambler, in Simmel's estimation, no longer experienced the proper emotional connection to money because they had reached a saturation point and were no longer capable of enjoyment.

Of course, Georg Simmel was not just interested in gambling, and his overall project centered on an exploration of money and its significance in a range of areas. Yet he was also aware of the special significance that money held for gamblers. In fact, money lent any game a special quality and elevated its psychological importance to the players. In this way, money and gambling represented a paradox. Money made gambling fun, but it also meant that money held a transformed importance to the gambler. Simmel writes in *Philosophy of Money*, "We have here one of those interesting cases in which the disease determines its own form of the cure. A money culture signifies such an enslavement of life in its means, that release from its weariness is also evidently sought in a mere means which conceals its final significance – in the fact of 'stimulation' as such."[42] Money stimulates, but it also enslaves – a duality that appears in a number of descriptions of gambling in the nineteenth century.

Simmel dealt with this dual quality of money in another section of the *Philosophy of Money* in which he notes the "relations between external stimuli and emotional responses in the field of money."[43] In particular, Simmel sought to probe the "threshold of the awareness of money," and he suggests that the emotional content of money is related to our awareness of it and its meaning to us in very localized ways. Emotions about money are essentially latent until some exogenous force – like a wager at the gambling table – crystallizes them and generates a form in which they are expressed (and this can be either positive or negative).[44] He explored this idea further in an essay published in 1904 titled "Fashion," in which he takes up the question of envy as an emotion related specifically to the possession of objects. Simmel describes the emotional dynamism of envy in the following way: "The moment we envy an object or a person, we are no longer absolutely excluded from it; some relation or other has been established – between both the same psychic content now exists – although in entirely different categories and forms of sensations."[45] While Simmel was not talking about gambling in the essay, his insight into the emotional power that objects exert over us remains a useful way to understand the lure that gambling held in the nineteenth century. In the emotional connections

---

[42] Simmel, *The Philosophy of Money*, 257.   [43] Simmel, *The Philosophy of Money*, 269.
[44] Simmel, *The Philosophy of Money*, 269–70.
[45] G. Simmel, *On Individuality and Social Forms* (University of Chicago Press, 1971), 304.

between players, or between players and the mechanical objects of the gambling hall, we see a tightly forged emotional connection. This connection was not always positive, and indeed it was not always reciprocal, but the powerful nature of games and play – and the social spaces in which these games were played – contributed much to the ways in which nineteenth-century observers noted the intensely emotional nature of gambling.

If players were often described as being overwhelmed by emotion, carried away on torrents of feeling that they could not control or at times even understand, the opposite affect was cultivated by the house. Time and again, nineteenth-century observers described the passionlessness of the house and noted its machine-like qualities. W. Fraser Rae called the roulette wheel "an ingenious device for inspiring a player with the prospect of gain, and for insuring that the player will contribute to maintain the keepers of the table. There is more excitement in playing at *roulette* than at *trente-et-quarante*, though the certainty of ultimate loss is the same at either."[46] In 1904, the Austrian journalist Viktor Silberer wrote, "In gambling, temper is stronger than reason. That is why men will always be far behind the Bank, which has no soul, no temper, no sentiments.... The human player is no match for a machine.... [T]o compete with the Bank on even terms they must be a machine like the Bank, they must have unlimited capital like the Bank, they must play every 'coup' like the Bank."[47] One aspect of system play, and one way to imagine the bank on the other side, is to consider how players attempted to form themselves into a type of artificial intelligence that could deliberately and systematically crush the opposition through a superior machine logic. Writing just before World War I, Stacpoole advanced a similar description of the casino at Monte Carlo.

> The bank never increases its stakes beyond those set forth in the schedule, and perhaps some philosophical brain may discover from the restraint on the part of the bank the origin of its success and of the fact that the bank always wins – in the long run. The bank is a machine without nerves, without passion, playing mechanically against human beings, and always winning. The chances are absolutely equal between the machine and the human beings, with the exception of the slight margin of profit given to the machine by zero. The Prince of Monaco, the Casino, the nine thousand attendants, the croupiers, the gold links and the management are not supported or built out of zero. Nor out of the fact that the bank's purse

---

[46] W. F. Rae, "Play and Players on the Riviera," *The Nineteenth Century*, 27/February (1890), 240–57, 249.
[47] H. S. Maxim, *Monte Carlo: Facts and Fallacies* (Grant Richards, 1904), 168.

is longer than the purse of each individual player. No; but out of the fact that the bank never plays "wild," whereas the human being does; human weakness is perhaps the true secret of the enormous profits of the inhuman game at which a machine pits itself against a human being.[48]

To beat the machine, become the machine. Stacpoole may have identified the secret logic of the twentieth century before it even really began.

The emotional history of gambling is a twisted one, to be sure. In descriptions of the interior drama of the wager, or of the game, or of the convoluted sequence of emotions suddenly untethered and allowed free expression, we see not only the ways that gambling generated emotional intensity in players but also how it invited closely detailed descriptions of emotions and the ways they were experienced. That these descriptions seem to have proliferated in the blooming of the bourgeois century is not especially surprising; we know that bourgeois Europeans cultivated their emotional lives in meticulous ways. But what is important here is the way in which play and the creation of Blanc-style casinos created a social space and a set of images of gambling that provided Europeans from differing backgrounds a common language of emotion. Feelings were certainly an important part of the story of nineteenth-century gambling, but so too were the psychological elements of gambling that so intrigued observers at the time. We turn now to the psychology of gambling as it developed in the nineteenth and early twentieth centuries.

---

[48] M. de V. Stacpoole, *Monte Carlo: A Novel* (Dodd, Mead and Co., 1913), 102–3.

CHAPTER 8

The Psychology of Gambling

We considered in previous chapters how nineteenth-century casino gambling affected the ways in which people experienced play in their bodies and how they felt in the course of play. We looked in particular at how the gambling body was included in larger discussions of evolution as well as changes adhering to the emotional landscape of the casino and the gambler. We turn now to the psychological dimensions of casino gambling in the nineteenth century. Gambling did not just affect the body and the emotions; it also affected the mental apparatus that people employed to understand the world around them as well as their own desires and compulsions. Gambling, I have argued, was both intensely physical and emotional. It was, as we saw at several points in earlier discussions, also intensely psychological, capable of transforming behaviors in dramatic ways.

Even before the nineteenth century, observers recognized the ways that gambling attracted people. Resorting to body metaphors like "itching" to describe the compulsion to play, observers noted the ways in which an anxious psychology of unsatisfiable desiring set in. One recurring motif in critiques of gambling consisted of the claim that gamblers had lost their capacity for reason and for considered action, and that they therefore lack some essential quality that makes them human. Gambling established a psychological dynamic seemingly perfectly calibrated to drive people to the edge of madness. The "storm" of despair generated by a loss, never compensated by a corresponding elation coming with a win, can overwhelm the player and leave them incapable of self-direction.

Early modern authors identified one consequence of gambling being a renewed psychological attachment to money: avarice. Others made a similar argument, noting the way that gamblers often possessed an intensified connection with money. Richard Hey, writing in the late eighteenth century, remarks that "when it is Money staked, all Limit seems to vanish."¹ The psychological dimension of the game is paramount, and the end goal of the player informs the approach to the game: "if he play without any distinct motive, through mere habit or blind infatuation, the same power which has carried him one length will carry him another, if he is weak enough to be carried on by it: there is not a check in the nature of the thing itself, as there is in other expenses."² E. T. A. Hoffmann's character the Chevalier is one such figure whose motivations were dominated by his relationship to money. Hoffmann writes that the Chevalier gambled not because he loved play but because he loved money: "It was not the gambling mania, no, it was the most hateful greed for money that Satan himself ignited in his inmost soul."³ If we understand avarice as a psychological and emotional force field in which a person is attracted to an unreasonable degree to money (or what money represents), then these ways of describing gambling that focus on the power of play to generate piles and piles of money remain a useful historical indicator of some of the ways that money exerted a psychological hold over people that could be satisfied through play.

If avarice was one way of summarizing the psychological dimension of gambling, the power of winning was another issue that nineteenth-century observers used to discuss the ways that gambling affected a person's mental state. George Sala explained that a handful of wins was all that was required to destroy a person's will, rendering them a slave to play, a powerful psychological dynamic that was conditioned in part on the manipulative effects of the casino environment. Sala examines how winning at the gambling table sets the stage for a prolonged and dismaying sequence of losses, and he directly compares gambling's punishment-reward cycle to other unpleasant physical sensations that teach people lessons. Sala writes

> The Demon of Play has him for his own, and he may go on playing and playing until he has lost every florin of his own, and as many of those belonging to other people as he can beg or borrow. Far more fortunate would it be for him in the long run if he met in the outset with a good swinging loss. The burnt child *does* dread the fire as a rule; but there is this capricious, almost preternatural feature of the physiology of gaming, that the young and the inexperienced generally win in the first instance. They are drawn on and on, and in and in. They begin to lose, and continue to

---

¹ R. Hey, *Three Dissertations; on the Pernicious Effects of Gaming, on Duelling and on Suicide* (J. Smith, 1812), 5.
² Hey, *Three Dissertations*, 5–6.
³ E. T. A. Hoffmann, *The Tales of Hoffmann* (Frederick Ungar Publishing Co., 1963), 223–24.

lose, and by the time they have cut their wise teeth they have neither sou nor silver wherewith to make their dearly-bought wisdom available.[4]

Sala does not use the term "addiction," but the psychological dynamic he describes resembles it. Employing a utilitarian theory of sensation – people avoid repeating painful episodes but seek to repeat pleasurable ones – Sala hints at what might be called today a behavioral understanding of gambling and its attractions.

Sala's mid-nineteenth-century insights into why people continue to play until they have lost everything are especially useful in understanding other contemporary sources. Dostoyevsky, for instance, has been described as "so excitable that when he entered the casino he became nervous and uncontrolled."[5] We saw in previous chapters the ways that Dostoyevsky described his own method of play, a system that left him inevitably impoverished. His correspondence is studded with descriptions like those of a letter sent in August 1863: "I spent four days or so in Wiesbaden, and I gambled, of course at roulette."[6] A week later, he ruefully writes, "I lost my shirt at roulette, absolutely, completely."[7] In a letter from August 1865, he notes, "I have been in Wiesbaden five days already and have lost everything, including my watch, and I am even in debt at the hotel."[8] Egon Corti, claiming that *The Gambler* is "frankly autobiographical," explains that the close descriptions appearing in the story of the psychological drama of gambling reveal something important about the time in which it was written.[9] Perhaps the most direct critique of the psychological and social effects of a gambling addiction comes near the conclusion of the novella, when the Gambler is confronted with the impoverished quality of his life. Dostoyevsky described his character in a letter sent in September 1863: "The main point is that all his life juices, energies, violence, boldness have gone *into roulette*. He is a gambler, and not an ordinary gambler."[10] The Gambler, having invested his "life juices" into the game, is left emotionally dead. Confronted by another character, Astley, the Gambler is told,

> "You've become apathetic," he [Astley] observed, "not only have you renounced life, your interests both personal and social, your duty as a

[4] G. A. Sala, *Make Your Game, or, The Adventures of the Stout Gentleman, the Slim Gentleman, and the Man with the Iron Chest: A Narrative of the Rhine and Thereabouts* (Ward and Lock, 1860), 190.
[5] E. C. Corti, *The Wizard of Monte Carlo* (E. P. Dutton, 1935), 210.
[6] F. Dostoyevsky, *Complete Letters* (Ardis, 1988), vol. 2, 57.
[7] Dostoyevsky, *Complete Letters*, 60.   [8] Dostoyevsky, *Complete Letters*, 165.
[9] Corti, *The Wizard of Monte Carlo*, 211.   [10] Dostoyevsky, *Complete Letters*, 70.

man and a citizen, your friends (and all the same you did have friends); not only have you renounced any goal whatsoever, apart from winning, you have even renounced your own memories. I remember you at an ardent and intense moment of your life; but I'm certain that you've forgotten all your best impressions of that time; your dreams, your most urgent desires now don't go further than *pair* and *impair*, *rouge*, *noir*, the twelve middle numbers and so forth and so on, I'm certain of it!"[11]

We should remember that *The Gambler* is a work of fiction. That said, Dostoyevsky's 1866 characterization of the psychological effects of addiction – not only how those behaviors were formed through repetition but also how they resulted in a person whose entire world had shrunk to just a tiny sliver of what it had been – certainly indicates how the machinery of Blanc-style casino gambling affected people in new and profound ways.

Dostoyevsky wrote *The Gambler* in a feverish burst of work, dictating the novella to his stenographer (and future wife) over the course of twenty-six days in 1866. John Venn published his *Logic of Chance* the same year. In it, he also reckoned with the psychological attractions of gambling, seeking to understand the hold that gambling exerted over people. Venn positioned gambling as a social practice in which people flirted with the notion of uncertainty. The desire to confront the mysteries of chance and uncertainty held an undeniable mental attraction to people, and this led to an intense desire to gamble. Venn writes, "I would not for a moment underrate the practical dangers which are found to attend the practice of gambling. It is remarked that the gambler . . . is under an almost irresistible impulse to increase his stakes, and so re-introduce the element of uncertainty. It is in fact this tendency to be thus led on, which makes the principal danger and mischief of the practice."[12] Venn, in a position perhaps characteristic of a certain social type of nineteenth-century man, suggests that people find something irresistible about the unknown. With his suggestion that by attempting to satisfy this desire through gambling people might run into extreme danger, Venn was merely giving voice to the idea that gambling might best be considered an ersatz form of exploration that focused a person's interest by heightening the sensations of excitement that they felt. Indeed, in another passage dealing with gambling, Venn argues that the "mischief" generated by gambling had the consequence of fostering both greed and loss. He writes that there "have

[11] F. Dostoyevsky, *The Gambler and Other Stories* (Penguin, 2010), 267.
[12] J. Venn, *The Logic of Chance: An Essay on the Foundations and Province of the Theory of Probability, with Especial Reference to Its Application to Moral and Social Science* (Macmillan, 1866), 378.

been a number of writers who, not content with dwelling upon the obvious moral and indirect mischief which result, in the shape of over-excitement, consequent greed, withdrawal from the steady business habits which alone insure prosperity in the long run, diversion of wealth into dishonest hands &c., have endeavoured to demonstrate the necessary loss caused by the practice."[13]

Dostoyevsky and Venn approached gambling from vastly different positions. Yet in 1866 they both agreed that gambling affected people in deeply psychological ways. And yet only the casino – not the friendly games of whist that Venn enjoyed – undermined a person's hold on reality or their ability to sustain normal social relationships. Dostoyevsky describes a person whose gambling has rendered him incapable of normal human relationships; Venn notes the ways that repeated immersion in a sea of uncertainty generates overexcitement, greed, and withdrawal from practices that were more likely to generate prosperity. Gambling, in other words, disrupted normal practice and encouraged a flight from reason. The inability to resist these impulses meant that players risked exposure to a deeply addictive practice that could sap both physical and mental energy. Andrew Steinmetz remarked that gambling exerted a special power over the mental lives of geniuses: "Men of intellect may rest assured that whether they win or lose at play, it will always be at the cost of their genius; the soul cannot support two passions together. The passion of play, although fatigued, is never satiated, and therefore it always leaves behind protracted agitation."[14] Steinmetz's account of a mind disrupted through the agitation of play provides one way of thinking through how observers categorized   the   mental   consequences   of   gambling   in   the nineteenth century.

Other reports from the early 1870s portray a similar account of the mental ramifications of gambling. One writer in 1873 claimed that the ubiquity of chance – and the consequent demise of agency or will over one's path in the world – left people unmoored and overwhelmed by their inability to affect change. He writes that "[e]vidently in spite of the clearest understanding of the chances of the game, the moral fallacy which attri-butes luck or ill-luck to something of capacity or gift, or incapacity and deficiency, in the individual player, must be profoundly ingrained in us."[15]

[13] Venn, *The Logic of Chance*, 383–84.
[14] A. Steinmetz, *The Gaming Table: Its Votaries and Victims*, 2 vols. (Tinsley Brothers, 1870), vol. 1, 287.
[15] Sala, "Saxon-les-bains: A Study in the Psychology of Gambling," *The Spectator* (1873), 1242–3, 1243.

These feelings of inadequacy, smallness in the face of fate, or inconsequential ability are profoundly distressing. This situation, in which people have no power but seek ways to convince themselves that they exert influence over events, is psychologically disruptive. The author writes,

> When you win at one time and lose at another, the mind is almost unable to realise steadily that there was no reason accessible to yourself why you won and why you lost. And so you invent – what you know perfectly well to be a fiction – the conception of some sort of inward-divining-rod which guided you right when you used it properly, and failed only because you did not attend adequately to its indications.[16]

Only by inventing a series of fantasies in which one convinces oneself of the reality of agency and will can the dismaying idea of a lack of agency be submerged. Even though he recognizes that this is a "fiction," the psychological importance of the maneuver remains impossible to deny.

To this point we have focused on the ways that gambling affected one's sense of self. We noted the inner psychological drama of addiction and the ways that people sought to develop tricks that would confirm the reality of their own agency. Other observers focused not on the interior consequences of gambling but on the ways it impacted relations between self and other. Richard Proctor wrote in 1887 that the personality of the gambler was one oriented around selfishness. Proctor explains: "First, gamblers pay little attention to the misfortunes of their fellows: the professed gambler is utterly selfish, and moreover he hates the sight of misfortune because it unpleasantly reminds him of his own risks."[17] Gambling not only produces, but also rewards, a heightened regard for self at the expense of others. In the zero-sum world of the gambling table, a mercantile logic sets in. Any profit comes from another, and any loss only enriches and emboldens other players. Proctor asserts that the psychological consequences of this environment include a relentless descent into unreality, superstition, and occult thinking. He writes that "the life-long gambler is familiar with games of chance, but utterly ignorant of the laws of chance."[18] In this way Proctor is able to argue that the selfishness of the gambler contributes to a flight from reality and a projection of a system of thought that is based on nonrational principles. He goes on to assert in another passage that gambling, unreason, and illogic go hand in hand, culminating in a malformed understanding of law, chance, reality, and

---

[16] Sala, "Saxon-les-bains: A Study in the Psychology of Gambling," 1243.
[17] R. A. Proctor, *Chance and Luck*, 2nd ed. (Longmans, Green, and Company, 1887), 37.
[18] Proctor, *Chance and Luck*, 30.

agency. Gambling, in short, promotes occult thinking and thus contributes to a type of social insanity.

Proctor was not alone in his view that gambling encouraged a disconnection of the player from reality. In his *Manual of Empirical Psychology*, Gustav Adolf Lindner wrote of the gambler that "In this sense the passionate man is not entirely sound mentally; because with him this reciprocal determinable character of the concepts is lost, and the passion concepts rule the whole consciousness, without allowing themselves to be adjusted by other concept groups, however important."[19] Norwood Young echoed Lindner's assertion, writing, "A peculiar mixture of reason and folly, however, is a characteristic of all gamblers; and those who have lived in intimacy with gamblers know well that their capacity for belief is without limit. The roulette wheel is to them the most potent of mesmeric instruments. Under its influence a man ceases to be a responsible being."[20] Young goes on to attack what he calls the "system-worship" of gamblers who attach blind faith to the occult logic of their particular system. Indeed, when a spectacular event takes place and the casino loses, it makes sure to advertise the fact wide and far with the knowledge that it will lure a new crop of customers, and the casinos encouraged the use of systems because they believed them ultimately to be ineffective. Because systems involve "superstition" at their base, they are completely arbitrary and culturally determined. Any sign must be converted by the faithful into a corresponding meaning: anything a "gambler's brain can imagine, may be converted into gambling terms by being assigned a number or a colour, and thus made the means of a wager."[21] Young notes the existence of "gambling dictionaries," a book listing the meaning of any conceivable sign and its conversion into black, red, even, odd, and so on. In this way, we can see that Young envisions the occult world as being the key to understanding the psychology of the gambler – the ability to read natural signs and to understand their occult meanings, and then to capitalize on one's skill at interpreting the signs, is the hallmark of the fin-de-siècle gambler. Importantly, the author connects a belief in the occult world directly to theosophy, explaining that the gambler, attuned to the proliferation of signs, "fluttered by such a succession of peculiar phenomena, ... has a sensation, or (as a Theosophist would say) a 'sending,' that he is in

---

[19] G. A. Lindner, *Manual of Empirical Psychology as an Inductive Science: A Text-Book for High Schools and Colleges* (D. C. Heath & Company, 1889), 230.
[20] N. Young, "Systems of Gambling," *National Review*, 18/29 (1892), 449–60, 451.
[21] Young, "Systems of Gambling," 453.

luck – *en vein*."²² And worse, perhaps, is the fact that this senseless wallowing in the astral plane corresponded to a disconnection from reality akin to old forms of magical knowledge that have been inappropriately revived by the modern state: "Such methods of divination by means of the dictionary oracle are extensively practised wherever the general tone of the community has been lowered by State lotteries."²³ Gambling, in short, encouraged practices that were evidence of disorder – both moral and psychological.

Gambling was thought to affect the sense of self, one's relations with others, and even the degree to which one apprehended the world around them in realistic ways that were free of psychoses. We have also considered the ways in which gambling – in that it represented a way to interact with the unknown – also facilitated a larger reckoning with the external world that was at once pleasurable and disturbing, thus reinforcing the attractiveness of the practice. But we also need to consider other ways that gambling facilitated a set of psychologically powerful connections in players. Money, perhaps unsurprisingly, was a key factor in the process of encouraging players to return to the gaming table. Georg Simmel notes in *Philosophy of Money*, "Money builds a bridge between such people and objects. In crossing the bridge, the mind experiences the attraction of their possession even if it does in fact not attain it."²⁴ Simmel goes on to argue that the act of payment exerts a stamp of ownership and personality on an object, but that money retains a special power because it is psychologically fluid. Money can represent anything. As Simmel explains,

> The greedy soul who seeks complete satisfaction and wants to penetrate the ultimate, innermost and absolute nature of things, is painfully rejected by them. Objects are, and remain, something for themselves which resists their complete integration into the sphere of the self and allows the most passionate ownership to end in dissatisfaction. The possession of money is free of this hidden contradiction that exists in all other kinds of possession.... It is only money that we own completely and without reservations; it is only money that merges completely into the function we assign to it.²⁵

Money, in other words, is the most psychologically satisfying medium because it can be converted into anything, and it therefore represents something special to the gambler. Writing two years after the publication of Simmel's *Philosophy of Money*, Clemens France noted that stakes were a

---

²² Young, "Systems of Gambling," 453.   ²³ Young, "Systems of Gambling," 453.
²⁴ G. Simmel, *The Philosophy of Money*, 3rd ed. (Routledge, 2004), 327.
²⁵ Simmel, *The Philosophy of Money*, 327–28.

vital psychological element in the attractiveness of gambling. Money made the game more interesting and more psychologically meaningful.[26] Money, in part because of its unlimited potential, makes the game more exciting and relevant. It also generates the conditions within which a train of emotions and instincts is made manifest.

To observers writing around the turn of the century, gambling represented a way to satisfy a range of psychic needs. A 1901 essay by University of Chicago sociologist W. I. Thomas published in the *American Journal of Sociology* addressed this point directly, suggesting that gambling developed because it gave physical expression to old psychological conflicts. Thomas, who had studied in Berlin and Göttingen with Wilhelm Wundt, proposes it is not the gambler but the bourgeois businessman who represents a historical novelty.[27] Accounting for the differences between the two – especially the psychological ones – allows Thomas not only to consider the gambler a social parasite but also to suggest that gambling is natural and an ersatz form of otherwise healthy activity. Indeed, Thomas notes the ubiquity of gambling and suggests that gamblers cannot be recognized as having some kind of psychological deficiency. He writes that the "gambler is distinguished by no particular psychic marks from other members of society."[28] And in fact, gamblers are perhaps especially well suited for success in the modern capitalist economy. Thomas argues, "There are among the bookmakers, card and confidence men, professional billiardists, and adventurers of Chicago men who by every psychological test have a very high grade of intelligence. They have excellent associative memories, capacity to see general relations amid details, to reach judgments quickly and surely, and to readjust themselves skillfully to changing situations."[29] His conclusion is that it is impossible to distinguish on the basis of psychological defect the existence of a class of gamblers. Arguing that while some gamblers are of unremarkable intellectual ability, others would have ascended the professional ranks, and there is no clear way to differentiate between the two groups. In short, "There is, in fact, psychologically no more a sporting class than there is a class of college men or a class of horse-breeders."[30]

Thomas explains that gambling is essentially natural. The people drawn to gambling are not inherently ill or otherwise deficient. They do,

[26] C. J. France, "The Gambling Impulse," *The American Journal of Psychology*, 13/3 (1902), 364–407, 386.
[27] W. I. Thomas, "The Gaming Instinct," *American Journal of Sociology*, 6/6 (1901), 750–63, 760–61.
[28] Thomas, "The Gaming Instinct," 761.   [29] Thomas, "The Gaming Instinct," 761.
[30] Thomas, "The Gaming Instinct," 762.

however, possess a stronger connection to what might be called natural man than the counterexample of the businessman. "The instincts of man are congenital," Thomas argues, "the arts and industries are acquired by the race and must be learned by the individual after birth. We have seen why the instinctive activities are pleasurable and the acquired habits irksome. The gambler represents a class of men who have not been weaned from their instinct."[31] Gamblers thus represent, as we saw previously, a type of atavism at the heart of the modern city and the modern economy. Psychologically, a gambler may not be different from anyone else, but he also offered social scientists like Thomas the chance to investigate the instinctual life of natural man.

The question of whether or not a gambler represented a prior stage of mental or psychological development was an unsettled one at the turn of the twentieth century.[32] Some, like Thomas, refused to see gambling as unnatural, yet he acknowledged its status as something that was highly instinctual (but still something that needed to be overcome). Other critics of gambling built on this critique, noting especially the embrace of superstition and the occult that they believed characterized the mental state of gamblers. Hiram Maxim, for instance, saw superstition as evidence of a false consciousness that peculiarly affected gamblers. He writes, "That gamblers are superstitious is proverbial, but in these hard, unsympathetic times of ours, we do not recognise hoodoos, fetishes, or good luck. It is simply a matter of plain, unsympathetic chance, and these chances are always and invariably in favour of the Bank."[33] Believing in the unbelievable was a form of self-delusion, an unhealthy psychological relationship with the world that allowed gamblers to hold the false belief that their actions mattered. Maxim continues, explaining,

> I found in conversing with the players that the greater number of them thought that the events which had taken place on the tables had some kind of an occult or ghostly influence on those which were about to take place.... On many occasions I attempted to ascertain why it was that they imagined that the events that had taken place would influence those that were to take place; as for myself, I could see no possible connection between the past and the future. None were able to tell me how the events of the past managed to get hold of the little ivory sphere and caused it to drop into

---

[31] Thomas, "The Gaming Instinct," 762.
[32] Indeed, the presence of atavistic practices and beliefs was an issue affecting a number of areas of European inquiry in the late nineteenth and early twentieth centuries. See H. Foster, *Prosthetic Gods* (MIT Press, 2004).
[33] H. S. Maxim, *Monte Carlo: Facts and Fallacies* (Grant Richards, 1904), 25–26.

the pocket that it would not have dropped into had these events not taken place.[34]

Not only do gamblers misunderstand history and causality, Maxim suggests, they also hold a fundamentally flawed view of the world, their connection to reality malformed.

We can read Maxim's critique of superstition as a larger attack on people who use the tools at their disposal to mitigate uncertainty. In this regard, Maxim was repeating aspects of Richard Proctor's arguments from two decades prior. Other social scientists from the turn of the century, however, fixated on different elements of the gambling problem in order to understand its attractions. Clemens France suggested that gambling found adherents in part because it could help resolve those feeling of uncertainty, but also – especially from the standpoint of observers – offered a form of entertainment and excitement that stemmed from the conversion of the uncertain into the certain. France writes that

> it is difficult to leave such a table after standing a few minutes merely to observe what number will win next. In any uncertain event there is the same attracting force, and although one may have no interest in either side, there is always a tendency to speculate on the outcome. This constitutes a large part of the philosophy of life, resolving the uncertainties into certainties.[35]

Indeed, the key psychological issue for the gambler was the attempt to convert the unknown into the known, to explore the uncertain and to render it certain. France thinks that this psychological approach to the world is in part what defines the gambler and their attempt to exert agency over the unknown. France argues that there is "a strong passion for certainty, a longing for the firm conviction of assurance for safety. The uncertain state is desired and entered upon, but ever with the denouement focal in mind."[36]

France understands the psychological appeal of gambling as being based in the opportunity it presents people to find security in certainty. France argues that "gambling is a struggle for the certain and the sure, i.e., the feeling of certainty. It is not merely a desire for uncertainty. We are here dealing with that same great passion for certitude which is the cornerstone of science, philosophy and religion – the desire to put the element of chance out of the game."[37] Especially significant when considering games

---

[34] Maxim, *Monte Carlo*, 27–28.   [35] France, "The Gambling Impulse," 385.
[36] France, "The Gambling Impulse," 397.   [37] France, "The Gambling Impulse," 397.

of chance like those played in the casino, France's conclusions about the psychological draw of gambling are bold statements about the motivations of people at the turn of the century. Indeed, the idea of defeating chance might be said to be the entire point of gambling. As France argues in a passage about games of chance, "It is because of this obscurity, because of the utter impossibility of prevision, that the player feels so utterly helpless before the unknown, in which there is not conception but that of chance as a deciding factor. On the side of chance is all the power and activity; on the side of the player all is impotence and passivity."[38] It is not that gamblers sought to wallow in the vagaries of chance; indeed, it may have been the opposite case. If France is correct, gamblers could be said to reject the idea that they were living in an "age of chance."

There is evidence for this argument when we consider Stacpoole's novel, in which she suggests that players feel a certain way – and then bet accordingly. We have already considered the ways that this emphasis on emotion contains a gesture to occult sensibility, but in this case, we consider the problem from the standpoint of agency. Stacpoole writes of when one character feels as if he is "in vein" and then assumes his intuition was a correct one: "'I knew it,' said he, 'black is going to turn up this time.' It did, and though he had not staked anything, his eyes sparkled with pleasure. 'How did you know?' 'I don't know. I seemed to get in the vein of it, I felt I could *make* it turn up.' 'Try again,' said Julia. He did, and he lost. 'The feeling has gone off me; one must keep on playing to keep it up.'"[39] Thorstein Veblen commented on a similar suite of ideas in a passage describing the relationships between sport and occult feeling:

> [I]t has appeared that the sense of an animistic propensity in material things and events is what affords the spiritual basis of the sporting man's gambling habit. For the economic purpose, this sense of propensity is substantially the same psychological element as expresses itself, under a variety of forms, in animistic beliefs and anthropomorphic creeds. So far as concerns those tangible psychological features with which economic theory has to deal, the gambling spirit which pervades the sporting element shades off by insensible gradations into that frame of mind which finds gratification in devout observances.[40]

Veblen, not content with a simple critique of instrumental religion, also argued that those with a sporting personality had a heightened belief in their

---

[38] France, "The Gambling Impulse," 397.
[39] M. de V. Stacpoole, *Monte Carlo: A Novel* (Dodd, Mead and Co., 1913), 35.
[40] T. Veblen, *The Theory of the Leisure Class: An Economic Study of Institutions* (Macmillan and Company, 1912), 294–95.

own ability to affect the sequence or the occurrence of events. "The sporting or gambling temperament ... comprises some of the substantial psychological elements that go to make a believer in creeds.... For the purpose of the gambling practice the belief in preternatural agency may be, and ordinarily is, less closely formulated, especially as regards the habits of thought and the scheme of life imputed to the preternatural agent; or, in other words, as regards his moral character and his purposes in interfering in events."[41] This type of person, in other words, is supremely confident in their ability to exert agency over unknown and unseen forces and therefore feels confident when taking risks.

We have considered in this chapter how gambling affected mental outlook and sense of self, and how it was integrated into theories of mental disorder. One of the striking things about gambling in the nineteenth century is the range of activities with which it was connected, and as we consider its impacts on the body, on emotion, and now on psychology it is clear that gambling represented many different things to many people. It could indicate disorder or the presence of a savage or barbarian mindset; gambling perhaps represented a way of understanding chance and uncertainty and of considering the significance of one's own existence or measuring the force of one's will. Perhaps more than anything else, gambling offered players the opportunity to engage in an activity that could – depending on one's outlook – either confirm or deny the power of one's self. If we accept that the modern self is partially a product of social and object relations, gambling presented more than just a leisure activity – it was implicated in existential questions of the highest order.

[41] Veblen, *The Theory of the Leisure Class*, 295.

CHAPTER 9

What Gambling Was

Gambling performed a variety of cultural work in the nineteenth and early twentieth centuries. The casinos were undeniably popular, and they presented a powerful indication of the fact that many thousands of people found the practice of gambling not only pleasurable but also devoid of any kind of moral taint. Its range of meanings meant that gambling could serve as a point of focus around which all sorts of social and cultural discussions unfolded. Gambling and play, like larger ruminations on how humans existed in a universe governed by chance (or in some cases ruled by luck), represented a unique field in human endeavor, tied to leisure, and they also provided the opportunity for gain. They were heterosocial but also threatened to scramble gender codes. They were exciting and fun, but also were attacked for generating social incoherence. Related to other attempts to monetize risk like insurance and stock-market speculation, gambling remained tainted by its older connections to vice, immorality, and "rascaldom."

Gambling in this period was never just about gambling; it always represented something else or spoke to some bigger set of concerns. Commenting on the desires that Monte Carlo was built to satisfy, Hiram Maxim suggested that Monaco was a system organized around exchange, but crafted in such a way as to permit an ersatz form of aggression. Maxim wrote in 1904,

> The Bank wants money, the players want play; there is an interchange of commodities. We belong to an aggressive and combative race. We have descended from ancestors who only a few hundred years ago were fierce and warlike barbarians. That we inherit many of the traits of these early ancestors is witnessed by the keen pleasure it gives us to catch fish and to chase and kill animals and birds. Many of us are quite willing to pay large sums for the sake of the gratification we experience pursuing and killing something. And so it is at Monte Carlo. We find keen enjoyment in contending with somebody or something. We like to attack, we like to

measure our strength and intelligence against that of some one else. And where can we find a better opportunity of gratifying our inherited instincts than in attacking and fighting the tiger at Monte Carlo? Fully three-quarters of the strikes that are so detrimental to British industry are brought about by the inherited instincts of the working man. He dislikes a steady, humdrum life; he seeks change or adventure. He is combative; he wishes to contend with some one; anything that offers a chance of a change or an opportunity to gratify his instincts is immensely interesting to him. And so at Monte Carlo our rich and leisured classes find a change from their painfully respectable and monotonous lives in the novelty and excitement of gambling. It is an extremely expensive kind of enjoyment, but the pleasures are so exquisite that they do not mind the expense. Moreover, to the vain it gives an opportunity to display their wealth and their disregard of gold.[1]

Maxim's statement unveils the ideas that we consider in this chapter. He suggests that gambling is a neutered form of aggression, made socially acceptable through the relentless power of the civilizing process but flowering in the novel context of the resort casino. He explains that workers and socialites both think about gambling – and the competitive urges it perhaps satisfies – as a way to connect to prior forms of existence. Gambling, in other words, not only represented a form of leisurely play, but also functioned as a substitute for socially unacceptable practices. This, as much as anything else, meant that gambling should be seen not as a harmless vice but rather as a harmful one that diminished the human condition. But it also could be the case that gambling – despite its dark reputation – could be a beacon of virtue in that it presented people an opportunity to safely participate in antisocial practices even as they promoted certain forms of sociability.

One way to understand this common appreciation for games of chance is to consider the way that late eighteenth- and early nineteenth-century players developed in a world conditioned in part by a romanticism that celebrated not only the influence of fate on people's lives but also the idea that humans had some sort of unseen and unspoken connection to the natural world. As Reith argues, romantics like Schiller promoted a view of the world in which "Play is . . . the highest manifestation of humanity: in it the true nature of the individual can be realised and expressed."[2] Play may be an ubiquitous element of the human experience, but it still is experienced in deeply historical ways. Blaise Pascal imagined play as a helpful

[1] H. S. Maxim, *Monte Carlo: Facts and Fallacies* (Grant Richards, 1904), 310–11.
[2] G. Reith, *The Age of Chance: Gambling in Western Culture* (Routledge, 1999), 3.

diversion from boredom, something that could bring pleasure and excitement to an otherwise tedious existence. And for Pascal gambling represented a heightened form of play, one that helped stimulate the imagination and generate the free flow of emotions.[3] Pascal's theory of play as a form of human activity and interaction that was especially important when it assumed the form of gambling tells us something important about play and its relationship to money in the seventeenth century. Play could be commodified in novel ways, but adding a money element to the mix only made its psychological and emotional significance more potent.

We see similar descriptions of play in other accounts from the seventeenth century. Charles Morton, author of the 1684 *The Gaming-Humour Considered and Reproved*, distinguished two goals of play: sport and gain. Morton was aware of the ways that money transformed play, although he was considerably more critical of the practice than Pascal was. Like Pascal, Morton saw a role for recreation, but he also made a distinction between gain derived from work and gain derived from play. But Morton denied that a profit motive could ever be included in a morally acceptable form of recreation. He writes that it must be denied that "*playing for money* is ever lawful; that is, to make the *Gain the end* of the Play. It perverts the order and nature of things so to do; it destroys the necessary Distinction between *Work* and *Play*; it crosses the Ordination of God, discovered in Scripture, who every where (that I can observe) assigns profit to be the product and fruit of *Labour*."[4] Morton's claim that play and work were two entirely different activities – and that gain should be derived only from work – is a valuable indication of the ways that religious principles inflected notions of leisure and labor in the early modern period. Profit, especially when it was derived from a source other than labor, could be spiritually dangerous, thus rendering play a threat to one's well-being.

The question of the morality of play did not disappear, of course, and by the nineteenth century in fact took on a heightened significance due to the changed economic circumstances generated by capitalism and the money economy. Andrew Steinmetz conflated the economic and the moral, suggesting that the two motives were in fact identical. Steinmetz argued, "We love play because it satisfies our avarice, – that is to say, our desire of having more; it flatters our vanity by the idea of preference that fortune

---

[3] B. Pascal, *Pensées and Other Writings* (Oxford University Press, 2008), 47.

[4] C. Morton, *The gaming-humor considered and reproved, or, The passion-pleasure and exposing money to hazard by play, lot or wager examined by a well-wisher to mankind.* (Tho. Cockerill, 1684), 32.

gives us, and of the attention that others pay to our success; it satisfies our curiosity, giving us a spectacle; in short, it gives us the different pleasures of surprise."[5] Steinmetz was prompted to explain the origins of play and to provide a description of the attractions that it may provide to people in the nineteenth century. Steinmetz dredged up a theory of play that focused on its emotional qualities. "Indolence and want of employment ... is the cause of the passion. It arises from a want of habitual employment in some material and regular line of conduct.... Something must be substituted to call forth the natural activity of the mind; and this is in no way more effectually accomplished, in all indolent pursuits, than by those *emotions and agitations* which gambling produces."[6] For Steinmetz, avarice and greed were key drivers of the passion to play: "Such is the source of the thing in our *nature*; but then comes the furious hankering after wealth – the desire to have it without *working* for it – which is the wish of so many of us; and *this* is the source of that hideous gambling which has produced the contemptible characters and criminal acts which are the burthen of this volume."[7] Despite the rhetoric Steinmetz employs, it is important to remember that the book is best understood as a pro-gambling text, thus rendering his theory that natural avarice is the foundation of play less derogatory than it might otherwise appear.

Steinmetz saw avarice as a natural desire, one that formed the emotional drive to gamble and play. He also understood play as something that crossed cultures and temporal boundaries, uniting humans in important ways. That said, Steinmetz also employed a racialist discourse that viewed the practice of gambling in highly localized and culturally specific ways. He suggested, for instance, that "the Asiatic gambler is desperate," and unlike Europeans who merely played for money, they would therefore stake anything, including loved ones and one's own liberty. Steinmetz's conflicted gesture toward a view of humanity united by certain drives but still different in the acceptable forms that wagering could assume perhaps speaks to the ways that play and gambling intersected with money in his culture. While Georg Simmel did not directly deal with gambling or play in his *Philosophy of Money*, it does still hold interest as a statement about the meaning of money to that society. Simmel argues that money represents unlimited potential and therefore is of special significance to an analysis of gambling. Simmel produced an analysis of intellectual effort as a proxy for emotion in the money economy, and his work allows us to

---

[5] A. Steinmetz, *The Gaming Table: Its Votaries and Victims*, 2 vols. (Tinsley Brothers, 1870), vol. 1, 23.
[6] Steinmetz, *The Gaming Table*, 22.   [7] Steinmetz, *The Gaming Table*, 22–23.

see how gaming joined play to the money economy and so had a dual function. Money is connected to both emotional and intellectual life in especially tight ways because of the risk-reward cycle. Simmel writes that "intellectual energy is the psychic energy which the specific phenomena of the money economy produces, in contrast to those energies generally denoted as emotions or sentiments which prevail in periods and spheres of interest not permeated by the money economy."[8] Money's fungibility allows it to transcend categorization in ways that permit its appearance as pure potential. Its magical qualities made it the perfect way to measure the value of a person, the worth of a commodity, or – in the form of gambling – to quantify and commodify the chance or the truth-value of a wager.

Simmel addressed these issues in *Philosophy of Money*, providing an explanation of how gambling represented a form of ersatz exchange. Gambling was a monetization of chance and luck – money could be used as a ruthless and merciless tool to quantify the random elements of the universe. As Simmel argues, "money is the purest reification of means . . . it is a pure instrument. The tremendous importance of money for understanding the basic motives of life lies in the fact that money embodies and sublimates the practical relation of man to the objects of his will, his power and his impotence; one might say, paradoxically, that man is an indirect being."[9] The idea that money achieves some kind of slippery status and can perform almost any type of cultural work is borne out in Simmel's analysis of the "calculating character of modern times," in which he asserts, "By and large, one may characterize the intellectual functions that are used at present in coping with the world and in regulating both individual and social relations as *calculative* functions. Their cognitive ideal is to conceive of the world as a huge arithmetical problem, to conceive events and the qualitative distinction of things as a system of numbers."[10] Simmel recognized that the conversion of the world into a set of monetized numerical functions was a novel departure from previous methods of ascertaining reality. He writes that this "psychological feature of our times which stands in such a decisive contrast to the more impulsive, emotionally determined character of earlier epochs seems to me to stand in a close causal relationship to the money economy. The money economy enforces the necessity of continuous mathematical operations in our daily transactions."[11] It is

---

[8] G. Simmel, *The Philosophy of Money*, 3rd ed. (Routledge, 2004), 429.
[9] Simmel, *The Philosophy of Money*, 211. [10] Simmel, *The Philosophy of Money*, 443–44.
[11] Simmel, *The Philosophy of Money*, 444.

only in the casino that the modern money economy is obscured and emotionalized, on the one hand, and deeply calculative, on the other. In the first case, the gambler and their somatic responses to gambling and the intense emotional investment in gambling unfold in an environment in which the usual markers of money have been removed through the use of proxy signifiers of money like chips. In the second case, money is used to quantify and rationalize probability and chance, and that is why the casino specifically and gambling generally appeal as a theoretical experimental space for statisticians.

An entry in the *Dictionary of Philosophy and Psychology* from 1901 explained that gambling "may be looked at both as a sport, a pastime, a recreation, and as a serious business, a passion."[12] The passage continues, noting the ways in which the very real chance of loss makes gambling a dramatic form of reality: "Certainly in most cases the hope of gain and the fear of loss bring an element of reality into the situation which is opposed to the make-believe or SEMBLANCE (q.v.) of play."[13] Gambling is not wrong because people must be allowed to spend their money as they see fit, and it is related to other forms of risk, like those associated with any business venture. However, even if gambling is "not ethically wrong," it is wrong in other ways. "It is serious – a passion, not a sport – and comes to supersede the regular forms of industry and business," so in its misuse becomes a problem.[14] Gambling also involves a loss of time, and "the man who gambles his time away as well as his money – taking both from his family – is ethically reprobate, not because he gambles, but because he is such a man."[15] In these ways gambling and play represented a form of action that was strongly related to external reality, but it also carried with it a set of concerns that no longer related to any kind of inherent immorality in seeking gain through play, but in the misuse of time or of the rejection of social responsibility that gambling could generate.

We have briefly covered some of the values that gambling and play represented to observers in the nineteenth century. It is also instructive to consider what gambling and play were not so that we can better see their presence by considering the negative space generated by their theoretical opposites. One common way of characterizing gambling was to isolate its differences from insurance. While both practices are oriented around

---

[12] J. M. Baldwin, ed., *Dictionary of Philosophy and Psychology* (Macmillan, 1901), 403.
[13] Baldwin, ed., *Dictionary of Philosophy and Psychology*, 403.
[14] Baldwin, ed., *Dictionary of Philosophy and Psychology*, 403.
[15] Baldwin, ed., *Dictionary of Philosophy and Psychology*, 403.

probability and chance, insurance and risk management suggest a different approach to the world. The *Dictionary of Philosophy and Psychology* suggests as much in the entry for insurance, explaining, "Insurance contracts and gambling contracts are both wagers, and may be exactly alike in form; but if such a contract is made for contingent gain, it results in loss of utility and in commercial demoralization; while if it is made to prevent contingent loss, it results in increase of utility in commercial security."[16] Later observers made a similar argument. One British mathematician writing in 1931 defined gambling as "an agreement between two parties whereby the transfer of something of value from one to the other is made dependent on an uncertain event in such a way that the gain of one party is balanced by the loss of another."[17] His colleagues accepted the definition, but lamented that it would include insurance under the rubric, and noted that "insurance is in principle the exact opposite of gambling."[18] Gambling was even divided by some critics into "trivial" gambling and what presumably informs the nontrivial variety. Thorstein Veblen, commenting on "church bazaars and raffles," argues that "these raffles, and the like trivial opportunities for gambling, seem to appeal with more effect to the common run of the members of religious organisations than they do to persons of a less devout habit of mind."[19]

There were different ways to imagine gambling and its relationship to other forms of risk. German psychologist Hugo Münsterberg contrasts market speculation and gambling with rational investing, and then seeks to understand the psychological foundations for the American style of capital accumulation. "A psychological problem appears only when such a course of wisdom is abandoned, and either the savings are hidden away instead of being made productive, or are thrown away in wildcat schemes."[20] Noting the foreign perceptions of Americans, Münsterberg suggests that

> Foreign visitors have indeed often noticed with surprise that the American public ... is more ready to throw its money into speculative abysses than the people of other lands. What is the reason? Those observers from abroad are usually satisfied with the natural answer that the Americans are gamblers, or that they have an indomitable desire for capturing money without working.[21]

---

[16] Baldwin, ed., *Dictionary of Philosophy and Psychology*, 557.
[17] "Gambling," *The Mathematical Gazette*, 15/212 (1931), 347–58, 347.   [18] "Gambling," 347.
[19] T. Veblen, *The Theory of the Leisure Class: An Economic Study of Institutions* (Macmillan and Company, 1912), 300–301.
[20] H. Münsterberg, *Psychology and Social Sanity* (Doubleday, Page & Co., 1914), 253–54.
[21] Münsterberg, *Psychology and Social Sanity*, 254.

Münsterberg concludes that market speculation in America replaces legal forms of gambling like those seen in state lotteries in Europe. In this way, a legal prohibition of gambling shapes risk behaviors that pop up in other contexts.

Münsterberg concedes that while some Europeans are "slaves" to lotteries, there are nonetheless important policy considerations that legal state-sanctioned gambling produces.[22] He explains that unlike the situation in the United States, which did not – at the time – employ public lotteries, "in the most civilized European countries, whenever a cathedral is to be built, or an exhibition to be supported, the state gladly sanctions big lottery schemes to secure the financial means."[23] Münsterberg supports these public forms of gambling because, as the Europeans had suggested, "a certain amount of gambling instinct is ingrained in human character, and that it is wiser to create a kind of official outlet by which it is held within narrow limits, and by which the results yielded are used for the public good."[24] Moreover, forbidding gambling merely makes the practice more attractive. Münsterberg claims that American interest in gambling dominates the tourist class, writing, "Every tourist remembers from the European casinos in the summer resorts the famous game with the little horses, a miniature Monaco scheme."[25] But because gambling remained prohibited in the United States, there are all sorts of covert practices that spring up to satisfy a natural desire: "Forbidden gambling houses are abundant, private betting connected with sport is flourishing everywhere; above all, the economic organization admits through a back door what is banished from the main entrance, by allowing stocks to be issued for very small amounts."[26] For respectable Americans, underground gambling may be off-putting, but as Münsterberg notes, there are other forms of gambling that retain legal sanction and indeed form the backbone of the modern American economy. He writes that the

> external framework of the stock market is here far more likely to tempt the man of small savings into the game, and the mere fact that this form has been demanded by public consciousness suggests that the spirit which craves lotteries is surely not absent in the new world, even though the lottery lists in the European newspapers are blackened over before they are

---

[22] Münsterberg, *Psychology and Social Sanity*, 255.
[23] Münsterberg, *Psychology and Social Sanity*, 255.
[24] Münsterberg, *Psychology and Social Sanity*, 255.
[25] Münsterberg, *Psychology and Social Sanity*, 256.
[26] Münsterberg, *Psychology and Social Sanity*, 257.

laid out in the American public libraries. A certain desire for gambling and quick returns evidently exists the world over.[27]

Münsterberg's recognition that gambling was a varied pursuit that could do different types of cultural work is also partially a pronounced realization that by the turn of the twentieth century gambling was never just a simple leisure activity. Instead, gambling represented for many observers a highly sophisticated – given the rules and social norms governing the interactions of players – stand-in for organized violence or as a necessary antidote to the boredom generated by modern society. Gambling, in short, was a form of primitive savagery that permitted forms of excitement and violence to be practiced in safety. As we saw in Chapter 6, gambling was integrated into larger theories of evolution. Descriptions of gambling in the highly organized and tightly controlled environment of the resort casino that envisioned it as a safe re-creation of old forms of violence or the search for excitement performed a similar intellectual task.

Other writers were more direct in their characterization of gambling as a modern form of primitive impulses. In his 1901 essay "The Gaming Instinct," University of Chicago sociologist W. I. Thomas explains that conflict and conflict situations are inherently interesting and pleasurable. He suggests in the piece that culture is barely active, and instinct is a much more important element in modern life than people typically realize. We see the importance of instinct at work in the prevalence of organized violence and warfare, in feuding, prize-fighting, and football. While aspects of Thomas's argument will remind readers of those produced later by Norbert Elias about the "civilizing process" or Freud's claims about "civilization and its discontents," Thomas includes a specifically racial component to the argument. It is "especially in the white race," Thomas explains, that "man found himself obliged to adjust himself to changed conditions or perish. Instead of slaughtering the ox, he fed it, housed it in the winter, bred from it, reared the calf, yoked it to a plow, plowed the fields, sowed seeds, dug out the weeds and gathered, threshed, and ground the grain."[28] Tracing the development of human civilization, Thomas argues that agricultural life was based on the systematic elimination of chance to whatever degree was possible. But the elimination of chance, Thomas argues, "was disagreeable, because the problematical and vicissitudinous element was eliminated or reduced to a minimum. Under the

---

[27] Münsterberg, *Psychology and Social Sanity*, 257–58.
[28] W. I. Thomas, "The Gaming Instinct," *American Journal of Sociology*, 6/6 (1901), 750–63, 757.

artificial system into which he was forced to obtain his food, sudden strains were not placed on the attention, emotional reactions did not follow, and the activities were habitual, dull, mechanical, irksome. This was labor."[29] The presumed tedium of agricultural labor was, in Thomas's mind, rejected by some members of society, and these people who remained unassimilated into the economic structures of agricultural life were important indicators of a desire for alternative forms of existence that embraced chance. "Not all individuals of our own race have made the adjustment, either. Tramps and criminals represent a repudiation of the new arrangement, and the rich man's son often shows how superficial are the race habits of industry."[30]

Thomas presents a racist view of development and historical change. The pleasures of conflict, rooted in instinctual behaviors, can nonetheless be translated into socially acceptable pursuits. The unassimilated white "tramp" could be integrated into modern society. "But some modern occupations are not irksome," Thomas writes, "and not all are irksome to the same degree; and an examination of them from this standpoint discloses a preference for those in which the element of uncertainty is pronounced, in which the problematical is present, or where, at least, the attention is intermittent."[31] Experiencing risk is the critical emotional issue for Thomas. He argues that "the risk is ... excessive; the element of uncertainty in the problem cannot be controlled. Economically it is a business, in the sense that it has a value in fixing prices and promoting exchange; but psychologically it is gambling."[32] Even some occupations, because they exist in an environment of "vicissitude," achieve social significance: "Politics is another illustration of the tendency of human nature to seek the more vicissitudinous pursuits, for political life involves little drudgery, and is, in fact, a series of problems, with rapid and violent emotional changes."[33] The gaming instinct, as Thomas presents it, is historically old, and it gives physical expression to those elements of society who cannot assimilate themselves to a boring job working in the fields or, worse, working at a desk. The constant search for excitement and the relentless hunt for risk were merely displaced into new professions and new forms of leisure, gambling being preeminent.

Thomas's theory of racially expressed development was not uncharacteristic of the period. What is more significant about his ideas is the fact

[29] Thomas, "The Gaming Instinct," 757.   [30] Thomas, "The Gaming Instinct," 757.
[31] Thomas, "The Gaming Instinct," 758.   [32] Thomas, "The Gaming Instinct," 758.
[33] Thomas, "The Gaming Instinct," 759.

that they suggested the existence of modern solutions to old problems. The tedium and lifelessness of steady work generated a type of person who continually sought risk and chance. Gambling was merely a modern variation on an old theme. Despite the attempts of people like Thomas to recognize gambling as the outgrowth of old tensions in human society, gambling was still often understood within a vice-virtue continuum. In the nineteenth century the language was perhaps more refined, and the gamblers perhaps better described, but the dangers remained remarkably similar. In the preface to *The Gaming Table*, Andrew Steinmetz writes that gambling "slinks and skulks away into corners and holes, like a poisoned rat. Therefore, public morality has triumphed, or, to use the card-phrase, 'trumped' over this dreadful abuse; and the law has done its duty, or has reason to expect congratulation for its success, in 'putting down' gaming houses."[34] George Sala offered a description of the unsavory elements that characterized mid-nineteenth-century gambling. "Roguery," he writes, "is very catholic."

> Rascaldom is of no citizenship but the world.... There is freemasonry among knaves – a system of signs, a code of laws, an universal language; and he who would cheat at the roulette wheel here, if he could, and sometimes does manage to claim a stake that is not his, is the same swindler who would decoy you, Mr. Greenhorn, into a skittle-alley in Shoreditch, and plunder you of your last shilling – is the same Mr. Softroe who would meet you at the liquor-bar of a Mississippi steamer, inveigle you to play "poker," cheat you, ay, and quickly bowie-knife you, if you discovered that it was through cheating you had lost your dollars; who would degenerate into a pure thief and pilferer, as a Neapolitan or a Chinese; and who, at Singapore or Manilla, would insinuate himself into your bed-room at night, nude, his body copiously and completely anointed with palm-oil – as slippery a thief and as difficult to lay hold of as a fraudulent bank-director – and steal the very teeth out of your head, in addition to your watch, clothes, and loose cash, while you slept.[35]

Cheating, dishonesty, drinking, murder, coded homosexuality, and of course thievery – these were the characteristics one could find in a gambler, at least until the Blanc-style casinos opened. The descriptions of gambling found in Sala and Steinmetz, it is important to remember, appeared in pro-

---

[34] Steinmetz, *The Gaming Table*, vol. 1, viii.
[35] G. A. Sala, *Make Your Game, or, The Adventures of the Stout Gentleman, the Slim Gentleman, and the Man with the Iron Chest: A Narrative of the Rhine and Thereabouts* (Ward and Lock, 1860), 199–200.

gambling texts. Strangely enough, those critics who opposed gambling were often more restrained in their writings.

Attacking gambling because it allowed players to derive money from sources other than work was one ploy used by those who addressed the issue. Another common source of concern could be found in the behaviors that various games encouraged. Among these, dishonesty was commonly identified by observers as a significant source of concern. When critics suggested that gambling promoted dishonesty, however, they did not typically suggest that gamblers were dishonest in their relationships with loved ones or employers; a more worrisome problem was found in the ways that players were dishonest with each other. Bluffing was especially concerning. The author of the *Dictionary of Philosophy and Psychology* entry on gambling declares that bluffing

> is wrong because ... it is in a large sense dishonest – a point which, to the present writer, is a valid ethical objection, and the only one, to gambling. To pretend to know, to guess at an issue, to give the "bluff" to fortune seriously – the money or any other value staked is the warrant of its seriousness, and so is the passion of gain – is the opposite of knowledge, of the careful estimation of evidence and probabilities, of the drawing of legitimate inferences, upon which all normal honestly acquired values rest.[36]

The point of bluffing, as the author notes, is to mislead an opponent and thereby to confuse the correct estimation of chance. Such an approach to other people, not to mention the world at large, was considered unethical. The author's conclusion was that "To gamble seriously is to rebel against moral law for a reward."[37] However, games that were truly chance-based were ethically neutral, because probability and chance are neither honest nor dishonest: "The law of probabilities, so far as it is exact, is a reasonable resort; and the morality of the use of it rests upon grounds foreign to those of gambling."[38] The conclusion was that bluffing in particular and gambling in general resulted in a form of antisocial behavior. "Reverting to the question of social utility, we have now the point of view, that being ethically wrong – on the ground that it involves dishonesty – gambling is also socially condemnable; for dishonesty of the sort described is antisocial."[39] Bluffing – a key element in many games – was antisocial.

---

[36] Baldwin, ed., *Dictionary of Philosophy and Psychology*, 403–4.
[37] Baldwin, ed., *Dictionary of Philosophy and Psychology*, 404.
[38] Baldwin, ed., *Dictionary of Philosophy and Psychology*, 404.
[39] Baldwin, ed., *Dictionary of Philosophy and Psychology*, 404.

Privileging the inauthentic and the ability to misdirect an opponent, bluffing was evidence of all sorts of divisive behaviors.

These examples were only a few of the ways that gambling was understood to constitute a form of vice. Gambling generated disorder; it facilitated forms of social collapse and encouraged antisocial behavior. Because it opened access to inappropriate sources of gain, gambling encouraged both avarice and income inequality. It established the conditions of physical decline and of gender confusion. For many critics, gambling represented a spiritual threat as well. The evidence we have considered here shows, in other words, that gambling was never going to be universally embraced or understood as being a value-neutral pursuit. Some critics were never going to see the practice as innocent play, because it was also doing some other type of cultural or spiritual work that was deeply threatening both to individuals and to the larger social order. And yet there were others who understood gambling in much more positive ways. We turn now to consider briefly those who presented gambling not as a vice but as a virtue.

James Romain provided the clearest example of the genre. Romain attacked religious critiques of gambling and suggested that gambling was morally neutral. He demanded that critics of gambling prove why a "wager is wrong" and then suggested that gambling generally was not prohibited in the Decalogue and therefore it was impossible to levy any kind of religious critique of gambling.[40] Romain emphasized the nature of gambling as an experiment with chance and suggested that therefore there was never any legitimate ethical or moral concern that could be used to make gambling illegal. He writes that "if the Bible is a divine production, how can appeals to chance be stigmatized as vicious or irreligious? Also, it is not to be denied that chance, or casualty, enters very largely into every department of human action."[41] By this logic, gambling and gaming should be considered essentially morally neutral, given the ubiquity of chance in everyday life. Romain argues that some "moralists admit the validity of a transaction, notwithstanding it may depend upon chance. They will concede there is no intrinsic wrong in any species of game, unless there exists an inequality of chance or skill."[42] The application of mathematics to the understanding of chance is seen by the author to be a type of appeal to some underlying morality of the equality of chance.

---

[40] J. H. Romain, *Gambling: Or, Fortuna, Her Temple and Shrine. The True Philosophy and Ethics of Gambling* (Craig Press, 1891), 55.
[41] Romain, *Gambling*, 60.   [42] Romain, *Gambling*, 62.

There simply are no favorites. Attacking the work of mathematicians, whom he felt drew similar conclusions as had the moralists, Romain suggests that probability studies had been employed to equate chance and luck and thereby offer another way to discredit gambling.[43] Romain, on the other hand, believes in the idea of luck but suggests that it is not something that can be attached to a specific person:

> No intelligent gambler is a believer in "luck" as a *personal quality*. He recognizes the phenomena of chance. *How* they will operate is not known to the mathematician more than to him; the "chances" may result favorably or unfavorably for a gambler; the law may so work as to benefit him, or it may not. Whether "chance" or "luck," is immaterial to the issue.[44]

Based on this position, Romain joined an attack on probability studies more generally, scoffing at its theoretical foundations: "A method of reasoning from the happening of an event to the *probabilities* of one or another cause . . . In its very nature this is a vain-glorious pretension, and upon what is it based?"[45]

Romain suggested that there were neither moral nor scientific bases to prohibit gambling. If neither the Bible nor the work of probabiliticians was a legitimate source of critique, then gambling must be allowed. This line of argumentation also revolved around the cross-cultural ubiquity of gambling. Shifting to an anthropological discussion of human cultural difference (based on a description of foodways, and then a critique of Puritans), the point of which was to highlight the diversity of human experience and therefore the absence of any single moral system, Romain predictably returned to the conclusion that gambling must be legalized. "Right and wrong are not *essentially* different," he explained:

> All moral distinctions are a matter of arbitrary establishment by the "powers that be." That which is statutory, customary, fashionable, or generally habitual, is fit and proper. Conduct is purely a question of majority and might. Place gambling in the ascendant to-morrow and it would be just; or, as the major part of humanity, gamesters would be respectable; for an opinion commonly accepted is the correct opinion. With this as a guide, can the state hold the gamester reprobate? Society keeps changing its sentiments with the centuries. Absolutely, we can never know when it is right or when it is wrong.[46]

Suggesting that gambling was not bad, of course, was not the same as arguing that it was good. Romain took up that issue by invoking political

---

[43] Romain, *Gambling*, 64.   [44] Romain, *Gambling*, 64–65.   [45] Romain, *Gambling*, 65.
[46] Romain, *Gambling*, 70.

economy. "The *morale* of gambling is not to be determined by political economy, which is not a part of moral philosophy. It is not founded on the imperations of duty, but upon the adequate footing of desirableness of self-interest."[47] Gambling found itself in close relationship to luxury, and as in the luxury debates of the eighteenth century, it could be used to argue that leisure practices were ultimately good.[48] Romain vigorously disputed the claim that gamblers were "idle and non-productive," and used this argument to launch into another one that centered on the claim – repeated in texts like the ones above – that viewed gambling as a practice that derived wealth from chance and not from labor. "What is meant here by idleness and non-production?" Romain asks. "Does it signify that *labor* is the proper basis of exchangeable value: the *only* just source of what is called wealth? If so, the condemnation includes all who obtain wealth without working for it.... What, then, of assumed rights, in the form of profits, dividends, rent and interest? If *true* wealth is the outcome of physical labor, are not banker, broker, middle man, landlord, capitalist, gentleman of leisure and gambler on the same footing"?[49] He continues this line of argumentation in another passage, asking rhetorically: "Now, some one may ask: 'Is not gambling immoral to the extent it may induce a reliance upon chance for a livelihood, instead of patient industry'?"[50] Romain concludes on the basis of this logic that gambling cannot be called "immoral, sinful, or irreligious," in part because "it is clear the propensity to gamble is as natural as the temperament or complexion."[51] Romain, in his roundabout way, makes an important point about the economic logic of the nineteenth century and the ways that gambling might be usefully understood as an equivalent to those who made their living from investments and not their own labor.

While many observers noted the ways that gambling had an affinal relationship to other forms of risk management (insurance) and speculative chance (stock market speculation), Romain equated the three. He writes, "Wherein, essentially, does gaming differ from speculation or insurance?... In neither instance can the result be foretold: the gamester may or may not win, the speculator may or may not realize a profit, the assured may or may not forfeit his life policy, or lose by fire. In every transaction, fortuity is the controlling element."[52] By this logic, gambling was no different from other pursuits deemed respectable, suggesting it was folly to label the pastime as a form of vice. Indeed, Romain denied that

---

[47] Romain, *Gambling*, 87. [48] Romain, *Gambling*, 88. [49] Romain, *Gambling*, 91.
[50] Romain, *Gambling*, 100. [51] Romain, *Gambling*, 135. [52] Romain, *Gambling*, 99.

gambling was a vice: "If a man chooses to risk his money, on a game of cards, he has a perfect right to do so, in the abstract, and no man, or any body of men, has a right to forbid him."[53] Turning to the legality of gambling, Romain's position was clear, if predictable. He took a libertarian approach, suggesting that one should be free to do what one wishes, and identifying gambling as natural and therefore legal: "The keepers of gambling resorts are denounced, as though they were responsible for the gambling propensity in mankind. Now, resorts for gambling do not cause the passion. It is a tendency to which all men are prone, more or less. 'The essential fact is the existence of this passion. There can never be any great difficulty in obtaining the means for its gratification.'"[54] A natural passion should not be legally suppressed, especially if no one was victimized by satisfying it. Defining vice as a crime against the self that therefore fell outside the realm of police supervision and control, Romain also refused to acknowledge the claims of the moralizers who depicted gambling as a grotesque violation of social norms. Suggesting that gambling was a social scenario in which all players were willing participants was a key to his argument. "To gamble with another," Romain writes, "is not to assault his person or property by main force. To wager or bet upon the laws of chance, deceit aside, is not to kill, maim, rob, or cheat your fellow man; the players freely participate in the hope of gain or for amusement. Then wherein is the action either felonious or tortious?"[55] When the participants in a free society, with equal knowledge of the potential outcomes, join a game, Romain argues, who can rightly call that a crime?

Romain's robust defense of gambling centered mainly on denying its status as a vice. He did not spend much effort providing an affirmative case for gambling that isolated or celebrated elements he considered positive. Others took up that position, even if they themselves embraced elements of an antigambling position. Clemens France, for instance, suggested that gambling created a type of self in which certain personality traits, including a gift for misdirection and a comfort with inauthenticity, were curated. He writes that the success of a gambler is based on the

> cultivation of a calm and passionate demeanor in moments of crisis, never displaying any emotion or hesitancy; the ability to recover quickly from defeat; being ever vigilant and attentive; acquiring the habit of studying your opponent most closely; few men being better "sizers up" of men than the gambler; a sufficient degree of caution tempering your boldness; the

---

[53] Romain, *Gambling*, 203–4.   [54] Romain, *Gambling*, 205.   [55] Romain, *Gambling*, 223.

learning how to bear sanely good fortune, as well as bad. These fit closely the essentials of any active, exploiting life. But for its costliness and dangers, no better education for life among men could be devised than the gambling table – especially the poker game.[56]

Later critics also suggested a positive role for gaming, but not for gambling. Writing in 1915, Lester Donahue wrote that "gaming as a means to an end is necessary and useful, since it affords a proper field for the activities of the tired mind or wearied body. Gambling, however, [is] a vicious outgrowth of gaming and [is] a practice to be avoided by all."[57] In this way gambling is fitted into a larger system of behaviors that align generally with the traits that also dominated the world of the bourgeois master of industry. Gaming and gambling, in other words, might cultivate certain habits of mind and various practices that could assist a person in their professional life.

Gambling represented to some observers a type a civilized proxy for much more dangerous and destructive pursuits. If gambling and play could be seen as an ersatz form of warfare, competition, and violence, then certainly its expression through a formalized and well-mannered black-tie solemnity could not be all bad. If gambling was simply a modernized and updated form of atavistic behaviors that all humans experienced, then it could not be taken as evidence of anything inherently or morally wrong. And given the way that gambling was represented as a common human expression, any localized suppression of the practice represented a fruitless attempt to shape human passions in impossible ways.

But gambling also always had its detractors. People hated gambling because it represented a way to make money that seemingly avoided labor. They hated it because it taught people to act in dishonest ways, or to misdirect and take advantage of the unequal skill or knowledge of others. The practice of bluffing generated widespread opprobrium. Some suggested that gambling's social consequences – the taking of profit from another person's work – made it impossible to incorporate gambling into any kind of social environment based on communitarian principles. And we should not ignore the voices of contemporaries who saw an undeniable seediness and sadness in gambling in the nineteenth century, and who connected it to addiction, an inability to navigate reality, and suicide. If Monte Carlo, as Somerset Maugham famously declared, was a "sunny

---

[56] C. J. France, "The Gambling Impulse," *The American Journal of Psychology*, 13/3 (1902), 364–407, 386.
[57] L. B. Donahue, "Psychology of Gambling," *America*, 12/24 (1915), 581–82, 582.

place for shady people," then gambling was the reason. Gambling, as we have seen in this chapter, was social, natural, and, more than anything, historical. Connecting these three areas of human experience allows us to see more clearly the ways that people at the time defined the essential qualities of what it meant to be a person.

Conclusion

Writing in 1669, the author of *The Nicker Nicked* equated the liminal status of the sailor with that of the gambler. The question was, "Whether Men, in Ships at Sea, were to be accounted amongst the Living or the Dead, because there were but few Inches betwixt them and Drowning? The same Query may be made of the great Gamesters, though their Estates be never so considerable, Whether they are to be esteemed poor or rich, since there are but a few Casts at Dice, betwixt a Person of Fortune (in that Circumstance) and a Beggar?"[1] Like an early modern version of Schrödinger's cat, the writer wondered whether a sailor could ever be judged accurately as alive or dead while unobservable and at sea. The same position on the wheel of fortune was occupied by the gambler, who could be both fortunate and unfortunate at the same moment. Only in hindsight – or through the lens of history – would we know for sure which state was occupied.

The passage points to one of the central arguments of this book: that early modern conceptions of indeterminacy and fate operated on a fundamentally different basis than nineteenth-century ones. Indeed, the nineteenth century was the pivotal period during which fate began to be rigorously tested and explored – not only in theory but also in practice. And the new casino was a prime location for that exploration.

Gambling was able to perform this work in the nineteenth century because of the way it leveraged three major developments. The first of these was political revolution. As we saw, the 1830 revolution in France culminated in an official prohibition of gambling in that country. This encouraged other states – first those along the Rhine in independent German polities like Bad Homburg and later Monte Carlo – to permit institutionalized forms of gambling, and even to support them financially, legally, and, to some small extent, militarily. The second development

---

[1] *The Nicker Nicked, or, The Cheats of Gaming Discovered*, 3rd ed. (1669), 96.

centers on the creation of new forms of transportation. The railroad not only revolutionized military and commercial transport, but also brought vast urban populations access to newly developed resorts in the Rhineland and the Riviera. Third, resorts took advantage of new communications structures – like the newspaper and magazine – to advertise the wonders available. Each of these transformations was significant, but together they allowed an institutionalized form of gambling – as we saw in Bad Homburg and Monte Carlo – to develop.

The casinos in the Rhineland and the Riviera tapped into new transportation and communication networks, and they were flexible enough to take advantage of the changing political map of Europe. The casinos found success amid these large structural transformations affecting the continent. But they also were successful for the experiences they offered. Nineteenth-century resort casinos, as we saw, projected a new type of sociability that exuded a sense of exclusivity *and* democracy at once. Entrance to the casino was carefully monitored and cultivated, but once inside, its economic logic was democratic and transparent. The money economy heightened – and flattened – the economic character of the clientele. The casino was also an environment that embraced social mixture. It allowed men and women entry to the gaming rooms, and as we saw, this component of the social environment encouraged interactions between people within a space that was no longer completely under the control of employer, church, or family. The casino also attracted a transnational and polyglot clientele, and impresarios like François Blanc used this fact to further heighten the reputation of their casinos. In all these ways, the nineteenth-century casino performed a novel type of cultural and social work. The casino, to put it simply, presented new opportunities for people to interact in fresh ways.

Nineteenth-century casinos were physical expressions of contemporary ideas about fate and agency. Gambling represented a systematic and intellectually ambitious attempt to come to terms with indeterminacy. Probability studies, which had always been oriented around gaming and play, found in the casino an incredible proliferation of laboratory experiments that were used to refine an understanding of chance. As we saw, probability studies developed in the nineteenth century as a language that existed at the crossroads of scientific and nonscientific preoccupation with agency. By attempting to understand probability, nineteenth-century gamblers were also seeking to understand the degree to which they were able to influence the course of events. There were few topics more significant in the nineteenth century than the issue of determining who could do what, and why. This question informed economics, colonization, the issue of political rights, and even revolutionary terrorism.[2] Gamblers in nineteenth-century casinos wrestled with the reality of their own agency with every wager. The intense debates about chance and luck, about the ability of "systems" to transform one's chances of exerting successfully some kind of influence over events, and about the occult logic of "evening" were nothing less than ruminations on the question of whether people had the power to change things. And in the nineteenth century, this meant that the question – and the answer – was posed in a peculiarly monetized form. The casino was simply the location within which that extended conversation took place, and the intensity with which a discussion of chance and luck revolved around those bigger questions indicates the significance of those categories to people at the time. Indeed, discussions about casino gambling provided a type of shorthand for the question of whether – as well as when, how, and under what circumstances – a person exerts influence on the universe.

When Fyodor Dostoyevsky wrote *The Gambler* in a terrifying burst of creativity in 1866, it came on the heels of the completion of *Crime and Punishment*, a novel that was itself interrupted by the attempted assassination of the Tsar. When Dostoyevsky's gambler feels "as if fate were urging me on," he was also expressing a larger question: How do people influence fate and the reality of their circumstances?[3] The gambler's fallacy may be fallacious, in other words, but the potency of the idea that a person could bend the curve of chance remained undeniably important, and it was only in the nineteenth-century casino that this concept could be so sharply – and at times tragically – expressed.

The nineteenth-century casino also occasioned a prolonged discussion of the body, feeling, and mind, and there is a wide recognition of culture's impact on the body. This impact not only was displayed in the descriptions of somatic reactions to gambling and play that populated nineteenth-century observations of gambling, but also could be seen in the lengthy depictions of how gambling had left its evolutionary mark on the human body: "Gambling, in some form, is a propensity of the general mind: an inclination now hereditary in the race."[4] The suggestion that gambling was a part of human evolutionary history, but one that perhaps could indicate degeneracy or was racially expressed in perverse ways, demonstrates the

[2] C. Verhoeven, *The Odd Man Karakozov: Imperial Russia, Modernity, and the Birth of Terrorism* (Cornell University Press, 2009).

[3] F. Dostoyevsky, *The Gambler and Other Stories* (Penguin, 2010), 241.

[4] J. H. Romain, *Gambling: Or, Fortuna, Her Temple and Shrine. The True Philosophy and Ethics of Gambling* (Craig Press, 1891), 132.

degree to which gambling – and the casino – were not external to nineteenth-century attempts to understand human development and racial categories, but inherent to them. It was impossible, in other words, to discuss gambling without talking about where it came from, why it developed, and who was susceptible to an inability to respect its limits. The democratic answer to those questions was to suggest that gambling had a long pedigree and universal quality. In its transcultural prominence, gambling might be one of those threads that joined the human family together. But it also contained darker elements, and perhaps suggested a primitive understanding of time, causality, and religious instrumentality. Even liberals like Thorstein Veblen could suggest that gambling promoted a belief in a type of occult agency.[5] But he also hinted at a conservative answer to the question of gambling's provenance that suggested it was linked to degeneracy, primitivity, and racial inferiority.

Those critics who situated gambling in a negative light often commented on the emotional and psychological demands it made on people. The recognition that gambling might generate a flood or a cascade of emotions in people, and that these emotions could be so intensely experienced that people could be rendered insensate or emotionally deadened, was a way to frame the experience of gambling as one directly tied to emotion. These emotional and psychological confrontations with indeterminacy – exhaustion, confusion, enervation – were frequently understood to be damaging or even a cause of insanity. In this way, nineteenth-century gambling should be seen as a practice that was implicated in the development of behavioral psychology in that it generated risk-reward cycles that influenced behavior in dramatic and predictable ways. Recognizing the effect that gambling had on players, nineteenth-century observers could consider how the self, the environment, and behavior all related to one another.

One conclusion that could be drawn – "To gamble would seem instinctive – inherent in the souls of mankind and fostered by the very nature of their environment" – indicates how gambling was inserted into the heart of the questions that nineteenth-century critics were asking about the nature of humanity and its origins.[6] The answer that one critic developed to these questions suggests that humanity was united in ways that were possible to discover only within the casino. "History reveals that all alike are possessed by this subtle passion – male and female, young and old, good and bad,

[5] T. Veblen, *The Theory of the Leisure Class: An Economic Study of Institutions* (Macmillan and Company, 1912), 295.
[6] Romain, *Gambling*, 22.

wise and unwise, rich and poor, the exalted and the lowly."[7] To claim in 1891 that gambling was universal and that its lessons could be applied in any corner of the earth was a revolutionary assertion. And the twofold lesson, that "Truth is not absolute but relative" and that "To live is to gamble.... Everywhere uncertainty is the rule and certainty the exception," could hardly have been more destabilizing to a social order built on enlightenment principles.[8]

[7] Romain, *Gambling*, 22.   [8] Romain, *Gambling*, 22–23.

Bibliography

Adorno, T. W., *The Stars Down to Earth and Other Essays on The Irrational in Culture* (Routledge, 2002)

Alaluf, Y. B., *The Emotional Economy of Holidaymaking: Health, Pleasure, and Class in Britain, 1870–1918* (Oxford University Press, 2021)

Appadurai, A. (ed.), *The Social Life of Things: Commodities in Cultural Perspective* (Cambridge University Press, 1986)

Bakhtin, M. M., *Rabelais and His World* (Indiana University Press, 1984)

Baldwin, J. M. (ed.), *Dictionary of Philosophy and Psychology* (Macmillan, 1901)

Baudelaire, C., *The Flowers of Evil* (New Directions Publishing, 1989)

Beard, G., "Neurasthenia, or Nervous Exhaustion," *The Boston Medical and Surgical Journal*, 80/13 (1869), 217–21

Blume, M., *Côte d'Azur: Inventing the French Riviera* (Thames & Hudson, 1992)

Braude, M., *Making Monte Carlo: A History of Speculation and Spectacle* (Simon & Schuster, 2016)

Brown, B., "Thing Theory," *Critical Inquiry*, 28/1 (2001), 1–22

Brown, B. (ed.), *Things* (University of Chicago Press, 2004)

Carter, E. J., "The Green Table: Gambling Casinos, Capitalist Culture, and Modernity in Nineteenth-Century Germany," PhD dissertation, University of Illinois at Urbana-Champaign, 2002

Chekhov, A. P., *Letters of Anton Chekhov to His Family and Friends* (Macmillan and Company, 1920)

Clark, C. M., *Iron Kingdom: The Rise and Downfall of Prussia, 1600–1947* (Allen Lane, 2006)

Confino, A., *The Nation as a Local Metaphor: Württemberg, Imperial Germany, and National Memory, 1871–1918* (University of North Carolina Press, 1997)

"The Congress at Baden," *The British Medical Journal*, 2/979 (1879), 556

Corti, E. C., *The Wizard of Monte Carlo* (E. P. Dutton, 1935)

Coy, J. P., *The Devil's Art: Divination and Discipline in Early Modern Germany* (University of Virginia Press, 2020)

Crowe, W., "The Game Season at Spürt," *Household Words*, 240 (1854), 262–64

Daston, L. (ed.), *Biographies of Scientific Objects* (University of Chicago Press, 2000)

Daston, L., *Classical Probability in the Enlightenment* (Princeton University Press, 1995)

Donahue, L. B., "Psychology of Gambling," *America*, 12/24 (1915), 581–82

Dostoyevsky, F., *Complete Letters* (Ardis, 1988), vol. 2

The Gambler and Other Stories (Penguin, 2010)

Foster, H., *Prosthetic Gods* (MIT Press, 2004)

France, C. J., "The Gambling Impulse," *The American Journal of Psychology*, 13/3 (1902), 364–407

Frevert, U., "Was haben Gefühle in der Geschichte zu suchen? (What Has History Got to Do with Emotions?)," *Geschichte und Gesellschaft*, 35/2 (2009), 183–208

Galison, P., *Einstein's Clocks and Poincaré's Maps: Empires of Time* (W. W. Norton, 2003)

"Gambling," *The Mathematical Gazette*, 15/212 (1931), 347–58

Geschiere, P., *The Modernity of Witchcraft: Politics and the Occult in Postcolonial Africa* (University Press of Virginia, 1997)

Gibbons, H. A., *Riviera Towns* (R. M. McBride & Co, 1920)

Hale, J. A. S., *The French Riviera: A Cultural History* (Oxford University Press, 2009)

Hey, R., *Three Dissertations; on the Pernicious Effects of Gaming, on Duelling and on Suicide* (J. Smith, 1812)

Hillard, D., H. Lempa, and R. A. Spinney (eds.), *Feelings Materialized: Emotions, Bodies, and Things in Germany, 1500–1950* (Berghahn Books, 2020)

Hoffmann, E. T. A., *The Tales of Hoffmann* (Frederick Ungar Publishing Co, 1963)

"Homburger Kur- und Bade-list: Die Quellen im Faksimile." www.lagis-hessen .de/de/klhg.

Huff, D., *How to Take a Chance* (W. W. Norton, 1959)

Hunt, L., *Inventing Human Rights: A History* (W. W. Norton & Co., 2008)

James, W., *The Will to Believe: And Other Essays in Popular Philosophy* (Longmans, Green, and Company, 1911)

Journal de Monaco. journaldemonaco.gouv.mc/Journaux/1863/Journal-0261.

Karl Baedeker (firm), *A Handbook for Travellers on The Rhine, from Holland to Switzerland* (K. Baedeker, 1864)

The Rhine from Rotterdam to Constance: Handbook for Travellers (Karl Baedeker, 1882)

Kavanagh, T. M., *Dice, Cards, Wheels: A Different History of French Culture* (University of Pennsylvania Press, 2005)

Enlightenment and the Shadows of Chance: The Novel and the Culture of Gambling in Eighteenth-Century France (The Johns Hopkins University Press, 1993)

Kern, S., *A Cultural History of Causality: Science, Murder Novels, and Systems of Thought* (Princeton University Press, 2004)

The Culture of Time and Space, 1880–1918 (Harvard University Press, 2003)

Keynes, J. M., *A Treatise on Probability* (Macmillan and Company, 1921)

Kingston, C., *The Romance of Monte Carlo* (J. L. the Bodley Head, 1925)

Koshar, R., *German Travel Cultures* (Berg, 2000)

Histories of Leisure (Berg, 2002)

Kroen, S., *Politics and Theater: The Crisis of Legitimacy in Restoration France, 1815–1830* (University of California Press, 2000)

Lears, T. J. J., *Something for Nothing: Luck in America* (Viking, 2003)

Ledger, S., and R. Luckhurst (eds.), *The Fin de Siècle: A Reader in Cultural History, c. 1880–1900* (Oxford University Press, 2000)

Lempa, H., *Spaces of Honor: Making German Civil Society, 1700–1914* (University of Michigan Press, 2021)

Lindner, G. A., *Manual of Empirical Psychology as an Inductive Science: A Text-book for High Schools and Colleges* (D. C. Heath & Company, 1889)

Macknik, S., and S. Martinez-Conde, *Sleights of Mind: What the Neuroscience of Magic Reveals about Our Brains* (Henry Holt, 2010)

Maxim, H. S., *Monte Carlo: Facts and Fallacies* (Grant Richards, 1904)

Morton, C., *The gaming-humor considered and reproved, or, The passion-pleasure and exposing money to hazard by play, lot or wager examined by a well-wisher to mankind* (Tho. Cockerill, 1684)

Morton, S., *At Odds: Gambling and Canadians, 1919–1969* (University of Toronto Press, 2003)

Müller, F., *Treatise on the Use of the Mineral Waters of Homburg*, 3rd ed. (Louis Schick, 1865)

Münsterberg, H., *Psychology and Social Sanity* (Doubleday, Page & Co., 1914)

The Nicker Nicked, or, The Cheats of Gaming Discovered, 3rd ed. (1669)

Nietzsche, F., *Twilight of the Idols* (Oxford University Press, 2008)

Pascal, B., *Pensées and Other Writings* (Oxford University Press, 2008)

Pearson, K., *The Chances of Death, and Other Studies in Evolution* (E. Arnold, 1897)

Pflanze, O., *The Unification of Germany, 1848–1871* (R. E. Krieger, 1979)

Pinkney, D. H., *French Revolution of 1830* (Princeton University Press, 1972)

Poincaré, H., "Chance," *The Monist*, 22/1 (1912), 31–52

Poley, J., *The Devil's Riches: A Modern History of Greed* (Berghahn Books, 2016)

Porter, T. M., *The Rise of Statistical Thinking, 1820–1900* (Princeton University Press, 1986)

Proctor, R. A., *Chance and Luck*, 2nd ed. (Longmans, Green, and Company, 1887)

Rae, W. F., "Play and Players on the Riviera," *The Nineteenth Century*, 27/ February (1890), 240–57

Reddy, W. M., *The Navigation of Feeling: A Framework for the History of Emotions* (Cambridge University Press, 2001)

Reith, G., *The Age of Chance: Gambling in Western Culture* (Routledge, 1999)

"Review of Chance and Luck: A Discussion of the Laws of Luck, Coincidences, Wagers, Lotteries, and the Fallacies of Gambling; With Notes on Poker and Martingales," *Science*, 10/233 (1887), 43–44

Romain, J. H., *Gambling: or, Fortuna, Her Temple and Shrine. The True Philosophy and Ethics of Gambling* (Craig Press, 1891)

Rosenwein, B. H., "Worrying about Emotions in History," *The American Historical Review*, 107/3 (2002), 821–45

Ryland, F., *Questions on Psychology, Metaphysics, and Ethics* (S. Sonnenschein, Lowrey & Company, 1887)

Saige, G., *Monaco, ses origines et son histoire; d'aprés les documents originaux* (Impr. de Monaco, 1897)

Sala, G. A., *Make Your Game, or, The Adventures of the Stout Gentleman, the Slim Gentleman, and the Man with the Iron Chest: A Narrative of the Rhine and Thereabouts* (Ward and Lock, 1860)

Sala, G. A., "Saxon-les-bains: A Study in the Psychology of Gambling," *The Spectator* (1873), 1242–43

Scheer, M., "Are Emotions a Kind of Practice (And Is That What Makes Them Have a History)? A Bourdieuian Approach to Understanding Emotion," *History and Theory*, 51/2 (2012), 193–220

Schivelbusch, W., *The Railway Journey: The Industrialization of Time and Space in the Nineteenth Century* (University of California Press, 2014)

Schooling, J. H., "Lotteries, Luck, Chance, and Gambling Systems. Part I – Lotteries," *Pall Mall Magazine*, 19/77 (1899), 543–52

"Lotteries, Luck, Chance, and Gambling Systems. Part II – Luck," *Pall Mall Magazine*, 20/81 (1900), 84–93

"Lotteries, Luck, Chance, and Gambling Systems. Part III – Chance," *Pall Mall Magazine*, 20/81 (1900), 262–72

"Lotteries, Luck, Chance, and Gambling Systems. Part IV – Gambling Systems," *Pall Mall Magazine*, 20/81 (1900), 377–86

Schwartz, D. G., *Roll the Bones: The History of Gambling* (Gotham Books, 2006)

"The Science of Chance," *The Saturday Review of Politics, Literature, Science, and Art*, 88 (1899), 97–98

Silver, N., *The Signal and the Noise: Why So Many Predictions Fail – But Some Don't* (Penguin Press, 2012)

Simmel, G., *On Individuality and Social Forms* (University of Chicago Press, 1971)

The Philosophy of Money, 3rd ed. (Routledge, 2004)

Smith, H. W., *Germany: A Nation in Its Time: Before, during, and after Nationalism, 1500–2000* (Liveright Publishing, 2022)

Smith, M. M., *Sensing the Past: Seeing, Hearing, Smelling, Tasting, and Touching in History* (University of California Press, 2007)

Stacpoole, M. de V., *Monte Carlo: A Novel* (Dodd, Mead and Co., 1913)

Stearns, P. N., *1848: The Revolutionary Tide in Europe* (Norton, 1974)

Stearns, P. N. and C. Z. Stearns, "Emotionology: Clarifying the History of Emotions and Emotional Standards," *The American Historical Review*, 90/4 (1985), 813–36

Steinmetz, A., *The Gaming Table: Its Votaries and Victims*, 2 vols. (Tinsley Brothers, 1870)

Stuart, K., *Defiled Trades and Social Outcasts: Honor and Ritual Pollution in Early Modern Germany* (Cambridge University Press, 1999)

Symonds, J. A., and H. F. Brown, *John Addington Symonds, a Biography*, 2nd ed. (Smith, Elder, & Co.; Charles Scribner's Sons, 1903)

Thomas, W. I., "The Gaming Instinct," *American Journal of Sociology*, 6/6 (1901), 750–63

Tijms, H., *Understanding Probability* (Cambridge University Press, 2012)

Twombly, C. G., "The Evil of Gambling: Cancer on Moral Life of Community," *Pennsylvania School Journal*, 56 (1908), 284–87

Veblen, T., *The Theory of the Leisure Class: An Economic Study of Institutions* (Macmillan and Company, 1912)

Venn, J., *The Logic of Chance: An Essay on the Foundations and Province of the Theory of Probability, with Especial Reference to Its Application to Moral and Social Science* (Macmillan, 1866)

Verhoeven, C., *The Odd Man Karakozov: Imperial Russia, Modernity, and the Birth of Terrorism* (Cornell University Press, 2009)

Weber, E., *Peasants into Frenchmen: The Modernization of Rural France, 1870–1914* (Stanford University Press, 1976)

Wilkins, W. H., and H. Vivian, *The Green Bay Tree: A Tale of To-day* (Hutchinson & Company, 1894)

Young, N., "Systems of Gambling," *National Review*, 18/29 (1892), 449–60

Index

addiction, 170
  psychological effects of, 170
advertisement, 14, 26, 42, 98, 200
agency, 8, 111, 173, 200, 201
  and luck, 149
aggression, 9
amnesia, 144
anti-Semitism, 37
anxiety, 159
aristocrats, 143
aristocrats
  Russian, 17
Arnauld, Antoine, 124
avarice, 154, 168, 169, 183, 193

Bad Homburg, 12, 199
  depictions of, 32–33
  description of casino, 48
  development of, 14–15
  development of casino at, 12
  as health spa, 40
  marketing, 16
  reading room, 57
  as resort, 31
  visitors to, 13, 18, 27
Baden-Baden, 11
Baedeker guides, 34, 69
Baker, Josephine, 37
Baudelaire, Charles, 67
Beard, George Miller, 75
behavior, 8
behavioralism, 154, 170, 202
Bénazet, Jacques, 11
Blanc, François, 10
  Blanc, Louis, 10
Blanc, François, 28, 39, 79, 102, 200
  early life, 10–11
  innovations to casino gambling, 13–14
  as transnational European, 28
Blanc, Louis
  death, 13

bluffing, 192
body, 8, 201
Bonaparte, Charles Lucien, 20
Braude, Mark, 6

California, 35
Cannes, 48
Cannon, Walter Bradford, 145
capitalism, 155, 183
Lametz, Maria Caroline Gibert de, Princess
      Consort of Monaco, 21
Carter, Everett John, 6, 45
casino
  architectural qualities of, 55
  and creative nonfiction, 31
  and emotion, 74
  as emotional space, 160
  employees described, 71
  as experience of the sublime, 77
  as experimental space, 89, 105, 106, 109, 200
  as heterosocial space, 200
  as inverted space, 54
  and money economy, 186
  and observation, 143
  and passion, 68
  as passionless, 157
  as place, 31
  resort, 2
  as sacred space, 55
  and sexual difference, 142
  soundscape, 70
  as space, 43
  spatial qualities of, 57
  and spirit, 77
  and untethered emotions, 77
causality, 6, 97, 98
causation, 89, 91, 94
  historical, 98
chance, 8, 91, 100, 102, 105, 106, 111, 191, 201
  culture of, 3
  history of, 113

chance (cont.)
　logic of, 112
　and mathematics, 114
　and morality, 113
　and novelty, 115
　and predictability, 114
chaos, 106, 108
Charles III, Prince of Monaco, 22
Chekhov, Anton, 39
class, 38–39, 83
　in Dostoyevsky, 38
climate, 39, 43
colonization, 200
communication, 8, 200
Congress of Vienna, 12
consumer revolution, 89
Corti, Egon, 11
court society, 43
courtship, 86
cures, 40

Daval, Pierre August, 22
decline, 193
democracy, 7, 200
development
　human, 9
dishonesty, 192
disorder, 193
divination, 133, 175
doctrine of averages, 92
doctrine of chances, 92, 96
Donahue, Lester, 197
Dostoyevsky, Fyodor, 7, 143, 201
　addiction in *The Gambler*, 170
　and chance, 114
　and fate, 116
　and the gambler's body, 144
　The Gambler, 20
　as gambler, 158, 170
　on luck, 129
　on pleasures of gambling, 157
dueling, 1, 140

earthquake, 54
egoism, 162
Elias, Norbert, 189
Ellis, Havelock, 47
emotion, 8, 202
　and ability to self-govern, 154
　and didacticism, 159
　and flux, 160
　and gambling before 1800, 153
　and gambling loss, 161
　and imagination, 159
　intensification of, 153

overstimulation of, 161
　utilitarian theory of, 154
empathy, 159
enlightenment, 3, 203
Ense, Karl August Varnagen von, 17
Erskine, Fitzroy S., 102
eugenics, 116
evening, 91, 95, 97, 101, 127
events
　dependent, 91, 94
　independent, 91, 95, 103
evolution, 108, 145, 147, 201
　and luck, 131, 149
excitement, 103
exclusivity, 24, 200
Eynaud, Adolphe, 22

fate, 8, 116, 199
Ferdinand, Landgrave of Hesse-Homburg, 27
fight or flight, 145
Flammarion, Nicolas Camille, 121
Florestan, Prince of Monaco, 22
Foster, Hal, 150
France
　ancien regime, 139
　gambling in, 11
France, Clemens J., 119, 133
　on certainty, 178
　on gambling and race, 147
　on luck, 148
　luck and psychological satisfaction, 136
　on pyschology of gambling, 175
　and psychology of uncertainty, 119
　on the self, 196
　universality of gambling, 147
Frankfurt Parliament, 18
Frederick William IV, King of Prussia, 20
Freud, Sigmund, 189
Frith, William Powell, 55

gambler professional, 87
　compared to sailor, 199
gambler's fallacy, 91, 94, 101, 201
gambling
　aleatory vs. agonistic, 15
　and anti-democratic practices, 81
　as anti-social, 155, 162, 192
　aristocracy, 16
　as atavistic, 150, 177
　bourgeoisie, 16
　casino, 5, 7
　as compulsion, 168
　and deadening of emotion, 158
　defense of, 196
　and democracy, 81

early modern critiques of, 154
effect on social relations, 172
eighteenth century, 15
emotional tension, 75
and emotional disconnection, 164
and emotional distress, 156
and emotional flux, 157
and emotional frenzy, 150
and emotional intensity, 158
and emotional stability, 154
and emotional violence, 163
and emotional wound, 162
as ersatz practice, 147
as ersatz violence, 189
ethical critique of, 186
and evolution, 145–51
evolution of, 8
and heterosociability, 141
how-to manuals, 69
and individualism, 163
industrial, 16, 35
and insanity, 168, 175
and legalization, 194
legality of, 19
legality of in Prussia, 27, 28
lure of, 67
as modern expression of primitive forms, 189
mania, 169
as morally neutral, 193
and natural selection, 147, 148
origins, 1
as passion, 186
philosophy of, 118
physical interactions during, 141
and pleasure, 162
as prior form of existence, 182
as proxy, 197
and psychosis, 175
and risk, 119
and the "savage", 146, 149
and sense of self, 173
somatic response to, 140–41, 144–45
state-sanctioned, 188
systems, 19, 87
and time, 186
as transational industry, 79
and transparency, 83
tutorials, 71
and typology, 86
universal, 1
versus stock market, 188
games
    social, 45
gaming tables
    descriptions of, 68, 70

gender, 83–86, 140, 142, 152, 193
    and risk, 120
Gibbons, Herbert, 36, 38
Gogol, Nicolai, 39
Gould, Jay, 102
greed, 153, 172, 184

happiness, 154
hatred, 164
health, 41–42, 140
    circulation, 41
hemorrhoids, 41
Hensel, Marie, 13, 79
heterosocialibility
    descriptions of, 80–81
Hey, Richard, 139, 154, 168
history, 99
Hoffmann, E. T. A., 7, 113, 141
    and chance, 113
    emotion in "Gambler's Luck",
        155–56
    on emotion, 155
    "Gambler's Luck", 43
honesty, 88, 89
honor, 132, 155
Huguelin, Magdeleine-Victoire, 12
Hunt, Lynn, 159
hysteria, 41

imagination
    of gambler, 133
indeterminacy, 4, 200, 202
industry
    health, 40
    leisure, 40
inheritance, 146
insanity, 161
insurance, 99, 187, 195
    versus gambling, 186

James, William, 118

Kavanagh, Thomas M., 5, 139
Kern, Stephen, 112
Keynes, John Maynard, 104, 109
Kingston, Charles, 48, 105, 135
Kisselev, Sophie, 86
knowledge, historical, 99

Law of Large Numbers, 91
Lears, Jackson, 2–3
    on luck, 124
leisure, 2, 43, 145
Lindner, Gustav Adolf, 163, 174
logic, industrial, 92

Louis III, Grand Duke of Hesse-Darmstadt, 27
Louis Napoleon, 19
Louis-Philippe, King of France, 11
luck, 7, 8, 105, 111, 150
    and agency, 129, 136
    Arnauld on, 124
    evolution of, 145
    as external force, 127
    and industrial logic, 127
    Montaigne on, 124
    Paracelsus on, 124
    representations of, 124
    and social science, 135
Ludwig, Landgrave of Hesse-Homburg, 12

magic, 123
Marbe, Karl, 109
market speculation
    versus gambling, 188
martingale, 94, 96, 100, 102, 106
Marx, Karl, 39
matchmaking, 142
mathematics, 102, 104
maturity of chances, 94, 99
Maugham, Somerset, 197
Maxim, Hiram, 8, 46, 81, 100, 105
    descriptions of gamblers, 87
    on gambling as aggression, 181
    on luck, 133
    on superstition, 177
    on systems, 100–6
Mediterranean, 8
modernity, 4
Monaco, 21
    as space, 35
    travel to, 23
monetization, 201
money economy, 200
Montaigne, Michel de, 124
Monte Carlo, 6
    architectural style, 57
    concert hall, 57
    development of, 21–26
    as paradise, 48
    psychology of isolation, 24
    as spectacle, 26
    vistors to, 26
Morton, Charles, 183
Müller, Frederick, 40
Münsterberg, Hugo, 151, 187
    on gambling and race, 151

neurasthenia, 75
Nietzsche, Friedrich, 97

occult, 92, 103, 133, 174, 201

Palais-Royale, 11
Paracelsus, 124
Pascal, Blaise, 182
passion, 55, 103
    and luck, 130
    and youth, 153
Pearson, Karl, 106, 109, 115
    on Monte Carlo, 106–9
permutation theory, 115
Phillip, Landgrave of Hesse-Homburg, 13
physiognomy, 143
play, 3, 9, 153, 183
    early modern theories of, 183
    morality of, 183
Poincaré, Henri, 115, 121
    and chance, 121
    and historical thinking, 121
    and laws of chance, 122
    and roulette, 122
poker, 132
Popular Front, 39
probability, 8, 96, 107, 154
    history of, 89, 109
Proctor, Richard, 95, 117, 127, 162, 173
    luck vs. superstition, 130
    on luck, 130, 132
    on the "savage mind", 146
professors, 87, 143
providence, 113
psychology, 8
    and uncertainty, 178
punting, 100

quantification, 90
quantum mechanics, 3

race, 37–38, 145, 190, 201
Rae, W. Fraser, 36, 97
    on emotion in gambling, 166
railways, 30, 32, 34, 35, 37, 200
Rae, W. Fraser, 142
Reith, Gerda, 3–4, 79, 89
    and luck, 122
resort, 5
revolution, 199
Revolutions of 1848, 18–20
Rhineland, 8, 12, 200
risk, 119, 191
    psychology of, 120
Riviera, 36, 200
    climate of, 40
Romain, James, 81, 96, 112

and philosophy of gambling, 118
and pro-gambling discourse, 193
romanticism, 182

Rosslyn, Lord. *See* St Clair-Erskine, James, Earl
    of Rosslyn
roulette, 16
    as "mesmeric", 174
    description of, 69, 70
    mechanics of, 70
runs, 89, 91–92, 98
Sala, George Augustus, 31, 93, 129, 141, 156
    on psychological effects of winning,
        169
Schooling, J. Holt, 98, 109, 115, 127
    on identifying the lucky, 128
    on luck, 127
Schwartz, David, 4
self-talk, 162
sensation, 170
senses, 48
Silberer, Viktor, 81, 166
Simmel, Georg, 7, 80, 137
    and "blasé attitude", 164
    and chance, 118
    on emotions and money, 175
    on envy, 165
    on instrumental quality of money,
        185
    on luck and status, 136
    on money, 165
    on money economy, 184
    on play, 45
    on quantification, 99
sociability, 45, 71, 79, 200
social mobility, 28
social science
    and risk, 119–21
social types, 71
Sociéte Anonyme des Bain de Mer et du Cercle
    des Étrangers à Monaco, 22
society, 7
sources, 7–8
space
    dream, 26
    heterosocial, 17
Spencer, Herbert, 162
St Clair-Erskine, James, Earl of Rosslyn, 102
Stacpoole, Margaret de Vere, 7, 30
    on casino as "machine", 166
    on luck, 134
    on psychology of gambling, 179
statistics, 90
Steinmetz, Andrew, 95, 112, 159, 160

on origins of play, 184
stock market, 195
suicide, 1, 78, 140, 145, 160, 161
suntanning, 39
superstition, 86, 97, 117–18, 129, 130, 132,
    174, 177, 178
Symonds, John Addington, 47, 69
    description of Monte Carlo, 47
    descriptions of casino staff, 75
    descriptions of gamblers, 74
    and sensory impressions, 76
systematizers, 92, 106
systems, 89, 92, 93–95, 97, 98, 99, 100, 105,
    114, 129, 174, 201
    and chance, 114
    computational, 115
    D'Alembert, 102, 106
    and luck, 129
    mathematical, 93

temptation, 103
terrorism, 201
theosophy, 116
thinking, historical, 91, 98
Thomas, W. I., 176, 189
    on gambling and civilization, 189
    on gambling as natural, 176
time, 6, 89, 91
tourism, 33, 36, 188
    as transformational force, 37
tourist guides, 34
transnational, 200
transportation, steam, 8, 34
Trent-et-Quarante, 16

unification
    German, 2, 20, 26
universality, 202

Veblen, Thorstein, 7
    on "barbarian temperament",
        150
    on "gambling temperament",
        179
    on luck, 135, 150
    on psychology of gambling,
        179
Venice, 11
Venn, John, 8, 94, 171
Versailles, 5
viatique, 79
Victoria, Queen of England, 87
Villemessant, Hippolyte de, 35
Vivian, Herbert, 48, 101

Wars, Napoleonic, 12
water, 14
    Bad Homburg, 40
    thermal, 43
wealth, 195
Weber, Eugen, 36
wheel of fortune, 16
Wilkins, William Henry, 48

winning
    psychology of, 169
witchcraft, 132
work, 145, 153, 183, 190, 191, 195
Wundt, Wilhelm, 151, 176

Young, Norwood, 97, 106, 143, 163,
    174

Printed in the USA
CPSIA information can be obtained
at www.ICGtesting.com
LVHW020725021123
762637LV00008B/244

9 781009 393546